VIOLATION OF HUMAN RIGHTS

VIOLATION OF HUMAN RIGHTS

PROF B.K. PANDA
DR SUKANTA SARKAR

KALPAZ

ISBN: 978-93-5128-159-7
Price : ₹ 1050

First Published, 2015

Published by

Kalpaz Publications
C-30, Satyawati Nagar,
Delhi-110052
Ph. : 9212142040
E-mail: kalpaz@hotmail.com

Printed at : G. Print Process, Delhi

Cataloging in Publication Data—DK

Courtesy: D.K. Agencies (P) Ltd. <docinfo@dkagencies.com>

Panda, B. K., author.

Violation of human rights / Prof. B.K. Panda, Dr. Sukanta Sarkar.

pages cm

Includes bibliographical references (pages) and index.

ISBN 9789351281597

1. Human rights—India. 2. Human rights. I. Sarkar, Sukanta, author. II. Title.

DDC 342.54085 23

Contents

Preface

Rights occupy an important place in man's life. Success of democracy depends on intelligent citizens. Rights enable citizens to take part in administration and this lead to the success of democracy. The philosophy of human rights is similar with that of the values. Human rights promotion is the work of all levels of society. Not only do the United Nations and international groups play a role, but so do national, state, and local governments. Human rights are moral principles or norms that describe certain standards of human behaviour, and are regularly protected as legal rights in national and international law. Human rights are rights inherent to all human beings, whatever our nationality, place of residence, sex, national or ethnic origin, colour, religion, language, or any other status. Human rights advocates agree that, sixty years after its issue, the Universal Declaration of Human Rights is still more a dream than reality. Violations exist in every part of the world. To protect human rights is to ensure that people receive some degree of decent humane treatment.

We desire to express our heartiest thank to Prof Md.A. Rahman, Department of Agriculture, International University of Business Agriculture and Technology, Dhaka, Bangladesh who despite his busy schedule and hectic academic engagements, all the time encouraged and supported us. We have also bebolden to Dr N.G. Pendse, Department of Economics, Rani Durgabati University, Jabalpur who's erudite and scholarly tidbits for preparing such a vast work are still fresh in our mind. We also thanks to Dr Pradeep Kumar Pandey, Centre of Judicial Studies, Dibrugarh University, Assam; Dr Suman Kalan Chaudhury, Department of Business Administration, Berhampur

University, Odisha; Dr Rakesh Joshi, Department of Economics, Saurashtra University, Gujarat; Dr D. Pulla Rao, Department of Economics, Andhra University; Dr Vibhuti Patel, Professor cum Director, Centre for Study of Social Exclusion and Inclusive Policy, SNDT Women's University, Mumbai; Dr Wakar Amin, Department of Social Work, University of Kashmir, J & K; Dr Shazia Manzoor, Assistant Professor, Department of Social Work, University of Kashmir, J & K; Dr. Pallab Kanti Ghoshal, Department of Commerce, Netaji Subhas College, Udaipur, for their valuable suggestions and moral support.

We are heartily grateful to Prof R. Prasad, Prof Ashish Kumar Shivastava and Prof L.S. Nigam, Pandit Ravishankar Shukla University, Raipur, Chhattisgarh who always encouraged us to carry on this constructive work. Further, we express our heartily thankfulness to each and every person who directly/indirectly helped us in preparing this work.

It is hoped that this book will be very useful to society in general and students of human rights in particular. Comments and suggestions are most welcome.

Prof B.K. Panda
Dr Sukanta Sarkar

Abbreviations

ADB	: Asian Development Bank
AMA	: American Medical Association
BCCI	: Board for Control of Cricket in India
BIS	: Bureau of Indian Standards
CEDAW	: Convention on Elimination of All Forms of Discrimination against Women
CGPDTM	: Controller General of Patents, Designs and Trade Marks
CIRM	: Central Industrial Relation Machinery
CMDM	: Cooked Mid-Day Meal
COPRS	: Country Operational Plan and Reporting Systems
CPCB	: Central Pollution Control Board
CRC	: Convention on Rights of the Child
DGFASLI	: Directorate General Factory Advice Service and Labour Institutes
DMCA	: Digital Millennium Copyright Act
DRM	: Digital Rights Management
DWCD	: Department of Women and Child Development's
ECOSOC	: Economic and Social Council
FAQ	: Fair Average Quality
IAEA	: International Atomic Energy Agency
ICCPR	: International Covenant on Civil and Political Rights
ICDS	: Integrated Child Development Services
ICESCR	: International Covenant on Economic, Social and Cultural Rights
ICPD	: International Conference on Population and Development
ILO	: International Labour Organisation
IPV	: Intimate Partner Violence

JSY	: Janani Suraksha Yojana
LGB	: Lesbian, Gay and Bisexual
MCH	: Maternal and Child Health Policy
MDGs	: Millennium Development Goals
MoU	: Memorandum of Understanding
MoWCD	: Ministry of Women and Child Development
MSIHC	: Manufacture, Storage, and Import of Hazardous Chemicals
MTP	: Medical Termination of Pregnancy
NACO	: National AIDS Control Organisation
NCDRC	: National Consumer Disputes Redressal Commission
NCL	: National Commission on Labour
NCLP	: National Child Labour Projects
NCW	: National Commission for Women
NII	: National Information Infrastructure
NRHM	: National Rural Health Mission
NSDP	: Net State Domestic Product
NSSO	: National Sample Survey Organisation
PLRA	: Prison Litigation Reform Act
PRI	: Panchayati Raj Institutions
RCH	: Reproductive and Child Health Policy
RTE	: Right to Education Act
SGA	: Sale of Goods Act
SPCB	: State Pollution Control Board
SRH	: Sexual and Reproductive Health
TFR	: Total Fertility Rate
TRIPS	: Intellectual Property Rights Agreement
UDHR	: Universal Declaration of Human Rights
UNAIDS	: United Nations Programme on AIDS
UNCHR	: United Nations Commission on Human Rights
UNCRPD	: UN Convention on the Rights of Persons with Disabilities
UNDAC	: United Nations Disaster Assessment and Coordination
UNFPA	: United Nations Population Fund
UNHCHR	: United Nations High Commissioner for Human Rights
UNHRC	: United Nations Human Rights Council
UNICEF	: United Nations Children's Fund
WCT	: WIPO Copyright Treaty
WIPO	: World Intellectual Property Organisation
WTO	: World Trade Organisation

1

Human Rights: An Overview

"I am disturbed by how states abuse laws on Internet access. I am concerned that surveillance programmes are becoming too aggressive. I understand that national security and criminal activity may justify some exceptional and narrowly-tailored use of surveillance. But that is all the more reason to safeguard human rights and fundamental freedoms."

- Ban Ki-moon

Introduction

Humans are uniquely adept at utilising systems of symbolic communication such as language and art for self-expression, the exchange of ideas, and organisation. They create complex social structures composed of many cooperating and competing groups, from families and kinship networks to states. They began to practice sedentary agriculture about 12,000 years ago, domesticating plants and animals, thus allowing for the growth of civilisation. Humans subsequently established various forms of government, religion, and culture around the world, unifying people within a region and leading to the development of states and empires.

Rights are legal, social, or ethical principles of freedom or entitlement; i.e. rights are the fundamental normative rules about what is allowed of people or owed to people, according to some legal system, social convention, or ethical theory. Rights are often considered fundamental to civilisation, being regarded as established pillars of society and culture, and the history of social conflicts can be found in the history of each right and its development. In one sense, a right is a permission to do something or an entitlement to a specific service or treatment, and these rights have been called positive rights. The general concept of rights is that they are possessed by individuals in the sense that they are permissions and entitlements to do things which other persons, or which governments or authorities, can not infringe. Rights are often included in the foundational questions that governments and politics have been designed to deal with. The specific enumeration of rights has differed greatly in different periods of history. In many cases, the system of rights promulgated by one group has come into sharp and bitter conflict with that of other groups.

Individual rights state explicitly the requirements for a person to benefit rather than suffer from living in a society. They codify man's protection from the initiation of force, as required by his rational nature. The right to life is the fundamental right, of which all other rights are corollaries. The right to life states that you own your own body. The right to liberty is a part of the right to life, specifically referring to your freedom of action. Property rights are an extension to the right to life. The right to the pursuit of happiness is freedom of action. The right to free speech is recognition that speech in itself if devoid of physical threats is not an initiation of force and does not warrant any retaliatory force. The right to defend yourself is a corollary to the right to life.

What are Human Rights?

Human rights are moral principles or norms that describe certain standards of human behaviour, and are regularly protected as legal rights in national and international law. Human rights are rights inherent to all human beings, whatever our nationality, place of residence, sex, national or ethnic origin, colour, religion, language, or any other status. We are all equally entitled to our human rights without discrimination. These rights are all interrelated, interdependent and indivisible. The Charter of the United Nations requires that all member states *"promote and encourage respect for human rights and for fundamental freedoms for all without distinction as to race, sex, language, or religion"*. In order to provide a common understanding of these rights, the Universal Declaration of Human Rights was adopted by the General Assembly of the United Nations on December 10, 1948. In simple language, it describes the rights shared by all human beings, and sets a common standard of achievement for all peoples and all nations. The Vienna Declaration affirmed the equal importance of all human rights, declaring them to be universal, indivisible and interdependent and interrelated.

The *Universal Declaration of Human Rights* reflects core human rights principles such as that human rights must be universal (for everyone), protected without discrimination, equitable, and indivisible (governments cannot protect some rights but not others). Human rights law provides standards and mechanisms to protect those rights necessary to ensure equality, dignity and freedom. In the arena of economic and social rights, human rights law includes:

(a) The right to education ensures access to quality schools and to an education that is directed towards the full development of the human personality. The aims of education must be directed toward the development of each child's personality and full potential, preparing children to participate in society and to do work that is rewarding and reasonably remunerative, and to continue learning throughout life.

(b) The human right to health means that everyone has the right to the highest attainable standard of physical and mental health, which includes access to all medical services, sanitation, adequate food, decent housing, healthy working conditions, and a clean environment. The human right to health care means that hospitals, clinics, medicines, and doctors' services must be accessible, available, acceptable, and of good quality for everyone, on an equitable basis, where and when needed. Healthcare must be accessible and provided without discrimination (in intent or effect) based on health status, race, ethnicity, age, sex, sexuality, disability, language, religion, national origin, income, or social status.

(c) The right to food guarantees freedom from hunger and access to safe and nutritious food. Any discrimination in access to food, as well as to means and entitlements for its procurement, on the grounds of race, colour, sex, language, age, religion, political or other opinion, national or social origin, property, birth or other status constitutes a violation of the right to food. Food should be secure, or accessible, for both present and future generations

(d) Everyone has a fundamental human right to housing, which ensures access to a safe, secure, habitable, and affordable home with freedom from forced eviction. This right must be provided to all persons irrespective of income or access to economic resources.

(e) The right to social security ensures that everyone, regardless of age or ability to work, is guaranteed the means necessary to procure basic needs and services. Social security must be provided without discrimination (in intent or effect) based on health status, race, ethnicity, age, sex, sexuality, disability, language, religion, national origin, income, or social status.

Importance of Human Rights

Rights occupy an important place in man's life. Success of democracy depends on intelligent citizens. Rights enable citizens to take part in administration and this lead to the success of democracy. Liberty and equality are the two pillars of democracy. They are necessary for its success. Enjoyment of rights by the individuals leads to them. Citizens are the backbone of a society. Human rights are important in the relationships that exist between individuals and the government that has power over them. The government exercises power over its people. States have to look after the basic needs of the people and protect some of their freedoms. Some basic human rights have been written down and agreed to by many states. The most famous text is the Universal Declaration of Human Rights (UDHR) which the UN General Assembly approved on 10 December 1948. International Human Rights Day is now celebrated on 10 December every year.

The philosophy of human rights is similar with that of the values. Values are one of the basic aspects of human rights. The strict adherence of human rights restores not only to values, but also in turn able to achieve peace, security and harmonious living community without any kind of discrimination that exist between individuals and nation-states. Dignity is another value that regulates the behaviour of individuals. Dignity is a relative term with regulatory nature. Liberty is another concept which plays a vital role in the promotion of human rights. The concept of liberty is the basics for the development of a right. Equality is another important component of human rights. From ancient to modern times, people are fighting to achieve this in terms of its practical application to each situation. To achieve the rigour of equality and to fill the gap especially on socio-economic and cultural grounds, the principles of international law of human rights provides for the necessary concessions to be extended, to people at the national level by states.

Human rights have little value if they are not implemented. States recovering from conflict or lacking human rights expertise often need help in implementing their human rights obligations by translating them into laws and practices. The Office of the High Commissioner for Human Rights devotes much of its resources through its Technical

Cooperation Programme to supporting States' efforts in this regard. The programme helps countries to apply international human rights norms at the national level. It provides practical assistance for the building and strengthening of institutions which have a direct impact on the promotion and protection of human rights and the rule of law. The economic empowerment of the world's poorest people will not happen unless their human rights are also considered. Navi Pillay, the UN High Commissioner for Human Rights, warned that the interrelation between freedom from want and freedom from fear must be central to the discussions of world leaders on how to achieve the Millennium Development Goals (MDGs) by their target date of 2015. Economic development and human rights have been considered by governments as separate issues to be tackled separately, with development treated as the overriding concern. Human rights principles such as equality, participation and accountability and the rule of law are instrumental for development to take firm root and be both equitable and sustainable.

Human rights promotion is the work of all levels of society. Not only do the United Nations and international groups play a role, but so do national, state, and local governments. Human rights are much more than well-meaning aspirations set to legal language. It is important for society to live human rights through its practices, behaviour, and attitudes. To live human rights values means to support the oppressed, embrace the excluded, advocate for the voiceless, and celebrate the diversity of our community. Around the world, peoples and nations have recognised the importance of human rights as a fundamental part of social justice. The idea of human rights also led to the creation of a system to monitor and oversee how governments around the world comply with human rights standards. While the United Nations has several functions, one of its core functions is promoting and protecting human rights around the world.

History of Human Rights

The history of human rights can be traced to past documents, particularly the Magna Carta (1215), the English Bill of Rights (1689), the French Declaration of the Rights of Man and of the Citizen (1789), and the Bill of Rights in the United States Constitution (1791). Magna Carta was the first document imposed upon a King of England by a group of his subjects, the feudal barons, in an attempt to limit his powers by law and protect their rights. The charter is widely known throughout the English speaking world as an important part of the protracted historical process that led to the rule of constitutional law in England and beyond. The Bill of Rights is an Act of the Parliament of England passed on 16 December 1689.

It was a restatement in statutory form of the Declaration of Right presented by the Convention Parliament to William and Mary in March 1689 (or 1688 by Old Style dating), inviting them to become joint sovereigns of England. The Declaration of the Rights of Man and of the Citizen, passed by France's National Constituent Assembly in August 1789, is a fundamental document of the French Revolution and in the history of human rights. Inspired in part by the American Revolution, the Declaration was a core statement of the values of the French revolution and had a major impact on the development of liberty and democracy in Europe and worldwide. The Declaration is introduced by a preamble describing the fundamental characteristics of the rights which are qualified as being natural, unalienable and sacred and consisting of simple and incontestable principles on which citizens could base their demands.

The earliest conceptualisation of human rights is credited to ideas about natural rights emanating from natural law. Natural rights are those not contingent upon the laws, customs, or beliefs of any particular culture or government, and therefore universal and inalienable. The concept of natural law is closely related to the concept of natural rights. The idea that certain rights are natural or inalienable also has a history dating back at least to the Stoics of late Antiquity and Catholic law of the early Middle Ages, and descending through the Protestant Reformation and the Age of Enlightenment to today. Natural law is a system of law that is determined by nature, and so is universal. The use of natural law, in its various incarnations, has varied widely through its history. There are a number of different theories of natural law, differing from each other with respect to the role that morality plays in determining the authority of legal norms. In the 19th century, human rights became a central concern over the issue of slavery. A number of reformers, notably British Member of Parliament William Wilberforce, worked towards the abolition of the slave trade and abolition of slavery. The establishment of the International Committee of the Red Cross, the 1864 Lieber Code and the first of the Geneva Conventions in 1864 laid the foundations of International humanitarian law, to be further developed following the two World Wars. The League of Nations was established in 1919 at the negotiations over the Treaty of Versailles following the end of World War I. The League's goals included disarmament, preventing war through collective security, settling disputes between countries through negotiation and diplomacy, and improving global welfare.

The Bill of Rights is the collective name for the first ten amendments to the United States Constitution. On June 8, 1789 Representative James Madison introduced a series of thirty-nine amendments to the constitution in the House of Representatives. The Bill of Rights reserves for the people any rights not specifically mentioned in the Constitution and reserves all powers not specifically granted to the federal government to the people or the States. The Constitution of the United States is the supreme law of the United States of America. Since the Constitution came into force in 1789, it has been amended twenty-seven times. The Constitution is interpreted, supplemented, and implemented by a large body of constitutional law. The Constitution of the United States was the first constitution of its kind, and has influenced the constitutions of other nations.

The idea of human rights, which is the simple but profound concept that each of us has basic rights by virtue of our humanity alone, was forcefully brought to the global stage in response to the atrocities of World War II. The foundation of human rights is the notion that every person should live in equality, dignity and freedom. The right to vote embodies the spirit of American democracy. The first major expansion of the right to vote occurred after the Civil War with the adoption of the Fifteenth Amendment to the United States Constitution which extended the right to vote to former African American slaves. However, from that time until the Voting Rights Act in 1965, many African American, Latino/a, Asian American and indigenous Indian communities were kept from the polls through overtly racist means. Although the passage of the Voting Rights Act of 1965 heralded a new beginning in providing racial and ethnic minority communities with access to the political process, the struggle for universal suffrage and political participation is far from over.

Human Rights and United Nations

The United Nations is an international organisation founded in 1945 after the Second World War by 51 countries committed to maintaining international peace and security, developing friendly relations among nations and promoting social progress, better living standards and human rights. The organisation is financed by assessed and voluntary contributions from its member states. Its objectives include maintaining international peace and security, promoting human rights, fostering social and economic development, protecting the environment, and providing humanitarian aid in cases of famine, natural disaster, and armed conflict. The United Nations' system is based on five principal organs: the General Assembly, the Security Council, the Economic and Social Council (ECOSOC), the Secretariat, and the International Court of Justice. A sixth principal organ, the Trusteeship Council, suspended operations in 1994, upon the independence of Palau, the last remaining UN trustee territory.

The United Nations Commission on Human Rights (UNCHR) was a functional commission within the overall framework of the United Nations from 1946 until it was replaced by the United Nations Human Rights Council in 2006. It was a subsidiary body of the UN Economic and Social Council, and was also assisted in its work by the Office of the United Nations High Commissioner for Human Rights (UNHCHR). It was the UN's principal mechanism and international forum concerned with the promotion and protection of human rights.

The Human Rights Council is an inter-governmental body within the United Nations system responsible for strengthening the promotion and protection of human rights around the globe and for addressing situations of human rights violations and make recommendations on them. It has the ability to discuss all thematic human rights issues and situations that require its attention throughout the year. It meets at the UN Office at Geneva. When creating the Human Rights Council in March 2006 the United Nations General Assembly decided that the Council's work and functioning should be reviewed five years after it had come into existence at the level of the General Assembly. The General Assembly can suspend the rights and privileges of any Council member that it decides has persistently committed gross and systematic violations of human rights during its term of membership. The UNHRC holds regular sessions three times a year, in March, June, and September. The first election of members was held on 9th May 2006.

Violation of Human Rights

Human rights advocates agree that, sixty years after its issue, the Universal Declaration of Human Rights is still more a dream than reality. Violations exist in every part of the world. To protect human rights is to ensure that people receive some degree of decent, humane treatment. To violate the most basic human rights, on the other hand, is to deny individuals their fundamental moral entitlements. Some of the gravest violations of the right to life are massacres, the starvation of entire populations, and genocide. The term "war crime" refers to a violation of the rules of jus in bello (justice in war) by any individual, whether military or civilian. Women and girls are often raped by soldiers or forced into prostitution.

For a long time, the international community has failed to address the problem of sexual violence during armed conflict. Sexual violence is sometimes viewed as a way to destroy male and community pride or humiliate men who cannot "protect" their women. Various lesser forms of political oppression are often enacted as well. Individuals who pose a threat to those in power or do not share their political views may be arbitrarily imprisoned, and either never brought to trial or subject to grossly unfair trial procedures. Violations of political and economic rights are the root causes of many crises. When rights to adequate food, housing, employment, and cultural life are denied, and large groups of people are excluded from the society's decision-making processes, there is likely to be great social unrest. In cases where extreme violations of human rights have occurred, reconciliation and peace building become much more difficult.

Female genital mutilation, in any form, is recognised internationally as a gross violation of human rights of girls and women. International human rights bodies have set standards which address FGM and the human rights it violates. These international and regional standards require countries to fulfill their human rights obligations by protecting women and girls at risk of FGM. A violation of economic, social and cultural rights occurs when a State fails in its obligations to ensure that they are enjoyed without discrimination or in its obligation to respect, protect and fulfill them. Often a violation of one of the rights is linked to a violation of other rights. While international law permits states to establish immigration policies and deportation procedures, it does not grant them discretion to violate human rights in the process. The United States regularly fails to uphold international human rights law in its immigration laws and enforcement policies, by violating the rights of immigrants to fair treatment at the hands of government, to proportional sanctions, to freedom from arbitrary detention, to respect for the right to family unity, and to protection from return to persecution.

Poverty is a brutal denial of human rights. This must be recognised at the outset by all policy-makers, including governments, donor agencies, international organisations and individual parliamentarians. Most people living in the Commonwealth today are poor. Too many of them are among the absolute poor. Poverty is a condition brought about by people and policies and is not a natural and normal condition. It can and must be changed as a matter of priority. The state of poverty itself, and not the act to eliminate it, is a violation of human rights. Poverty reduction efforts have traditionally been guided by the paternalist 'welfare' approach where the State becomes the benefactor of the poor who must wait upon the generosity and goodwill of the giver. Most Commonwealth parliamentarians, whether indirectly as donors or directly as representatives are closely associated with designing policies, that are aimed at rapid economic development and poverty eradication.

Conclusion

Human rights are moral principles or norms that describe certain standards of human behaviour, and are regularly protected as legal rights in national and international law. Human rights principles such as equality, participation and accountability and the rule of law are instrumental for development to take firm root and be both equitable and sustainable. Human rights promotion is the work of all levels of society. Not only do the United Nations and international groups play a role, but so do national, state, and local governments. Human rights are much more than well-meaning aspirations set to legal language. The *Universal Declaration of Human Rights* reflects core human rights principles such as that human rights must be universal (for everyone), protected without discrimination, equitable, and indivisible (governments cannot protect some rights but not others).

The United Nations is an international organisation founded in 1945 after the Second World War by 51 countries committed to maintaining international peace and security, developing friendly relations among nations and promoting social progress, better living standards and human rights. Human rights advocates agree that, sixty years after its issue, the Universal Declaration of Human Rights is still more a dream than reality. Violations exist in every part of the world. Sexual violence is sometimes viewed as a way to destroy male and community pride or humiliate men who cannot "protect" their women. Poverty is a brutal denial of human rights.

References

1. *A human rights violations,* Retrieved from http://www.endfgm.eu/en/female-genital-mutilation/a-human-rights-violation/
2. Bernard Grofman, Chandler Davidson (2009), *Controversies in Minority Voting: The Voting Rights Act in Perspective*, Brookings Institution Press.
3. Carsten K. W. De Dreu, Nanne K. De Vries (2001), *Group Consensus and Minority Influence: Implications for Innovation,* Wiley.
4. Curtis Francis Doebbler (2004), *International Human Rights Law: Cases and Materials*, CD Pub.
5. D. L. Sheth, Gurpreet Mahajan (1999), *Minority Identities and the Nation-state*, Oxford University Press.
6. Daniel Moeckli, Sangeeta Shah, Sandesh Sivakumaran, David Harris (2013), *International Human Rights Law,* Oxford University Press.
7. David Carpenter (1990), *The Minority of Henry III*, University of California Press.
8. European Centre for Minority Issues (2004), *Mechanisms for the Implementation of Minority Rights,* European Centre for Minority Issues.
9. Guofang Li, Lihshing Wang (2008), *Model Minority Myth Revisited: An Interdisciplinary Approach to Demystifying Asian American Educational Experiences*, IAP.
10. *Harish Babu* (2014), Importance of Rights can be discovered under the following heads
11. *Human* (2014), Retrieved from http://en.wikipedia.org/wiki/Human
12. *Human Rights* (2014), Retrieved from http://en.wikipedia.org/wiki/Human_rights
13. *Human rights in action* (2015), Retrieved from http://www.ohchr.org/Documents/Countries/terrain.pdf
14. *Human Rights: A Global Vision* (2015), Retrieved from http://www.nesri.org/human-rights/human-rights-a-global-vision
15. Hurst Hannum (1993), *Basic Documents on Autonomy and Minority Rights,* Martinus Nijhoff Publishers.
16. Importance of Human Rights, Retrieved from http://www.pearsonpublishing.co.uk/education/samples/S_497198.pdf
17. *Importance of the Right to Vote* (2015), Retrieved from http://www.law.seattleu.edu/centers-and-institutes/korematsu-center/importance-of-the-right-to-vote

18. *Introduction to human rights and duties* (2015), Retrieved from http://www.unipune.ac.in/pdf_files/Final%20Book_03042012.pdf
19. Jack Donnelly (2012), *International Human Rights*, International Human Rights.
20. Javaid Rehman (2003), *International Human Rights Law: A Practical Approach,* Longman.
21. Javaid Rehman (2011), *International Human Rights Law,* Longman/Pearson.
22. Jay A. Sigler (1983), *Minority Rights: A Comparative Analysis,* Greenwood Press.
23. Jean-Marc Coicaud, Michael W. Doyle, Anne-Marie Gardner (2003), *The Globalisation of Human Rights,* United Nations University Press.
24. John David Skrentny (2002), *The Minority Rights Revoluation*, Harvard University Press.
25. John E. Farley (2004), *Majority-minority Relations*, Edition 4, Prentice Hall.
26. Leo Grebler, Joan W. Moore, Ralph C. Guzmán, Jeffrey Lionel Berlant (1970), *The Mexican-American people: the Nation's second largest minority*, Free Press.
27. Louisa Schein (2000), *Minority Rules: The Miao and the Feminine in China's Cultural Politics*, Duke University Press.
28. Marc Weller (2007), *Universal Minority Rights: A Commentary on the Jurisprudence of International Courts and Treaty Bodies*, Oxford University Press.
29. Michelle Maiese, *Human Rights Violations,* Retrieved from http://www.beyondintractability.org/essay/human-rights-violations
30. Nalini Rajan (2008), *Democracy and the Limits of Minority Rights*, SAGE Publications.
31. Nicole J. Beger (2004), *Tensions in the Struggle for Sexual Minority Rights in Europe: Que(e)rying Political Practices*, Manchester University Press.
32. Patrick Thornberry, María Amor Martín Estébanez (2004), *Minority Rights in Europe: A Review of the Work and Standards of the Council of Europe*, Council of Europe.
33. Peter Cumper, Steven Charles Wheatley (1999), *Minority Rights in the "new" Europe: The Hague,* Martinus Nijhoff Publishers.
34. Peter Davies (1988), *Human Rights,* Routledge.
35. Peter Skerry (1993), *Mexican Americans: The Ambivalent Minority*, Free Press.
36. Retrieved from http://www.preservearticles.com/2012011620880/importance-of-rights-can-be-discovered-under-the-following-heads.html

37. Richard Pierre Claude, Burns H. Weston (2006), *Human Rights in the World Community: Issues and Action,* University of Pennsylvania Press.
38. *Rights* (2014), Retrieved from http://en.wikipedia.org/wiki/Rights
39. *Rights* (2014), Retrieved from http://www.importanceofphilosophy.com/Politics_Rights.html
40. Stephen Harold Riggins (1992), *Ethnic Minority Media: An International Perspective*, SAGE Publications.
41. Stephen May (2008), *Language and minority rights: ethnicity, nationalism and the politics of language,* Routledge.
42. Stephen May, Tariq Modood, Judith Squires (2004), *Ethnicity, Nationalism, and Minority Rights,* Cambridge University Press.
43. Student Services, Inc (1998), *The Minority and Women's Complete Scholarship Book*, Sourcebooks.
44. Tawhida Ahmed (2011), *The Impact of EU Law on Minority Rights,* Hart.
45. Tessa J. Bartholomeusz, Chandra Richard De Silva (1998), *Buddhist Fundamentalism and Minority Identities in Sri Lanka,* SUNY Press.
46. *The importance of human rights* (2014), Retrieved from http://ww2.gazette.net/stories/11242010/montlet184258_32548.php
47. Thomas A. LaVeist (2011), *Minority Populations and Health: An Introduction to Health Disparities in the United States,* John Wiley & Sons.
48. Tim Wise (2002), *Dear White America: Letter to a New Minority*, City Lights Publishers.
49. *UN official stresses the importance of human rights in overcoming poverty* (2014), Retrieved from http://www.un.org/apps/news/story.asp? NewsID =35536#.VFTuSjtQHFw
50. *Unfair immigration policy* (2014), Retrieved from http://www.hrw.org/united-states/us-program/unfair-immigration-policies
51. Unit: 2, *The Importance of Human Rights to Democracy, Governance and Development,* Retrieved from http://www.parliamentary strengthening.org/humanrightsmodule/pdf/humanrightsunit2.pdf
52. *United Nations Commission on Human Rights* (2014), Retrieved from http://en.wikipedia.org/wiki/United_Nations_Commission_ on_ Human_Rights
53. *What are examples of violations of economic, social and cultural rights?* (2014), Retrieved from http://www.ohchr.org/EN/Issues/ESCR/Pages/Whatare examples ofviolationsofESCR.aspx
54. *What Are Human Rights?* (2014), Retrieved from http://www.international.gc.ca/rights-droits/human_rights-droits_personne.aspx?lang=eng

55. *What is the Human Right to Education?* (2014), Retrieved from http://www.nesri.org/programs/what-is-the-human-right-to-education
56. *What is the Human Right to Food?* (2014), Retrieved from http://www.nesri.org/programs/what-is-the-human-right-to-food
57. *What is the Human Right to Health and Health Care?* (2014), Retrieved from http://www.nesri.org/programs/what-is-the-human-right-to-health-and-health-care
58. *What is the Human Right to Housing?* (2014), Retrieved from http://www.nesri.org/programs/what-is-the-human-right-to-housing
59. *What is the Human Right to Social Security?* (2014), Retrieved from http://www.nesri.org/programs/what-is-the-human-right-to-social-security
60. Will Kymlicka (1995), *Multicultural Citizenship: A Liberal Theory of Minority Rights*, Oxford University Press.
61. Will Kymlicka (1997), *The New Debate Over Minority Rights, Robert F. Harney Professorship and Program in Ethnic Immigration and Pluralism Studies*, University of Toronto.

2

United Nations and Human Rights

"Governments that block the aspirations of their people, that steal or are corrupt, that oppress and torture or that deny freedom of expression and human rights should bear in mind that they will find it increasingly hard to escape the judgement of their own people, or where warranted, the reach of international law."

- William Hague

Introduction

The United Nations is an intergovernmental organisation established on 24 October 1945 to promote international co-operation. A replacement for the ineffective League of Nations, the organisation was created following the Second World War to prevent another such conflict. In the century prior to the UN's creation, several international treaty organisations and conferences had been formed to regulate conflicts between nations, such as the International Committee of the Red Cross and the Hague Conventions of 1899 and 1907. The United Nations was formulated and negotiated among the delegations from the Soviet Union, the UK, the US and China in Dumbarton Oaks Conference.

The Dumbarton Oaks Conference constituted the first important step taken to carry out paragraph 4 of the Moscow Declaration of 1943, which recognised the need for a post-war international organisation to succeed the League of Nations. The conversations were held in two phases, since the Soviets were unwilling to meet directly with the Chinese. In the first phase, representatives of the Soviet Union, the United Kingdom, and the United States convened between August 21 and September 28. In the second, representatives of Republic of China, the United Kingdom, and the United States held discussions between September 29 and October 7.

The United Nations' system is based on five principal organs: the General Assembly, the Security Council, the Economic and Social Council, the Secretariat, and the International Court of Justice. The General Assembly meets under its president or Secretary-General in regular yearly sessions the main part of which lasts from September to December and resumed part from January until all issues are addressed. The General Assembly votes on many resolutions brought forth by sponsoring states. The General Assembly also approves the budget of the United Nations, and decides how much money each member state must pay to run the organisation. The General Assembly may take action on maintaining international peace and security if the United Nations Security Council is unable, usually due to disagreement among the permanent members, to exercise its primary responsibility. Security Council powers include the establishment of peacekeeping operations, the establishment of international sanctions, and the authorisation of military action through Security Council resolutions. The Security Council held its first session on 17th January 1946. Security Council resolutions are typically enforced by UN peacekeepers, military forces voluntarily provided by member states and funded independently of the main UN budget.

The ECOSOC serves as the central forum for discussing international economic and social issues, and for formulating policy recommendations addressed to member states and the United Nations system. It is responsible for coordinating the economic, social and related work of 14 UN specialised agencies, their functional commissions and five regional commissions. The UN Secretariat is headed by the Secretary-General, assisted by a staff of international civil servants worldwide. The Secretary-General is appointed by the General Assembly, after being recommended by the Security Council, where the permanent members have veto power. The International Court of Justice is the primary judicial branch of the United Nations. The ICJ is composed of fifteen judges elected to nine-year terms by the UN General Assembly and the UN Security Council from a list of persons nominated by the national groups in the Permanent Court of Arbitration. As stated in Article 93 of the UN Charter, all 193 UN members are automatically parties to the Court's statute. Article 94 establishes the duty of all UN members to comply with decisions of the Court involving them.

Needs of United Nations

The United Nations is an international organisation of countries. It was created for many reasons: (a) There should be peace and security in the world after the Second World War; (b) Countries should be friendly to each other; (c) Countries should help each other solve problems; (d) Human rights should be respected everywhere in the world. The Security Council makes very important decisions and all the countries have to obey them. It tries to keep peace in the world and also tries to solve conflicts that endanger world peace. It also sends peacekeepers to countries where there is trouble. The United Nations also has many other organisations. The International Atomic Energy Agency (IAEA) tries to find out if countries have atomic weapons. The World Health Organisation is a UN programme to help control diseases all over the world. UNICEF is an organisation to help children in need in poor countries.

United Nations Children's Fund

UNICEF was created by the United Nations General Assembly on December 11, 1946, to provide emergency food and healthcare to children in countries. Most of UNICEF's work is in the field, with staff in over 190 countries and territories. UNICEF's programme emphasise developing community-level services to promote the health and well-being of children. UNICEF was awarded the Nobel Peace Prize in 1965 and the Prince of Asturias Award of Concord in 2006. To raise money to support its Education and Literacy Programmes, UNICEF collaborates with companies worldwide and encompassing international as well as small- and medium-sized businesses. UNICEF works directly with companies to improve their business practices, bringing them in line with obligations under international law, and ensuring that they respect children's rights in the realms of the marketplace, workplace and the community. UNICEF Ambassadors are leaders in the entertainment industry, representing the fields of film, television, music, sports and beyond. UNICEF Innocenti Research Centre in Florence, Italy, was established in 1988, to strengthen the research capability of the United Nations Children's Fund and to support its advocacy for children worldwide.

United Nations Disaster Assessment and Coordination

The United Nations Disaster Assessment and Coordination (UNDAC) is part of the international emergency response system for sudden-onset emergencies. It is designed to help the United Nations and governments of disaster-affected countries during the first phase of a sudden-onset emergency. The UNDAC system has three regional teams: Europe/ Africa/ Middle East, the Americas (including the Caribbean) and Asia-Pacific. UNDAC was created in 1993. It is designed to help the United Nations and governments of disaster-affected countries during the first phase of a sudden-onset emergency. UNDAC, as a tool of OCHA, also assists in the coordination of incoming international relief at national level and/or at the site of the emergency.

United Nations Human Rights Council

The United Nations Human Rights Council (UNHRC) is a United Nations System inter-governmental body whose 47-member states are responsible for promoting and protecting human rights around the world. The UNHRC has addressed conflicts including the Israeli-Palestinian conflict and also addresses rights-related situations in countries such as in Burma, Guinea, North Korea, Côte d'Ivoire, Kyrgyzstan, Syria, Libya, Iran, and Sri Lanka. The UN General Assembly elects the members who occupy the UNHRC's 47 seats. The UNHRC holds regular sessions three times a year, in March, June, and September. The UNHRC can decide at any time to hold a special session to address human rights violations and emergencies, at the request of one-third of the member states.

World Health Organisation

The WHO Constitution states that its objective is the attainment by all people of the highest possible level of health. WHO works to reduce morbidity and mortality and improve health during key stages of life, including pregnancy, childbirth, the neonatal period, childhood and adolescence, and improve sexual and reproductive health and promote active and healthy aging for all individuals. WHO works to improve nutrition, food safety and food security and to ensure this has a positive effect on public health and sustainable development. The organisation develops and promotes the use of evidence-based tools, norms and standards to support member states to inform health policy options.

United Nations Disarmament Commission

Its goal is to promote nuclear disarmament and non-proliferation and the strengthening of the disarmament regimes in respect to other weapons of mass destruction, chemical and biological weapons. It also promotes disarmament efforts in the area of conventional weapons, especially landmines and small arms, which are often the weapons of choice in contemporary conflicts. The United Nations Office for Disarmament Affairs had originally been established as a department in 1982 upon the recommendation of the General Assembly's second special session on disarmament. UNODA supports the development and implementation of practical disarmament measures after a conflict, such as disarming and demobilising former combatants and helping them to reintegrate in civil society.

United Nations High Commissioner for Refugees

It is a United Nations agency mandated to protect and support refugees at the request of a government or the UN itself and assists in their voluntary repatriation, local integration or resettlement to a third country. The UNHCR has won two Nobel Peace Prizes, once in 1954 and again in 1981. UNHCR was established on 14 December 1950 and succeeded the earlier United Nations Relief and Rehabilitation Administration. The agency is mandated to lead and co-ordinate international action to protect refugees and resolve refugee problems worldwide. Since 1954, the UNHCR Nansen Refugee Award has been annually awarded to a person or an organisation in recognition of outstanding service to the cause of refugees, displaced or stateless people.

Millennium Development Goals

The Millennium Development Goals (MDGs) are eight international development goals that were established following the Millennium Summit of the United Nations in 2000, following the adoption of the United Nations Millennium Declaration. The MDGs originated from the United Nations Millennium Declaration. The Declaration asserted that every individual has dignity; and hence, the right to freedom, equality. It is a basic standard of living that includes freedom from hunger and violence and encourages tolerance and solidarity. The MDG emphasised three areas: human capital, infrastructure and human rights (social, economic and political), with the intent of increasing living standards.

United Nations Population Fund

The United Nations Population Fund (UNFPA), formerly the United Nations Fund for Population Activities, is a UN organisation.

The work of the UNFPA involves promotion of the right of every woman, man and child to enjoy a life of health and equal opportunity. UNFPA began operations in 1969 as the United Nations Fund for Population Activities (the name was changed in 1987) under the administration of the United Nations Development Fund. Its stated mission is to promote the right of every woman, man and child to enjoy a life of health and equal opportunity. UNFPA is the world's largest multilateral source of funding for population and reproductive health programmes.

United Nations Commission on Human Rights

The United Nations Commission on Human Rights was a functional commission within the overall framework of the United Nations from 1946 until it was replaced by the United Nations Human Rights Council in 2006. It was a subsidiary body of the UN Economic and Social Council, and was also assisted in its work by the Office of the United Nations High Commissioner for Human Rights. The Sub-Commission on the Promotion and Protection of Human Rights was the main subsidiary body of the Commission on Human Rights. The Commission on Human Rights established 30 special procedures, or mechanisms, to address specific country situations or thematic issues such as freedom of expression and opinion, torture, the right to food, and the right to education.

The United Nations Democracy Fund

The United Nations Democracy Fund (UNDEF) was established by United Nations Secretary-General Kofi Annan in July 2005 at the African Union Summit in Sirte, Libya, as a United Nations General Trust Fund under his authority. The fund provides assistance to governmental, non-governmental, national, regional, and international organisations, including relevant United Nations departments, offices, funds, programmes and agencies. The United Nations Democracy Fund, UNDEF, supports projects to strengthen democratic development in more than 100 countries. The fund complements current UN efforts to strengthen and expand democracy worldwide.

Universal Declaration of Human Rights

The Universal Declaration of Human Rights (UDHR) is a declaration adopted by the United Nations General Assembly on 10th December 1948 at the Palais de Chaillot, Paris. The adoption of the Universal Declaration is a significant international commemoration marked each year on 10th December, and is known as Human Rights Day or International Human Rights Day. The Declaration consists of thirty articles which have been elaborated in subsequent international treaties, regional human rights instruments, national constitutions, and other laws. The Declaration was commissioned in 1946 and was drafted over two years by the Commission on Human Rights.

United Nations Convention on the Rights of the Child

The United Nations Convention on the Rights of the Child is a human rights treaty which sets out the civil, political, economic, social, health and cultural rights of children. The Convention defines a child as any human being under the age of eighteen, unless the age of majority is attained earlier under a state's own domestic legislation. The Convention deals with the child-specific needs and rights. It requires that states act in the best interests of the child. The Convention obliges states to allow parents to exercise their parental responsibilities. The Convention forbids capital punishment for children.

Universal Declaration of Human Rights

Article	*Statement*
1	All human beings are born free and equal in dignity and rights. They are endowed with reason and conscience and should act towards one another in a spirit of brotherhood.
2	Everyone is entitled to all the rights and freedoms set forth in this Declaration, without distinction of any kind, such as race, colour, sex, language, religion, political or other opinion, national or social origin, property, birth or other status. Furthermore, no distinction shall be made on the basis of the political, jurisdictional or international status of the country or territory to which a person belongs, whether it be independent, trust, non-self-governing or under any other limitation of sovereignty
3	Everyone has the right to life, liberty and security of person.
4	No one shall be held in slavery or servitude; slavery and the slave trade shall be prohibited in all their forms.
5	No one shall be subjected to torture or to cruel, inhuman or degrading treatment or punishment.

(Contd.)

(Contd. Table)

Article	*Statement*
6	Everyone has the right to recognition everywhere as a person before the law.
7	All are equal before the law and are entitled without any discrimination to equal protection of the law. All are entitled to equal protection against any discrimination in violation of this Declaration and against any incitement to such discrimination.
8	Everyone has the right to an effective remedy by the competent national tribunals for acts violating the fundamental rights granted him by the constitution or by law.
9	No one shall be subjected to arbitrary arrest, detention or exile.
10	Everyone is entitled in full equality to a fair and public hearing by an independent and impartial tribunal, in the determination of his rights and obligations and of any criminal charge against him.
11	(1) Everyone charged with a penal offence has the right to be presumed innocent until proved guilty according to law in a public trial at which he has had all the guarantees necessary for his defence. (2) No one shall be held guilty of any penal offence on account of any act or omission which did not constitute a penal offence, under national or international law, at the time when it was committed. Nor shall a heavier penalty be imposed than the one that was applicable at the time the penal offence was committed.
12	No one shall be subjected to arbitrary interference with his privacy, family, home or correspondence, nor to attacks upon his honour and reputation. Everyone has the right to the protection of the law against such interference or attacks.
13	(1) Everyone has the right to freedom of movement and residence within the borders of each state. (2) Everyone has the right to leave any country, including his own, and to return to his country.
14	(1) Everyone has the right to seek and to enjoy in other countries asylum from persecution. (2) This right may not be invoked in the case of prosecutions genuinely arising from

(Contd.)

(Contd. Table)

Article	*Statement*
	non-political crimes or from acts contrary to the purposes and principles of the United Nations.
15	(1) Everyone has the right to a nationality. (2) No one shall be arbitrarily deprived of his nationality nor denied the right to change his nationality.
16	(1) Men and women of full age, without any limitation due to race, nationality or religion, have the right to marry and to found a family. They are entitled to equal rights as to marriage, during marriage and at its dissolution. (2) Marriage shall be entered into only with the free and full consent of the intending spouses. (3) The family is the natural and fundamental group unit of society and is entitled to protection by society and the State.
17	(1) Everyone has the right to own property alone as well as in association with others. (2) No one shall be arbitrarily deprived of his property.
18	Everyone has the right to freedom of thought, conscience and religion; this right includes freedom to change his religion or belief, and freedom, either alone or in community with others and in public or private, to manifest his religion or belief in teaching, practice, worship and observance.
19	Everyone has the right to freedom of opinion and expression; this right includes freedom to hold opinions without interference and to seek, receive and impart information and ideas through any media and regardless of frontiers.
20	(1) Everyone has the right to freedom of peaceful assembly and association. (2) No one may be compelled to belong to an association.
21	(1) Everyone has the right to take part in the government of his country, directly or through freely chosen representatives. (2) Everyone has the right of equal access to public service in his country. (3) The will of the people shall be the basis of the authority of government; this will shall be expressed in periodic and genuine elections which shall be by universal and equal suffrage and shall be held by secret vote or by equivalent free voting procedures.

(Contd.)

(Contd. Table)

Article	*Statement*
22	Everyone, as a member of society, has the right to social security and is entitled to realisation, through national effort and international co-operation and in accordance with the organisation and resources of each State, of the economic, social and cultural rights indispensable for his dignity and the free development of his personality.
23	(1) Everyone has the right to work, to free choice of employment, to just and favourable conditions of work and to protection against unemployment. (2) Everyone, without any discrimination, has the right to equal pay for equal work. (3) Everyone who works has the right to just and favourable remuneration ensuring for himself and his family an existence worthy of human dignity, and supplemented, if necessary, by other means of social protection. (4) Everyone has the right to form and to join trade unions for the protection of his interests.
24	Everyone has the right to rest and leisure, including reasonable limitation of working hours and periodic holidays with pay.
25	(1) Everyone has the right to a standard of living adequate for the health and well-being of himself and of his family, including food, clothing, housing and medical care and necessary social services, and the right to security in the event of unemployment, sickness, disability, widowhood, old age or other lack of livelihood in circumstances beyond his control. (2) Motherhood and childhood are entitled to special care and assistance. All children, whether born in or out of wedlock, shall enjoy the same social protection.
26	(1) Everyone has the right to education. Education shall be free, at least in the elementary and fundamental stages. Elementary education shall be compulsory. Technical and professional education shall be made generally available and higher education shall be equally accessible to all on the basis of merit. (2) Education shall be directed to the full development of the human personality and to the strengthening of respect for human rights and fundamental freedoms. It shall promote understanding, tolerance and

(Contd.)

(Contd. Table)

Article	*Statement*
	friendship among all nations, racial or religious groups, and shall further the activities of the United Nations for the maintenance of peace. (3) Parents have a prior right to choose the kind of education that shall be given to their children.
27	(1) Everyone has the right freely to participate in the cultural life of the community, to enjoy the arts and to share in scientific advancement and its benefits. (2) Everyone has the right to the protection of the moral and material interests resulting from any scientific, literary or artistic production of which he is the author.
28	Everyone is entitled to a social and international order in which the rights and freedoms set forth in this Declaration can be fully realised.
29	(1) Everyone has duties to the community in which alone the free and full development of his personality is possible. (2) In the exercise of his rights and freedoms, everyone shall be subject only to such limitations as are determined by law solely for the purpose of securing due recognition and respect for the rights and freedoms of others and of meeting the just requirements of morality, public order and the general welfare in a democratic society. (3) These rights and freedoms may in no case be exercised contrary to the purposes and principles of the United Nations.
30	Nothing in this Declaration may be interpreted as implying for any State, group or person any right to engage in any activity or to perform any act aimed at the destruction of any of the rights and freedoms set forth herein.

Source: http://www.un.org/en/documents/udhr/#atop

International Covenant on Civil and Political Rights

The *International Covenant on Civil and Political Rights* (ICCPR) was adopted by the United Nations General Assembly on 16th December 1966. The ICCPR was to take effect ten years later in all nations that had become state parties. A sufficient number of states had become parties so the ICCPR took effect as planned in 1976. The United States Senate ratified the ICCPR in June 1992.

(Contd. Table)

Article	*Statement*
	PART 1
1	All peoples have the right of self-determination. By virtue of that right they freely determine their political status and freely pursue their economic, social and cultural development. All peoples may, for their own ends, freely dispose of their natural wealth and resources without prejudice to any obligations arising out of international economic co-operation, based upon the principle of mutual benefit, and international law. In no case may a people be deprived of its own means of subsistence. The States Parties to the present Covenant, including those having responsibility for the administration of Non-Self-Governing and Trust Territories, shall promote the realisation of the right of self-determination, and shall respect that right, in conformity with the provisions of the Charter of the United Nations.
	PART II
2	Each State Party to the present Covenant undertakes to respect and to ensure to all individuals within its territory and subject to its jurisdiction the rights recognised in the present Covenant, without distinction of any kind, such as race, colour, sex, language, religion, political or other opinion, national or social origin, property, birth or other status. Where not already provided for by existing legislative or other measures, each State Party to the present Covenant undertakes to take the necessary steps, in accordance with its constitutional processes and with the provisions of the present Covenant, to adopt such laws or other measures as may be necessary to give effect to the rights recognised in the present Covenant.Each State Party to the present Covenant undertakes: (a) To ensure that any person whose rights or freedoms as herein recognised are violated shall have an effective remedy, notwithstanding that the violation has been committed by persons acting in an official capacity; (b) To ensure that any person claiming such a remedy shall have his right thereto determined by competent judicial, administrative or legislative authorities, or by any other competent authority

(Contd.)

(Contd. Table)

Article	*Statement*
	provided for by the legal system of the State, and to develop the possibilities of judicial remedy; To ensure that the competent authorities shall enforce such remedies when granted.
3	The States Parties to the present Covenant undertake to ensure the equal right of men and women to the enjoyment of all civil and political rights set forth in the present Covenant.
4	In time of public emergency which threatens the life of the nation and the existence of which is officially proclaimed, the States Parties to the present Covenant may take measures derogating from their obligations under the present Covenant to the extent strictly required by the exigencies of the situation, provided that such measures are not inconsistent with their other obligations under international law and do not involve discrimination solely on the ground of race, colour, sex, language, religion or social origin.Any State Party to the present Covenant availing itself of the right of derogation shall immediately inform the other States Parties to the present Covenant, through the intermediary of the Secretary-General of the United Nations, of the provisions from which it has derogated and of the reasons by which it was actuated. A further communication shall be made, through the same intermediary, on the date on which it terminates such derogation.
5	Nothing in the present Covenant may be interpreted as implying for any State, group or person any right to engage in any activity or perform any act aimed at the destruction of any of the rights and freedoms recognised herein or at their limitation to a greater extent than is provided for in the present Covenant. There shall be no restriction upon or derogation from any of the fundamental human rights recognised or existing in any State Party to the present Covenant pursuant to law, conventions, regulations or custom on the pretext that the present Covenant does not recognise such rights or that it recognises them to a lesser extent.

(Contd.)

(Contd. Table)

Article	*Statement*
	PART III
6	Every human being has the inherent right to life. This right shall be protected by law. No one shall be arbitrarily deprived of his life. In countries which have not abolished the death penalty, sentence of death may be imposed only for the most serious crimes in accordance with the law in force at the time of the commission of the crime and not contrary to the provisions of the present Covenant and to the Convention on the Prevention and Punishment of the Crime of Genocide. This penalty can only be carried out pursuant to a final judgement rendered by a competent court. When deprivation of life constitutes the crime of genocide, it is understood that nothing in this article shall authorise any State Party to the present Covenant to derogate in any way from any obligation assumed under the provisions of the Convention on the Prevention and Punishment of the Crime of Genocide. Anyone sentenced to death shall have the right to seek pardon or commutation of the sentence. Amnesty, pardon or commutation of the sentence of death may be granted in all cases. Sentence of death shall not be imposed for crimes committed by persons below eighteen years of age and shall not be carried out on pregnant women. Nothing in this article shall be invoked to delay or to prevent the abolition of capital punishment by any State Party to the present Covenant.
7	No one shall be subjected to torture or to cruel, inhuman or degrading treatment or punishment. In particular, no one shall be subjected without his free consent to medical or scientific experimentation.
8	No one shall be held in slavery; slavery and the slave-trade in all their forms shall be prohibited.
9	Everyone has the right to liberty and security of person. No one shall be subjected to arbitrary arrest or detention. No one shall be deprived of his liberty except on such grounds and in accordance with such procedure as are established by law. Anyone who is arrested shall be informed, at the time of arrest, of the reasons for his arrest and shall be promptly

(Contd.)

(Contd. Table)

Article	*Statement*
	informed of any charges against him. Anyone arrested or detained on a criminal charge shall be brought promptly before a judge or other officer authorised by law to exercise judicial power and shall be entitled to trial within a reasonable time or to release. It shall not be the general rule that persons awaiting trial shall be detained in custody, but release may be subject to guarantees to appear for trial, at any other stage of the judicial proceedings, and, should occasion arise, for execution of the judgement. Anyone who is deprived of his liberty by arrest or detention shall be entitled to take proceedings before a court, in order that that court may decide without delay on the lawfulness of his detention and order his release if the detention is not lawful. Anyone who has been the victim of unlawful arrest or detention shall have an enforceable right to compensation.
10	All persons deprived of their liberty shall be treated with humanity and with respect for the inherent dignity of the human person. Accused persons shall, save in exceptional circumstances, be segregated from convicted persons and shall be subject to separate treatment appropriate to their status as unconvicted persons. Accused juvenile persons shall be separated from adults and brought as speedily as possible for adjudication. The penitentiary system shall comprise treatment of prisoners the essential aim of which shall be their reformation and social rehabilitation. Juvenile offenders shall be segregated from adults and be accorded treatment appropriate to their age and legal status.
11	No one shall be imprisoned merely on the ground of inability to fulfil a contractual obligation.
12	Everyone lawfully within the territory of a State shall, within that territory, have the right to liberty of movement and freedom to choose his residence. Everyone shall be free to leave any country, including his own. The above-mentioned rights shall not be subject to any restrictions except those which are provided by law, are necessary to protect national security, public order (ordre public), public health or morals

(Contd.)

(Contd. Table)

Article	*Statement*
	or the rights and freedoms of others, and are consistent with the other rights recognised in the present Covenant. No one shall be arbitrarily deprived of the right to enter his own country.
13	An alien lawfully in the territory of a State Party to the present Covenant may be expelled there from only in pursuance of a decision reached in accordance with law and shall, except where compelling reasons of national security otherwise require, be allowed to submit the reasons against his expulsion and to have his case reviewed by, and be represented for the purpose before, the competent authority or a person or persons especially designated by the competent authority.
14	All persons shall be equal before the courts and tribunals. In the determination of any criminal charge against him, or of his rights and obligations in a suit at law, everyone shall be entitled to a fair and public hearing by a competent, independent and impartial tribunal established by law. The press and the public may be excluded from all or part of a trial for reasons of morals, public order (ordre public) or national security in a democratic society, or when the interest of the private lives of the parties so requires, or to the extent strictly necessary in the opinion of the court in special circumstances where publicity would prejudice the interests of justice; but any judgement rendered in a criminal case or in a suit at law shall be made public except where the interest of juvenile persons otherwise requires or the proceedings concern matrimonial disputes or the guardianship of children.
15	No one shall be held guilty of any criminal offence on account of any act or omission which did not constitute a criminal offence, under national or international law, at the time when it was committed. Nor shall a heavier penalty be imposed than the one that was applicable at the time when the criminal offence was committed. If, subsequent to the commission of the offence, provision is made by law for the imposition of the lighter penalty, the offender shall benefit thereby. Nothing

(Contd.)

(Contd. Table)

Article	*Statement*
	in this article shall prejudice the trial and punishment of any person for any act or omission which, at the time when it was committed, was criminal according to the general principles of law recognised by the community of nations.
16	Everyone shall have the right to recognition everywhere as a person before the law.
17	No one shall be subjected to arbitrary or unlawful interference with his privacy, family, home or correspondence, nor to unlawful attacks on his honour and reputation. Everyone has the right to the protection of the law against such interference or attacks.
18	Everyone shall have the right to freedom of thought, conscience and religion. This right shall include freedom to have or to adopt a religion or belief of his choice, and freedom, either individually or in community with others and in public or private, to manifest his religion or belief in worship, observance, practice and teaching. No one shall be subject to coercion which would impair his freedom to have or to adopt a religion or belief of his choice. Freedom to manifest one's religion or beliefs may be subject only to such limitations as are prescribed by law and are necessary to protect public safety, order, health, or morals or the fundamental rights and freedoms of others. The States Parties to the present Covenant undertake to have respect for the liberty of parents and, when applicable, legal guardians to ensure the religious and moral education of their children in conformity with their own convictions.
19	Everyone shall have the right to hold opinions without interference. Everyone shall have the right to freedom of expression; this right shall include freedom to seek, receive and impart information and ideas of all kinds, regardless of frontiers, either orally, in writing or in print, in the form of art, or through any other media of his choice. The exercise of the rights provided for in paragraph 2 of this article carries with it special duties and responsibilities.

(Contd.)

(Contd. Table)

Article	*Statement*
20	Any propaganda for war shall be prohibited by law. Any advocacy of national, racial or religious hatred that constitutes incitement to discrimination, hostility or violence shall be prohibited by law.
21	The right of peaceful assembly shall be recognised. No restrictions may be placed on the exercise of this right other than those imposed in conformity with the law and which are necessary in a democratic society in the interests of national security or public safety, public order (ordre public), the protection of public health or morals or the protection of the rights and freedoms of others.
22	Everyone shall have the right to freedom of association with others, including the right to form and join trade unions for the protection of his interests. No restrictions may be placed on the exercise of this right other than those which are prescribed by law and which are necessary in a democratic society in the interests of national security or public safety, public order (ordre public), the protection of public health or morals or the protection of the rights and freedoms of others. This article shall not prevent the imposition of lawful restrictions on members of the armed forces and of the police in their exercise of this right. Nothing in this article shall authorise States Parties to the International Labour Organisation Convention of 1948 concerning Freedom of Association and Protection of the Right to Organise to take legislative measures which would prejudice, or to apply the law in such a manner as to prejudice, the guarantees provided for in that Convention.
23	The family is the natural and fundamental group unit of society and is entitled to protection by society and the State. The right of men and women of marriageable age to marry and to found a family shall be recognised. No marriage shall be entered into without the free and full consent of the intending spouses. States Parties to the present Covenant shall take appropriate steps to ensure equality of rights and

(Contd.)

(Contd. Table)

Article	*Statement*
	responsibilities of spouses as to marriage, during marriage and at its dissolution. In the case of dissolution, provision shall be made for the necessary protection of any children.
24	Every child shall have, without any discrimination as to race, colour, sex, language, religion, national or social origin, property or birth, the right to such measures of protection as are required by his status as a minor, on the part of his family, society and the State. Every child shall be registered immediately after birth and shall have a name. Every child has the right to acquire a nationality.
25	Every citizen shall have the right and the opportunity, without any of the distinctions mentioned in article 2 and without unreasonable restrictions: (a) To take part in the conduct of public affairs, directly or through freely chosen representatives; (b) To vote and to be elected at genuine periodic elections which shall be by universal and equal suffrage and shall be held by secret ballot, guaranteeing the free expression of the will of the electors; (c) To have access, on general terms of equality, to public service in his country.
26	All persons are equal before the law and are entitled without any discrimination to the equal protection of the law. In this respect, the law shall prohibit any discrimination and guarantee to all persons equal and effective protection against discrimination on any ground such as race, colour, sex, language, religion, political or other opinion, national or social origin, property, birth or other status.
27	In those States in which ethnic, religious or linguistic minorities exist, persons belonging to such minorities shall not be denied the right, in community with the other members of their group, to enjoy their own culture, to profess and practise their own religion, or to use their own language.
	PART IV
28	There shall be established a Human Rights Committee (hereafter referred to in the present Covenant as the Committee). It shall consist of eighteen members and shall carry out the functions hereinafter provided. The Committee

(Contd.)

(Contd. Table)

Article	*Statement*
	shall be composed of nationals of the States Parties to the present Covenant who shall be persons of high moral character and recognised competence in the field of human rights, consideration being given to the usefulness of the participation of some persons having legal experience. The members of the Committee shall be elected and shall serve in their personal capacity.
29	The members of the Committee shall be elected by secret ballot from a list of persons possessing the qualifications prescribed in article 28 and nominated for the purpose by the States Parties to the present Covenant. Each State Party to the present Covenant may nominate not more than two persons. These persons shall be nationals of the nominating State. A person shall be eligible for renomination.
30	The initial election shall be held no later than six months after the date of the entry into force of the present Covenant. At least four months before the date of each election to the Committee, other than an election to fill a vacancy declared in accordance with article 34, the Secretary-General of the United Nations shall address a written invitation to the States Parties to the present Covenant to submit their nominations for membership of the Committee within three months.The Secretary-General of the United Nations shall prepare a list in alphabetical order of all the persons thus nominated, with an indication of the States Parties which have nominated them, and shall submit it to the States Parties to the present Covenant no later than one month before the date of each election. Elections of the members of the Committee shall be held at a meeting of the States Parties to the present Covenant convened by the Secretary General of the United Nations at the Headquarters of the United Nations. At that meeting, for which two thirds of the States Parties to the present Covenant shall constitute a quorum, the persons elected to the Committee shall be those nominees who obtain the largest number of votes and an absolute majority of the votes of the representatives of States Parties present and voting.

(Contd.)

(Contd. Table)

Article	*Statement*
31	The Committee may not include more than one national of the same State. In the election of the Committee, consideration shall be given to equitable geographical distribution of membership and to the representation of the different forms of civilisation and of the principal legal systems.
32	The members of the Committee shall be elected for a term of four years. They shall be eligible for re-election if renominated. However, the terms of nine of the members elected at the first election shall expire at the end of two years; immediately after the first election, the names of these nine members shall be chosen by lot by the Chairman of the meeting referred to in article 30, paragraph 4.
33	If, in the unanimous opinion of the other members, a member of the Committee has ceased to carry out his functions for any cause other than absence of a temporary character, the Chairman of the Committee shall notify the Secretary-General of the United Nations, who shall then declare the seat of that member to be vacant. In the event of the death or the resignation of a member of the Committee, the Chairman shall immediately notify the Secretary-General of the United Nations, who shall declare the seat vacant from the date of death or the date on which the resignation takes effect.
34	When a vacancy is declared in accordance with article 33 and if the term of office of the member to be replaced does not expire within six months of the declaration of the vacancy, the Secretary-General of the United Nations shall notify each of the States Parties to the present Covenant, which may within two months submit nominations in accordance with article 29 for the purpose of filling the vacancy. The Secretary-General of the United Nations shall prepare a list in alphabetical order of the persons thus nominated and shall submit it to the States Parties to the present Covenant. The election to fill the vacancy shall then take place in accordance with the relevant provisions of this part of the present Covenant. A member of the Committee elected to fill a vacancy declared in accordance with article 33 shall hold office for

(Contd.)

(Contd. Table)

Article	*Statement*
	the remainder of the term of the member who vacated the seat on the Committee under the provisions of that article.
35	The members of the Committee shall, with the approval of the General Assembly of the United Nations, receive emoluments from United Nations resources on such terms and conditions as the General Assembly may decide, having regard to the importance of the Committee's responsibilities.
36	The Secretary-General of the United Nations shall provide the necessary staff and facilities for the effective performance of the functions of the Committee under the present Covenant.
37	The Secretary-General of the United Nations shall convene the initial meeting of the Committee at the Headquarters of the United Nations. After its initial meeting, the Committee shall meet at such times as shall be provided in its rules of procedure. The Committee shall normally meet at the Headquarters of the United Nations or at the United Nations Office at Geneva.
38	Every member of the Committee shall, before taking up his duties, make a solemn declaration in open committee that he will perform his functions impartially and conscientiously.
39	The Committee shall elect its officers for a term of two years. They may be re-elected. The Committee shall establish its own rules of procedure, but these rules shall provide, inter alia, that: (a) Twelve members shall constitute a quorum; Decisions of the Committee shall be made by a majority vote of the members present.
40	The States Parties to the present Covenant undertake to submit reports on the measures they have adopted which give effect to the rights recognised herein and on the progress made in the enjoyment of those rights: (a) Within one year of the entry into force of the present Covenant for the States Parties concerned; (b) Thereafter whenever the Committee so requests. All reports shall be submitted to the Secretary-General of the United Nations, who shall transmit them to the Committee for consideration. Reports shall indicate the factors and difficulties, if any, affecting the implementation of the present

(Contd.)

(Contd. Table)

Article	*Statement*
	Covenant. The Secretary-General of the United Nations may, after consultation with the Committee, transmit to the specialised agencies concerned copies of such parts of the reports as may fall within their field of competence. The Committee shall study the reports submitted by the States Parties to the present Covenant. It shall transmit its reports, and such general comments as it may consider appropriate, to the States Parties. The Committee may also transmit to the Economic and Social Council these comments along with the copies of the reports it has received from States Parties to the present Covenant. The States Parties to the present Covenant may submit to the Committee observations on any comments that may be made in accordance with paragraph 4 of this article.
41	A State Party to the present Covenant may at any time declare under this article that it recognises the competence of the Committee to receive and consider communications to the effect that a State Party claims that another State Party is not fulfilling its obligations under the present Covenant. Communications under this article may be received and considered only if submitted by a State Party which has made a declaration recognising in regard to itself the competence of the Committee.
42	If a matter referred to the Committee in accordance with article 41 is not resolved to the satisfaction of the States Parties concerned, the Committee may, with the prior consent of the States Parties concerned, appoint an ad hoc Conciliation Commission (hereinafter referred to as the Commission). The good offices of the Commission shall be made available to the States Parties concerned with a view to an amicable solution of the matter on the basis of respect for the present Covenant. The Commission shall consist of five persons acceptable to the States Parties concerned. If the States Parties concerned fail to reach agreement within three months on all or part of the composition of the Commission, the members of the Commission concerning whom no agreement has been

(Contd.)

(Contd. Table)

Article	*Statement*
	reached shall be elected by secret ballot by a two-thirds majority vote of the Committee from among its members.
43	The members of the Committee, and of the ad hoc conciliation commissions which may be appointed under article 42, shall be entitled to the facilities, privileges and immunities of experts on mission for the United Nations as laid down in the relevant sections of the Convention on the Privileges and Immunities of the United Nations.
44	The provisions for the implementation of the present Covenant shall apply without prejudice to the procedures prescribed in the field of human rights by or under the constituent instruments and the conventions of the United Nations and of the specialised agencies and shall not prevent the States Parties to the present Covenant from having recourse to other procedures for settling a dispute in accordance with general or special international agreements in force between them.
45	The Committee shall submit to the General Assembly of the United Nations, through the Economic and Social Council, an annual report on its activities.
	PART V
46	Nothing in the present Covenant shall be interpreted as impairing the provisions of the Charter of the United Nations and of the constitutions of the specialised agencies which define the respective responsibilities of the various organs of the United Nations and of the specialised agencies in regard to the matters dealt with in the present Covenant.
47	Nothing in the present Covenant shall be interpreted as impairing the inherent right of all peoples to enjoy and utilise fully and freely their natural wealth and resources.
	PART VI
48	The present Covenant is open for signature by any State Member of the United Nations or member of any of its specialised agencies, by any State Party to the Statute of the International Court of Justice, and by any other State which has been invited by the General Assembly of the United Nations to become a Party to the present Covenant. The

(Contd.)

(Contd. Table)

Article	*Statement*
	present Covenant is subject to ratification. Instruments of ratification shall be deposited with the Secretary-General of the United Nations.
49	The present Covenant shall enter into force three months after the date of the deposit with the Secretary-General of the United Nations of the thirty-fifth instrument of ratification or instrument of accession. For each State ratifying the present Covenant or acceding to it after the deposit of the thirty-fifth instrument of ratification or instrument of accession, the present Covenant shall enter into force three months after the date of the deposit of its own instrument of ratification or instrument of accession.
50	The provisions of the present Covenant shall extend to all parts of federal States without any limitations or exceptions.
51	Any State Party to the present Covenant may propose an amendment and file it with the Secretary-General of the United Nations. The Secretary-General of the United Nations shall thereupon communicate any proposed amendments to the States Parties to the present Covenant with a request that they notify him whether they favour a conference of States Parties for the purpose of considering and voting upon the proposals. In the event that at least one third of the States Parties favours such a conference, the Secretary-General shall convene the conference under the auspices of the United Nations. Any amendment adopted by a majority of the States Parties present and voting at the conference shall be submitted to the General Assembly of the United Nations for approval. Amendments shall come into force when they have been approved by the General Assembly of the United Nations and accepted by a two-thirds majority of the States Parties to the present Covenant in accordance with their respective constitutional processes. 3. When amendments come into force, they shall be binding on those States Parties which have accepted them, other States Parties still being bound by the provisions of the present Covenant and any earlier amendment which they have accepted.

(Contd.)

(Contd. Table)

Article	Statement
52	Irrespective of the notifications made under article 48, paragraph 5, the Secretary-General of the United Nations shall inform all States referred to in paragraph 1 of the same article of the following particulars: (a) Signatures, ratifications and accessions under article 48; (b) The date of the entry into force of the present Covenant under article 49 and the date of the entry into force of any amendments under article 51.
53	The present Covenant, of which the Chinese, English, French, Russian and Spanish texts are equally authentic, shall be deposited in the archives of the United Nations. The Secretary-General of the United Nations shall transmit certified copies of the present Covenant to all States referred to in article 48.

Source: http://www.ohchr.org/EN/ProfessionalInterest/Pages/CCPR.aspx

International Covenant on Economic, Social and Cultural Rights

It is a multilateral treaty adopted by the United Nations General Assembly on 16th December 1966, and in force from 3rd January 1976 (International Covenant on Economic, Social and Cultural Rights, 2014). The Covenant is monitored by the UN Committee on Economic, Social and Cultural Rights. The ICESCR has its roots in the same process that led to the Universal Declaration of Human Rights.

Article	Statement
1	All peoples have the right of self-determination. By virtue of that right they freely determine their political status and freely pursue their economic, social and cultural development. All peoples may, for their own ends, freely dispose of their natural wealth and resources without prejudice to any obligations arising out of international economic co-operation, based upon the principle of mutual benefit, and international law. In no case may a people be deprived of its own means of subsistence. The States Parties to the present Covenant,

(Contd.)

(Contd. Table)

Article	*Statement*
	including those having responsibility for the administration of Non-Self-Governing and Trust Territories, shall promote the realisation of the right of self-determination, and shall respect that right, in conformity with the provisions of the Charter of the United Nations.
2	Each State Party to the present Covenant undertakes to take steps, individually and through international assistance and co-operation, especially economic and technical, to the maximum of its available resources, with a view to achieving progressively the full realisation of the rights recognised in the present Covenant by all appropriate means, including particularly the adoption of legislative measures. The States Parties to the present Covenant undertake to guarantee that the rights enunciated in the present Covenant will be exercised without discrimination of any kind as to race, colour, sex, language, religion, political or other opinion, national or social origin, property, birth or other status. Developing countries, with due regard to human rights and their national economy, may determine to what extent they would guarantee the economic rights recognised in the present Covenant to non-nationals.
3	The States Parties to the present Covenant undertake to ensure the equal right of men and women to the enjoyment of all economic, social and cultural rights set forth in the present Covenant.
4	The States Parties to the present Covenant recognise that, in the enjoyment of those rights provided by the State in conformity with the present Covenant, the State may subject such rights only to such limitations as are determined by law only in so far as this may be compatible with the nature of these rights and solely for the purpose of promoting the general welfare in a democratic society.
5	Nothing in the present Covenant may be interpreted as implying for any State, group or person any right to engage in any activity or to perform any act aimed at the destruction of any of the rights or freedoms recognised herein, or at

(Contd.)

(Contd. Table)

Article	*Statement*
	their limitation to a greater extent than is provided for in the present Covenant. No restriction upon or derogation from any of the fundamental human rights recognised or existing in any country in virtue of law, conventions, regulations or custom shall be admitted on the pretext that the present Covenant does not recognise such rights or that it recognises them to a lesser extent.
6	The States Parties to the present Covenant recognise the right to work, which includes the right of everyone to the opportunity to gain his living by work which he freely chooses or accepts, and will take appropriate steps to safeguard this right. The steps to be taken by a State Party to the present Covenant to achieve the full realisation of this right shall include technical and vocational guidance and training programmes, policies and techniques to achieve steady economic, social and cultural development and full and productive employment under conditions safeguarding fundamental political and economic freedoms to the individual.
7	The States Parties to the present Covenant recognise the right of everyone to the enjoyment of just and favourable conditions of work which ensure, in particular: (a) Remuneration which provides all workers, as a minimum; (b) Safe and healthy working conditions; (c) Equal opportunity for everyone to be promoted in his employment to an appropriate higher level, subject to no considerations other than those of seniority and competence; (d) Rest, leisure and reasonable limitation of working hours and periodic holidays with pay, as well as remuneration for public holidays.
8	The States Parties to the present Covenant undertake to ensure: (a) The right of everyone to form trade unions and join the trade union of his choice, subject only to the rules of the organisation concerned, for the promotion and protection of his economic and social interests. No restrictions may be placed on the exercise of this right other than those prescribed by law and which are necessary in a democratic society in

(Contd.)

(Contd. Table)

Article	*Statement*
	the interests of national security or public order or for the protection of the rights and freedoms of others; (b) The right of trade unions to establish national federations or confederations and the right of the latter to form or join international trade-union organisations; (c) The right of trade unions to function freely subject to no limitations other than those prescribed by law and which are necessary in a democratic society in the interests of national security or public order or for the protection of the rights and freedoms of others; (d) The right to strike, provided that it is exercised in conformity with the laws of the particular country.This article shall not prevent the imposition of lawful restrictions on the exercise of these rights by members of the armed forces or of the police or of the administration of the State. 3. Nothing in this article shall authorise States Parties to the International Labour Organisation Convention of 1948 concerning Freedom of Association and Protection of the Right to Organise to take legislative measures which would prejudice, or apply the law in such a manner as would prejudice, the guarantees provided for in that Convention.
9	The States Parties to the present Covenant recognise the right of everyone to social security, including social insurance.
10	The States Parties to the present Covenant recognise that: (a) The widest possible protection and assistance should be accorded to the family, which is the natural and fundamental group unit of society, particularly for its establishment and while it is responsible for the care and education of dependent children. Marriage must be entered into with the free consent of the intending spouses. (b) Special protection should be accorded to mothers during a reasonable period before and after childbirth. During such period working mothers should be accorded paid leave or leave with adequate social security benefits. (c) Special measures of protection and assistance should be taken on behalf of all children and young persons without any discrimination for reasons of parentage or other conditions. Children and young persons should be protected

(Contd.)

(Contd. Table)

Article	*Statement*
	from economic and social exploitation. Their employment in work harmful to their morals or health or dangerous to life or likely to hamper their normal development should be punishable by law. States should also set age limits below which the paid employment of child labour should be prohibited and punishable by law.
11	The States Parties to the present Covenant recognise the right of everyone to an adequate standard of living for himself and his family, including adequate food, clothing and housing, and to the continuous improvement of living conditions. The States Parties will take appropriate steps to ensure the realisation of this right, recognising to this effect the essential importance of international cooperation based on free consent. The States Parties to the present Covenant, recognising the fundamental right of everyone to be free from hunger, shall take, individually and through international co-operation, the measures, including specific programmes, which are needed: (a) To improve methods of production, conservation and distribution of food by making full use of technical and scientific knowledge, by disseminating knowledge of the principles of nutrition and by developing or reforming agrarian systems in such a way as to achieve the most efficient development and utilisation of natural resources; (b) Taking into account the problems of both food-importing and food-exporting countries, to ensure an equitable distribution of world food supplies in relation to need.
12	The States Parties to the present Covenant recognise the right of everyone to the enjoyment of the highest attainable standard of physical and mental health. The steps to be taken by the States Parties to the present Covenant to achieve the full realisation of this right shall include those necessary for: (a) The provision for the reduction of the stillbirth-rate and of infant mortality and for the healthy development of the child; (b) The improvement of all aspects of environmental and industrial hygiene; (c) The prevention, treatment and control of epidemic, endemic, occupational and other diseases;

(Contd.)

(Contd. Table)

Article	*Statement*
	(d) The creation of conditions which would assure to all medical service and medical attention in the event of sickness
13	The States Parties to the present Covenant recognise the right of everyone to education. They agree that education shall be directed to the full development of the human personality and the sense of its dignity, and shall strengthen the respect for human rights and fundamental freedoms. They further agree that education shall enable all persons to participate effectively in a free society, promote understanding, tolerance and friendship among all nations and all racial, ethnic or religious groups, and further the activities of the United Nations for the maintenance of peace.
14	Each State Party to the present Covenant which, at the time of becoming a Party, has not been able to secure in its metropolitan territory or other territories under its jurisdiction compulsory primary education, free of charge, undertakes, within two years, to work out and adopt a detailed plan of action for the progressive implementation, within a reasonable number of years, to be fixed in the plan, of the principle of compulsory education free of charge for all.
15	The States Parties to the present Covenant recognise the right of everyone: (a) To take part in cultural life; (b) To enjoy the benefits of scientific progress and its applications; (c) To benefit from the protection of the moral and material interests resulting from any scientific, literary or artistic production of which he is the author. The steps to be taken by the States Parties to the present Covenant to achieve the full realisation of this right shall include those necessary for the conservation, the development and the diffusion of science and culture. The States Parties to the present Covenant undertake to respect the freedom indispensable for scientific research and creative activity. The States Parties to the present Covenant recognise the benefits to be derived from the encouragement and development of international contacts and co-operation in the scientific and cultural fields.

(Contd.)

(Contd. Table)

Article	*Statement*
16	The States Parties to the present Covenant undertake to submit in conformity with this part of the Covenant reports on the measures which they have adopted and the progress made in achieving the observance of the rights recognised herein.
17	The States Parties to the present Covenant shall furnish their reports in stages, in accordance with a programme to be established by the Economic and Social Council within one year of the entry into force of the present Covenant after consultation with the States Parties and the specialised agencies concerned.
18	Pursuant to its responsibilities under the Charter of the United Nations in the field of human rights and fundamental freedoms, the Economic and Social Council may make arrangements with the specialised agencies in respect of their reporting to it on the progress made in achieving the observance of the provisions of the present Covenant falling within the scope of their activities. These reports may include particulars of decisions and recommendations on such implementation adopted by their competent organs.
19	The Economic and Social Council may transmit to the Commission on Human Rights for study and general recommendation or, as appropriate, for information the reports concerning human rights submitted by States in accordance with articles 16 and 17, and those concerning human rights submitted by the specialised agencies in accordance with article 18.
20	The States Parties to the present Covenant and the specialised agencies concerned may submit comments to the Economic and Social Council on any general recommendation under article 19 or reference to such general recommendation in any report of the Commission on Human Rights or any documentation referred to therein.
21	The Economic and Social Council may submit from time to time to the General Assembly reports with recommendations of a general nature and a summary of the information received from the States Parties to the present Covenant and the

(Contd.)

(Contd. Table)

Article	*Statement*
	specialised agencies on the measures taken and the progress made in achieving general observance of the rights recognised in the present Covenant.
22	The Economic and Social Council may bring to the attention of other organs of the United Nations, their subsidiary organs and specialised agencies concerned with furnishing technical assistance any matters arising out of the reports referred to in this part of the present Covenant which may assist such bodies in deciding, each within its field of competence, on the advisability of international measures likely to contribute to the effective progressive implementation of the present Covenant.
23	The States Parties to the present Covenant agree that international action for the achievement of the rights recognised in the present Covenant includes such methods as the conclusion of conventions, the adoption of recommendations, the furnishing of technical assistance and the holding of regional meetings and technical meetings for the purpose of consultation and study organised in conjunction with the Governments concerned.
24	Nothing in the present Covenant shall be interpreted as impairing the provisions of the Charter of the United Nations and of the constitutions of the specialised agencies which define the respective responsibilities of the various organs of the United Nations and of the specialised agencies in regard to the matters dealt with in the present Covenant.
25	Nothing in the present Covenant shall be interpreted as impairing the inherent right of all peoples to enjoy and utilise fully and freely their natural wealth and resources.
26	The present Covenant is open for signature by any State Member of the United Nations or member of any of its specialised agencies, by any State Party to the Statute of the International Court of Justice, and by any other State which has been invited by the General Assembly of the United Nations to become a party to the present Covenant.

(Contd.)

(Contd. Table)

Article	*Statement*
27	The present Covenant shall enter into force three months after the date of the deposit with the Secretary-General of the United Nations of the thirty-fifth instrument of ratification or instrument of accession. For each State ratifying the present Covenant or acceding to it after the deposit of the thirty-fifth instrument of ratification or instrument of accession, the present Covenant shall enter into force three months after the date of the deposit of its own instrument of ratification or instrument of accession.
28	The provisions of the present Covenant shall extend to all parts of federal States without any limitations or exceptions.
29	Any State Party to the present Covenant may propose an amendment and file it with the Secretary-General of the United Nations. The Secretary-General shall thereupon communicate any proposed amendments to the States Parties to the present Covenant with a request that they notify him whether they favour a conference of States Parties for the purpose of considering and voting upon the proposals. In the event that at least one third of the States Parties favours such a conference, the Secretary-General shall convene the conference under the auspices of the United Nations. Any amendment adopted by a majority of the States Parties present and voting at the conference shall be submitted to the General Assembly of the United Nations for approval.
30	Irrespective of the notifications made under article 26, paragraph 5, the Secretary-General of the United Nations shall inform all States referred to in paragraph 1 of the same article of the following particulars: (a) Signatures, ratifications and accessions under article 26; (b) The date of the entry into force of the present Covenant under article 27 and the date of the entry into force of any amendments under article 29.
31	The present Covenant, of which the Chinese, English, French, Russian and Spanish texts are equally authentic, shall be deposited in the archives of the United Nations.

Source: http://www.ohchr.org/Documents/ProfessionalInterest/cescr.pdf

Conclusion

The United Nations is an international organisation of countries. It was created for many reasons: (a) There should be peace and security in the world after the Second World War; (b) Countries should be friendly to each other; (c) Countries should help each other solve problems; (d) Human rights should be respected everywhere in the world. UNICEF was created by the United Nations General Assembly on December 11, 1946, to provide emergency food and healthcare to children in countries. The United Nations Disaster Assessment and Coordination is part of the international emergency response system for sudden-onset emergencies. It is designed to help the United Nations and governments of disaster-affected countries during the first phase of a sudden-onset emergency. The United Nations Human Rights Council is a United Nations System inter-governmental body whose 47-member states are responsible for promoting and protecting human rights around the world.

The WHO Constitution states that its objective is the attainment by all people of the highest possible level of health. The Millennium Development Goals are eight international development goals that were established following the Millennium Summit of the United Nations in 2000, following the adoption of the United Nations Millennium Declaration. The United Nations Population Fund is a UN organisation. The United Nations Commission on Human Rights was a functional commission within the overall framework of the United Nations from 1946 until it was replaced by the United Nations Human Rights Council in 2006. The United Nations Convention on the Rights of the Child is a human rights treaty which sets out the civil, political, economic, social, health and cultural rights of children.

References

1. *Dumbarton Oaks Conference* (2015), Retrieved from http://en.wikipedia.org/wiki/Dumbarton_Oaks_Conference
2. *International Court of Justice* (2015), Retrieved from http://en.wikipedia.org/wiki/International_Court_of_Justice
3. International Gay and Lesbian Human Rights Commission (2014), Retrieved from https://www.linkedin.com/company/international-gay-and-lesbian-human-rights-commission

4. *International Lesbian, Gay, Bisexual, Trans and Intersex Association* (2015), Retrieved from http://en.wikipedia.org/wiki/International_Lesbian,_Gay,_Bisexual,_Trans_and_Intersex_Association
5. *International Society for Human Rights* (2015), Retrieved from http://en.wikipedia.org/wiki/International_Society_for_Human_Rights
6. *Millennium Development Goals* (2015), Retrieved from http://en.wikipedia.org/wiki/Millennium_Development_Goals
7. *The United Nations Democracy Fund* (2015), Retrieved from http://en.wikipedia.org/wiki/United_Nations_Democracy_Fund
8. *UN Office for Disarmament Affairs* (2015), Retrieved from http://en.wikipedia.org/wiki/United_Nations_Office_for_Disarmament_Affairs
9. *United Nations* (2015), Retrieved from http://en.wikipedia.org/wiki/United_Nations
10. *United Nations* (2015), Retrieved from http://www.english-online.at/government/united-nations/un.htm
11. *United Nations Children's Fund* (2014), Retrieved from http://en.wikipedia.org/wiki/UNICEF
12. *United Nations Commission on Human Rights* (2014), Retrieved from http://en.wikipedia.org/wiki/United_Nations_Commission_ on_Human_Rights
13. *United Nations Convention on the Rights of the Child* (2014), *Retrieved from http://en.wikipedia.org/wiki/Convention_on_the_Rights_of_the_Child*
14. *United Nations Disaster Assessment and Coordination* (2015), Retrieved from http://en.wikipedia.org/wiki/United_Nations_ Disaster_ Assessment_and_Coordination
15. *United Nations Disaster Assessment and Coordination* (2015), Retrieved from http://reliefweb.int/report/world/united-nations-disaster-assessment-and-coordination-undac
16. *United Nations Economic and Social Council* (2015), Retrieved from http://en.wikipedia.org/wiki/United_Nations_Economic_and_Social_Council
17. *United Nations General Assembly* (2015), Retrieved from http://en.wikipedia.org/wiki/United_Nations_General_Assembly
18. *United Nations High Commissioner for Refugees* (2015), Retrieved from http://en.wikipedia.org/wiki/United_Nations_High_Commissioner_for_Refugees
19. *United Nations Human Rights Council* (2015), Retrieved from http://en.wikipedia.org/wiki/United_Nations_Human_Rights_Council
20. *United Nations Population Fund* (2015), Retrieved from http://en.wikipedia.org/wiki/United_Nations_Population_Fund
21. *United Nations Security Council* (2015), Retrieved from http://en.wikipedia.org/wiki/United_Nations_Security_Council

22. Universal Declaration of Human Rights (2015), Retrieved from http://en.wikipedia.org/wiki/Universal_Declaration_of_Human_Rights
23. *World Health Organisation* (2015), *Retrieved from http://en.wikipedia.org/wiki/World_Health_Organisation*

3

Children Rights

"The Charter of the United Nations expresses the noblest aspirations of man: abjuration of force in the settlement of disputes between states; the assurance of human rights and fundamental freedoms for all without distinction as to race, sex, language or religion; the safeguarding of international peace and security."

-Haile Selassie

Introduction

The United Nations Convention on the Rights of the Child defines *child* as "a human being below the age of 18 years unless under the law applicable to the child, majority is attained earlier". This is ratified by 192 of 194 member countries. Biologically, a child is generally anyone between birth and puberty or in the developmental stage of childhood, between infancy and adulthood. Every child goes through many stages of social development. An infant or very young child will play alone happily. There are many social issues that affect children. They are such as childhood education, bullying, child poverty, dysfunctional families and in developing countries, hunger. Social attitudes toward children differ around the world in various cultures. These attitudes have changed over time. Data from UNICEF indicate that in 2011, 57 million children were out of school; and more than 20 per cent of African children have never attended primary school or have left without completing primary education.

Rights are what should have or be able to do to have the best start in life. These rights are listed in the UN Convention on the

Rights of the Child. All rights are equally important and are connected to each other. Human are born with these rights, and no one can take them away. Many adults are responsible to help protect their rights and do what is best for you. Governments have the main responsibility to make sure the rights of children in the Convention on the Rights of the Child are protected and provided for. All citizens have responsibilities to respect the rights of children as well. Children can show their respect for the rights of others in different ways.

What is Children Rights?

United Nations in 1989 adopted a historic agreement: the Convention on the Rights of the Child (CRC). The Convention defines a child as a human being up to the age of 18. The idea that children have special needs has now given way to the conviction that children have the same spectrum of rights as adults: civil and political, social, cultural and economic. Under the Convention, children's rights should be implemented without discrimination of any kind, all actions and policies should be guided by the best interests of the child, the participation of children should always be sought and all actions should aim at the promotion of the survival and development of children. The Convention clearly states that all children have rights that are inherent human rights, and that these should not be perceived as optional, as a question of favour or kindness to children, or as an expression of charity. These rights generate obligations and responsibilities.

All children have the right to protection. They have the right to survive, to be safe, to belong, to be heard, to receive adequate care and to grow up in a protective environment. A family is the first line of protection for children. Parents or other caregivers are responsible for building a protective and loving home environment. Schools and communities are responsible for building a safe and child-friendly environment outside the child's home. Millions of children are not fully protected. Many of them deal with violence, abuse, neglect, exploitation, exclusion and/or discrimination every day.

Importance of Children in Society

Children are our future. What happens to children in their first days, months and years of life affects their development, the development of our society, and the development of our world. Children are important because they are the future leaders. Some may become nation leaders while others may become leaders in the sense that they will be the ones who will nurture the next generation. Leaders, be it as the nation's top administrator or a husband/wife are leaders all the same. The most apparent issues concerning children nowadays are issues of low self-esteem. Kids emulate everything they see, hear and things that adults do. Children are the greatest gift to humanity and childhood is an important and impressionable stage of human development as it holds the potential to the future development of any society. Children who are brought up in an environment, which is conducive to their intellectual, physical and social health, grow up to be responsible and productive members of society. Every nation links its future with the present status of its children.

Child development refers to the changes that occur as a child grows and develops in relation to being physically healthy, mentally alert, emotionally sound, socially competent and ready to learn. The first five years of a child's life are fundamentally important. They are the foundation that shapes children's future health, happiness, growth, development and learning achievement at school, in the family and community, and in life in general. Children are the ones who are very vital for deciding how the world will go in future. Education has to be aimed at the overall development of child. Rural areas have been major victim of lack of educational facilities, that's where most of the children are deprived of even the basic education. And coming to the urban life it's totally insane. Children are a means of cheap labour who rarely speak against their masters. Lack of basic education has been a hindrance to many and at most occasion's uneducated people get cheated easily.

Investing financial resources to help children survive and develop to their full potential is, first and foremost, a moral imperative. But investing in children is also important on practical grounds. It yields positive benefits to economies and societies. Since the foundation of an individual's health and well-being is laid in early childhood, the most opportune time to break the cycle of poverty, or prevent it from beginning, is during that time. Children are born ready to learn and interested in the world around them. It is natural for them to use all their abilities to learn. From birth, children are learning about themselves, other people and the world around them, and playing an active role in their own learning and development. Health and physical wellbeing are the basis for all learning and development. Such areas as eating habits, attitudes towards exercise and self-care routines build from the child's earliest experiences.

The tradition of family life is broken. Children frequently grow up in a broken family structure. Children today often must learn to survive at a very early age. Many times they are alone in their struggles. Their isolation often forces children to rely on their inner resources, which seems to have contributed to the spiritual awareness. In order to make the crucial contact which makes learning, teaching and the exchange of ideas possible, the teacher or facilitator must understand the background of each child. He must understand that every member of society feels validated in some places and invalidated in others. The upper class child feels invalidated by the lower class child. The lower class child feels invalidated by the upper class child. Learning must concern itself with the opening of consciousness, not the closing of minds. Teachers must be open to individuals different from themselves regardless of background or race. Learning begins with an awareness of the existence of people, places, ideas and beliefs different from oneself and one's own. The term childcare includes all types of education and care provided for young children. The term is also used more specifically for the supplemental care of children from birth to age eight years by persons other than parents. Childcare is used for a variety of reasons, and programmes vary by the number and age of children.

Child Labour

Child labour refers to the employment of children in any work that deprives children of their childhood, interferes with their ability to attend regular school, and that is mentally, physically, socially or morally dangerous and harmful. In developing countries, with high poverty and poor schooling opportunities, child labour is still prevalent. In 2010, sub-Saharan Africa had the highest incidence rates of child labour; with several African nations witnessing over 50 per cent of children aged 5–14 working. During the Industrial Revolution, children as young as four were employed in production factories with dangerous, and often fatal, working conditions. In the early 1900s, thousands of boys were employed in glass making industries. Karl Marx was an outspoken opponent of child labour, saying British industries, could but lives by sucking blood and children's blood too, and that U.S. capital was financed by the capitalised blood of children. An estimated 1.7 million children under the age of fifteen were employed in American industry by 1900. Systematic use of child labour was common place in the colonies of

European powers between 1650 to 1950. In Africa, colonial administrators encouraged traditional kin-ordered modes of production that is hiring a household for work not just the adults.

Child labour is most concentrated in Asia and Africa, which together account for more than 90 per cent of total child employment. Though there are more child workers in Asia than anywhere else, a higher percentage of African children participate in the labour force. Asia is led by India which has 44 million child labourers, giving it the largest child workforce in the world. In Pakistan, 10 per cent are of all workers. The lack of enforcement of labour restrictions perpetuates child labour. This is manifested in different ways. The number of enforcement officials is very low, especially in developing countries where the immediate priority of subsistence takes precedence over anything else. There are also inconsistencies in legislation, which may pose problems are between the ages of 10 and 14 years.

Children work for a variety of reasons. The most important is poverty. Children work to ensure the survival of their family and themselves. Though children are not well paid, they still serve as major contributors to family income in developing countries. Schooling problems also contribute to child labour. Many times children seek employment simply because there is no access to schools (distance, no school at all). When there is access, the low quality of the education often makes attendance a waste of time for the students. Schools in many developing areas suffer from problems such as overcrowding, inadequate sanitation and apathetic teachers. When children drop out of school, it is not necessarily because of irresponsible parenting; it may be due to the family's financial situation. When these children leave school, they become potential workers. Traditional factors are also important. The established female role in certain countries dictates that women will not fit into traditional roles if they become educated. There is a pervasive notion in some nations that educated females will not get married nor have children. Often parents in developing countries assign different roles to their children. This has been called child specialisation, and may increase the number of working children. Rapid rural-to-urban migration is the cause for the increasing rate of child labour in urban areas of developing countries.

Child Labour in India

The magnitude of child labour in India has been witnessing enormous decline in the last two decades, both in terms of magnitude and workforce participation rates. Evidence drawn from the National Sample Survey data suggest that India's child workforce during 2004-05 was estimated at little over nine million (9.07 million) as against twenty-one and half million (21.55 million) in 1983. As per the Census 2001, there are 1.26 crores economically active children in the age-group of 5-14 years. It was 1.13 crores in the 1991 Census. Among the states, Uttar Pradesh accounts for a larger share of close to one fourth of all child labour in India followed by Andhra Pradesh. According to the Census 2001 figures there are 1.26 crore working children in the age group of 5-14 as compared to the total child population of 25.2 crore. There are approximately 12 lakhs children working in the hazardous occupations/processes which are covered under the Child Labour (Prohibition and Regulation) Act i.e. 18 occupations and 65 processes. As per survey conducted by National Sample Survey Organisation (NSSO) in 2004-05, the number of working children is estimated at 90.75 lakh. As per Census 2011, the number of working children in the age group of 5-14 years has further reduced to 43.53 lakh. It shows that the efforts of the Government have borne the desired fruits.

Absence of compulsory education at the primary level, parental ignorance regarding the bad effects of child labour, the lack of implementation of child labour laws and penalties, non-availability and non-accessibility of schools, boring and unpractical school curriculum and cheap child labour are some other factors which lead to child labour. Child labour in India is mostly practiced in restaurants, roadside stalls; matches, fireworks and explosives industry; glass and bangles factories; beedi-making; carpet-making; lock-making; brassware; export-oriented garment units; gem polishing export industry; slate mines and manufacturing units; leather units; diamond industry; building and construction industry; brick kilns, helpers to mechanics, masons, carpenters, painters, plumbers, cooks, etc. The Indian Constitution says that child labour is a wrong practice and standards should be set by law to eliminate it. The Child Labour Act of 1986 implemented by the government of India makes child labour illegal in many regions and sets the minimum age of employment at 14 years. Due to economic factors, many of the law's goals are difficult to meet. The law, for example, does nothing to protect children who perform domestic or unreported labour. In almost all Indian industries girls are unrecognised labourers because they are seen as helpers and not workers. Girls are thus not protected by the law.

Who are Bonded Labour?

Bonded labour is probably the least known form of slavery today, and yet it is the most widely used method of enslaving people. A person becomes a bonded labourer when their labour is demanded as a means of repayment for a loan. The person is then tricked or trapped into working for very little or no pay. Bonded labourers are forced to work to repay debts their employer says they owe, and they are not allowed to work for anyone else. Debt bondage has been described by the United Nations as a form of modern day slavery and the Supplementary Convention on the Abolition of Slavery seeks to abolish the practice. Debt bondage was very common in Ancient Greece. In ancient Athens, Solon forbade taking out loans using oneself as a security and ended such debt.

Bonded Labour in India

The most inhuman form of child exploitation is the age old practice of bonded labour in India. Here children are sold to the buyer like a commodity for a certain period of time. The labour that the child is subjected to is treated as collateral security and exploiters "buy" them for small sums at exorbitant interest rates. There are many reasons for child labour. Poverty is the biggest reason for child labour in India. The small income of child labourers is also absorbed by their families. Despite the statutory prohibition, bonded labour is widely practiced. The worst affected are the children and women particularly those from the Dalit community. It was reported in the *Hindu* news paper on 19/10/2012 that a person had sold himself and his wife as bonded labourers against a loan of Rs 45,000 four years ago to the village landlord. He died this August leaving behind the unpaid debt.

Debt bondage in India was legally abolished in 1976 but it remains prevalent, with weak enforcement of the law by governments. Bonded labour involves the exploitive interlinking of credit and labour agreements that devolve into slave-like exploitation due to severe power imbalances between the lender and the borrower. Estimates of the problem vary. Official figures include a 1993 estimate of 251,000 bonded labourers, while the Bandhua Mukti Morcha says there are over 20 million bonded labourers. A 2003 project by Human Rights Watch has reported a major problem with bonded child labour in the silk industry. The Ministry of Labour, Government of India has initiated a Centrally Sponsored Scheme under which Rs 20,000 is provided for the rehabilitation of each bonded labourer, to be equally contributed by the Centre and the State Governments.

Legal Provision or Commissions for Children Rights in India

India has all along followed a proactive policy in addressing the problem of child labour and has always stood for constitutional, statutory and developmental measures that are required to eliminate child labour. The Constitution of India has relevant provisions to secure compulsory universal primary education. The Constitutional guarantees are reflected in the policies, plans, laws and schemes on child labour. As per Article 24 of the Constitution, no child below the age of 14 years is to be employed in any factory, mine or any hazardous employment. Further, Article 39 requires the States to direct its policy towards ensuring that the tender age of children is not abused and that they are not forced by economic necessity to enter avocations unsuited to their age or strength. Recently, with the insertion of Article 21A, the State has been entrusted with the task of providing free and compulsory education to all the children in the age group of 6-14 years. Child Labour (Prohibition and Regulation) Act (1986) was the culmination of efforts and ideas that emerged from the deliberations and recommendations of various committees on child labour. Significant among them were the National Commission on Labour (1966-1969), the Gurupadaswamy Committee on Child Labour (1979) and the Sanat Mehta Committee (1984).

The Government is emphasising enhancement of resource allocation and full utilisation of allocated resources for the schemes and programmes for children. A child budgeting review has been initiated for proper governance and accountability. The key objectives of child budgeting are to analyse budgetary provisions on the social sector, to identify the magnitude of budgetary allocations made by the Centre/State Governments on schemes meant for addressing specific needs of children, to examine the trend in child specific expenditure etc. Various schemes and programmes are being implemented by different Ministries and Departments for the benefit of children at the Central level. Children's issues are being addressed by the Government in different ways. There are Constitutional provisions, legislations, policies, plans of action, schemes and programmes for children. Child abuse and violence against children was found to be one of the sectors in which there was little data available in the country. Hence it was decided to conduct a national level survey on child abuse.

India is a large country, administered at the Union and State levels. Children's issues are being handled at the Union level by different Ministries and Departments and at state level by State

Governments and UT Administrations. All these partners are jointly and independently working for the welfare and betterment of children in the country. The joint efforts of Government, non-Government organisations and the community result in effective impact. UNICEF projects are being implemented in India through a Master Plan of Operations, which is an agreement prepared after mutual consultation and consensus within the framework of the Basic Agreement signed between India and UNICEF in 1978. Child participation is now being emphasised by the Government in the process of policy formulation and other initiatives taken for the benefit of children.

India's Labour Policy is mainly centred towards various labour laws. These laws have evolved over a period of time in response to two main needs. In the first place, they reflected certain needs of individuals; society and the nation based on the Fundamental Rights guaranteed by the Constitution. For example, Article 19 guarantees freedom of speech and expression, freedom to form Association or Unions and freedom to practice any profession or to carry on any occupation, trade or business, subject to reasonable restrictions that may be imposed by law on the exercise of these freedoms. Article 23 prohibits traffic in human beings and forced labour and Article 24 prohibits employment of children in factories etc. These are constitutionally binding and are reflected in the labour laws. In addition, the Directive Principles of State Policy in Part IV of the Constitution are fundamentals in the governance of the country and it shall be the duty of the State to apply these principles in making laws. The Principles enshrined in Articles 39, 41, 42, 43, 43-A are the basic pillars for formulating the policy for our workers. In order to bring labour reforms, Government of India constituted the Second National Commission on Labour under the Chairmanship of Hon'ble Shri Ravindra Varma on 15.10.1999. The Commission was given a two-point terms of reference (i) to suggest rationalisation of existing laws relating to labour in the organised sector; and (ii) to suggest 'umbrella' legislation for ensuring a minimum level of protection to the workers in the unorganised sector.

The first protective legislation for child labour in India was seen in 1881 in the form if Indian Factories Act which had the provisions prohibiting employment of children below seven years, limiting the working hours for children to nine hours a day and providing four holidays in a month and rest hours. This was actually made by the ruling British Government to decrease the production in Indian industries through some legal restrictions. Besides Constitutional provisions, there are several legislative enactments which provide legal protection to children in various occupations.

1. The Children (Pledging of Labour) Act, 1933
2. The Employment of Children Act, 1938
3. The Minimum Wages, Act 1948
4. The Factories Act, 1948
5. The Plantations Labour Act, 1951
6. The Mines Act, 1952
7. The Merchant Shipping Act, 1958
8. The Apprentices Act, 1961
9. The Atomic Energy Act, 1962
10. The Beedi and Cigar Workers (Conditions of Employment) Act, 1966
11. The Shops and Establishment Act in Various States, and
12. Child Labour (Prohibition and Regulation) Act, 1986

Conclusion

Children are our future. Child development is the changes that occur as a child grows and develops in relation to being physically healthy, mentally alert, emotionally sound, socially competent and ready to learn. Investing financial resources to help children survive and develop to their full potential is, first and foremost, a moral imperative. Child labour to the employment of children in any work that deprives children of their childhood interferes with their ability to attend regular school, and that is mentally, physically, socially or morally dangerous and harmful. It is most concentrated in Asia and Africa, which together account for more than 90 per cent of total child employment. Children work for a variety of reasons. The most important is poverty. Children work to ensure the survival of their family and themselves.

Bonded labour is probably the least known form of slavery today, and yet it is the most widely used method of enslaving people. A person becomes a bonded labourer when their labour is demanded as a means of repayment for a loan. Debt bondage in India was legally abolished in 1976 but it remains prevalent, with weak enforcement of the law by governments. Bonded labour involves the exploitive interlinking of credit and labour agreements that devolve into slave-like exploitation due to severe power imbalances between the lender and the borrower. The Constitution of India has relevant provisions to secure compulsory universal primary education. The Constitutional guarantees are reflected in the policies, plans, laws and schemes on child labour. The Government is emphasising enhancement of resource allocation and full utilisation of allocated resources for the Schemes and programmes for children. India's Labour Policy is mainly centred towards various labour laws. These laws have evolved over a period of time in response to two main needs. In the first place, they reflected certain needs of individuals; society and the nation based on the Fundamental Rights guaranteed by the Constitution.

References

1. *About child labour* (2014), Retrieved from http://labour.gov.in/content/division/child-labour.php
2. *Central Board for Workers Education* (2014), Retrieved from http://www.cbwe.gov.in/about-us.aspx
3. *Child* (2014), Retrieved from http://en.wikipedia.org/wiki/Child
4. *Child care* (2014), Retrieved from http://family.jrank.org/pages/226/Childcare.html
5. *Child development and early learning* (2014), Retrieved from http://www.factsforlifeglobal.org/03/
6. *Child Labour* (2013), Retrieved from http://164.100.47.134/intranet/childlabour.pdf
7. *Child labour* (2014), Retrieved from http://en.wikipedia.org/wiki/Child_labour
8. *Child Labour (Prohibition & Regulation) Act, 1986,* Retrieved from http://business.gov.in/legal_aspects/child_labour.php
9. *Child Labour (Prohibition & Regulation).Act, 1986,* Retrieved from http://bba.org.in/sites/default/files/Child%20Labour% 20_Prohibition% 20_%20Regulation_%20Act,%201986.pdf
10. *Child labour free India* (2014), Retrieved from http://bba.org.in/campaigns/CLFI/
11. *Children are our future* (2014), Retrieved from http://www.bernard vanleer.org /files/crc/1.B%20Peter_Laugharn_(BVLF).pdf
12. *Children rights* (2014), Retrieved from http://www.un.org/cyberschoolbus/briefing/children/children.pdf
13. *Children rights and responsibility* (2014), Retrieved from http://www.e-activist.com/ea-campaign/action.retrievefile.do?ea_fileid=14129
14. *Children: how importances are they for the world?* (2013), Retrieved from http://blog.sanaulla.info/2008/07/10/children-and-world/

15. *Convention on the Rights of the Child* (2009), Retrieved from http://www.coe.int/t/dg3/children/participation/CRC-C-GC-12.pdf
16. Debt bondage (2015), Retrieved from http://en.wikipedia.org/wiki/Debt_bondage
17. *Debt bondage in India* (2015), Retrieved from http://en.wikipedia.org/wiki/Debt_bondage_in_India
18. Deodhar et al (2010), *An evaluation of midday meal scheme*, Retrieved from http://www.iimahd.ernet.in/ ~ satish/MDMJISPEPaper(2).pdf
19. *Fact sheet: A summary of the rights under the Convention on the Rights of the Child* (2014), Retrieved from http://www.unicef.org/crc/files/Rights_overview.pdf
20. Faraaz Siddiqi and Harry Anthony Patrinos (2014), *Child: Labour: Issues, causes and interventions*, Retrieved from http://siteresources.worldbank.org/EDUCATION/Resources/278200-1099079877269/547664-109907 99344 75/547667-1135281552767/Child_Labour_issues.pdf
21. *Importance of investing in children* (2014), Retrieved from http://www.unicef.org/socialpolicy/index_53294.ht
22. *Integrated Child Development Services* (2014), Retrieved from http://en.wikipedia.org/wiki/Integrated_Child_Development_Services_(India)
23. *Integrated Child Development Services schemes in brief* (2014), Retrieved from http://cdf.ifmr.ac.in/wp-content/uploads/2011/03/ICDS-Scheme-Brief.pdf
24. *Key notes address on Bonded labour* (2015), Retrieved from http://nhrc.nic.in/Documents/SPEECH_2012_10_25.pdf
25. *Mid Day Meal Programme - A Historical Perspective* (2014), Chapter 1. Retrieved from http://nutritionfoundationofindia.res.in/Evaluation/Evaluation
26. *Mid Day Meal Scheme* (2014),Retrieved from http://en.wikipedia.org/wiki/Midday_Meal_Scheme
27. *Mid Day Meal Scheme in India: Origin and Implementation* (2014), chapter 2, Retrieved from http://shodhganga.inflibnet.ac.in/bitstream/10603/4244/11/11_chapter%202.pdf
28. *Ministry of Women and Child Development* (2015), Retrieved from http://en.wikipedia.org/wiki/Ministry_of_Women_and_Child_Development
29. *National Report on "A World Fit for Children"* (2007), Retrieved from http://www.unicef.org/worldfitforchildren/files/India_WFFC5_Report.pdf
30. *Over 60 million child labourers in India* (2014), Retrieved from http://www.indiatribune.com/index.php?option=com_content&id=2884:over-60-million-child-labourers-in-india&Itemid=400

31. *Performance Evaluation of Cooked Mid-Day Meal (CMDM),* Retrieved from http://planningcommission.gov.in/reports/peoreport/peoevalu/peo_cmdm0106.pdf
32. Priyanka Khanna (2014), *Combating Child Labour in India*, Retrieved from http://www.unicef.org/india/child_protection_1726.htm
33. *Programmes for Women* (2014), Retrieved from http://wcd.nic.in/ar0708/English/Chapter-2.pdf
34. *The Integrated Child Development Services* (2014), Retrieved from http://www.unicef.org/india/media_2640.htm
35. *The Integrated Child Development Services* (2014), Retrieved from http://siteresources.worldbank.org/SOUTHASIAEXT/Resources/223546-1147272668285/undernourished_chapter_2.pdf
36. *The Times of India* (Aug 07, 2014), UP among worst performers in kids malnutrition, Retrieved from http://timesofindia.indiatimes.com/city/lucknow/UP-among-worst-performers-in-kids-malnutrition/articleshow/39786370.cms
37. *The Times of India* (Sep 05, 2014), HC notice to Gujarat govt, Centre over lack of facilities in crèches, Retrieved from http://timesofindia.indiatimes.com/city/ahmedabad/hc-notice-to-gujarat-govt-centre-over-lack-of-facilities-in-creches/articleshow/41774600.cms
38. Thurman E. Scott (2014), *Children's Contribution to Society, Creative Process and the Young Peoples Creative Workshop,* Retrieved from http://www.actorstheatreworkshop.com/about/tes_essay3.php

4

Rights of Intellectual Property

"Human rights, of course, must include the right to religious freedom, understood as the expression of a dimension that is at once individual and communitarian - a vision that brings out the unity of the person while clearly distinguishing between the dimension of the citizen and that of the believer."

-Pope Benedict XVI

Introduction

Rights are legal, social, or ethical principles of freedom or entitlement; that is, rights are the fundamental normative rules about what is allowed of people or owed to people, according to some legal system, social convention, or ethical theory. Rights are often included in the foundational questions that governments and politics have been designed to deal with. Many diverse things are claimed as rights: *"A right to life, a right to choose; a right to vote, to work, to strike; a right to one phone call, to dissolve parliament, to operate a forklift, to asylum, to equal treatment before the law, to feel proud of what one has done; a right to exist, to sentence an offender to death, to launch a nuclear first strike, to carry a concealed weapon, to a distinct genetic identity; a right to believe one's own eyes, to pronounce the couple husband and wife, to be left alone, to go to hell in one's own way."* Natural rights are rights which are "natural" in the sense of "not artificial, not man-made", as in rights deriving from deontic logic, from human nature, or from the edicts of a god. A right is a permission to do something or an entitlement to a specific service or treatment from others, and these rights have been called *positive rights*.[1]

Property rights are theoretical constructs in economics for determining how a resource is used and owned. Resources can be owned by individuals, associations or governments. Property rights to a good must be defined, their use must be monitored, and possession of rights must be enforced.[2] Intellectual property is a legal term that refers to creations of the mind. Examples of intellectual property include music, literature, and other artistic works; discoveries and inventions; and words, phrases, symbols, and designs.

Intellectual property rights are the rights given to persons over the creations of their minds. They usually give the creator an exclusive right over the use of his/her creation for a certain period of time. Intellectual property rights include patents, copyright, industrial design rights, trademarks, trade dress, and in some jurisdictions trade secrets. The stated objective of most intellectual property law (with the exception of trademarks) is to "Promote progress."[3] Intellectual property rights are customarily divided into two main areas: Copyright and rights related to copyright and Industrial property.[4] Established in 1970, the World Intellectual Property Organisation (WIPO) is an international organisation dedicated to helping ensure that the rights of creators and owners of intellectual property are protected worldwide, and that inventors and authors are therefore recognised and rewarded for their ingenuity.[5]

The Trade Related Aspects of Intellectual Property Rights Agreement (TRIPS) culminated at the end of seven years of negotiations from 1986 to 1993, as part of the Uruguay Round of Multilateral Trade Negotiations of the GATT.[6] IPR are largely territorial rights except copyright, which is global in nature in the sense that it is immediately available in all the members of the Berne Convention. These rights are awarded by the State and are monopoly rights implying that no one can use these rights without the consent of the right holder.[7]

What are Intellectual Property Rights?

Intellectual property refers to creations of the mind: inventions; literary and artistic works; and symbols, names and images used in commerce. Intellectual property rights are like any other property right. They allow creators, or owners, of patents, trademarks or copyrighted works to benefit from their own work or investment in a creation. The importance of intellectual property was first recognised in the Paris Convention for the Protection of Industrial Property (1883) and the Berne Convention for the Protection of Literary and Artistic Works (1886). Both treaties are administered by the World Intellectual Property Organisation (WIPO).[8]

According to WIPO (World Intellectual Property Organisation), "intellectual property (IP) refers to creations of the mind: inventions, literary and artistic works, and symbols, names, images, and designs used in commerce." Divided into two categories, IP includes industrial property and copyright. And both are equally as valuable since the ramifications of not protecting these assets can be serious.[9]

One can broadly classify the various forms of IPRs into two categories: (a) IPRs that stimulate inventive and creative activities (patents, utility models, industrial designs, copyright, plant breeders' rights and layout designs for integrated circuits) and (b) IPRs that offer information to consumers (trademarks and geographical indications).[10] Intellectual property (IP) contributes enormously to our national and state economies. Dozens of industries across our economy rely on the adequate enforcement of their patents, trademarks, and copyrights, while consumers use IP to ensure they are purchasing safe, guaranteed products.[11]

Patents

Patent is an exclusive right granted for an invention – a product or process that provides a new way of doing something, or that offers a new technical solution to a problem. It is an exclusive right granted by a country to an inventor, allowing the inventor to exclude others from making, using or selling his or her invention in that country during the life of the patent.[12] Patent provides patent owners with protection for their inventions. Protection is granted for a limited period, generally 20 years. Patent protection means an invention cannot be commercially made, used, distributed or sold without the patent owner's consent.[13] The procedure for granting patents, requirements placed on the patentee, and the extent of the exclusive rights vary widely between countries according to national laws and international agreements. Primary incentives embodied in the patent system include incentives to invent in the first place; to disclose the invention once made; to invest the sums necessary to experiment, produce and market the invention; and to design around and improve upon earlier patents. One effect of modern patent usage is that a small-time inventor can use the exclusive right status to become a licensor.[14]

Patents provide incentives to individuals by offering them recognition for their creativity and material reward for their marketable inventions. These incentives encourage innovation, which assures that the quality of human life is continuously enhanced. A patent owner has the right to decide who may or may not use the patented invention for the period in which the invention is protected. The patent owner may give permission to, or license, other parties to use the invention on mutually agreed terms.[15] Patents promote innovation and dissemination of information by obliging the owner to publicly disclose the information which enriches the total technical knowledge in the world; the public knowledge promotes creativity to others; patents provide not only protection to the owner but the valuable information for future generations of research and inventors; patents provide the means of licensing of technology at all levels.[16]

Patents have emerged as a major area of business competence. It has become as important as understanding innovation, technology, marketing, finance, corporate governance, industrial economics and strategy. They provide insights on technology, business and competition, and have the potential to affect key decisions, such as those related to the R&D and business strategies of a company, research organisations and universities.[17]

The present Patents Act, 1970 came into force in the year 1972, amending and incorporating the existing laws relating to Patents and Designs Act 1911 in India. The Patent (amendment) Act 2005 came into force from 1st January 2005, which brought changes in the previous patent system of India wherein product patent was extended to all subjects of technology consisting of food, drugs, chemicals and micro organisms.[18] The Indian Patent Office is administered by the Office of the Controller General of Patents, Designs and Trade Marks (CGPDTM). This is a subordinate office of the Indian government and administers the Indian law of Patents, Designs and Trade Marks. The patent office is headquartered at Kolkata with branches in Chennai, New Delhi and Mumbai, but the office of the CGPDTM is in Mumbai[19].

Copyright

Copyright laws grant authors, artists and other creator's protection for their literary and artistic creations, generally referred to as "works". The creators of works protected by copyright, and their heirs and successors, have certain basic rights under copyright law. Copyright and related rights protection is an essential component in fostering human creativity and innovation.[20] It is a legal right created by the law of a country that grants the creator of an original work exclusive right to its use and distribution, usually for a limited time, with the intention of enabling the creator to receive compensation for their intellectual effort. It is a form of intellectual property, applicable to any expressed representation of a creative work. The usual justification of copyright is to enable creators of intellectual wealth to financially support themselves and give them a motive to continue publishing their creations. Copyright came about with the invention of the printing press and with wider literacy.[21]

Copyright is described under the umbrella term intellectual property along with rights and trade name. Copyright can to apply for any work, it must be an original idea or literature that is put to use. The idea alone cannot be protected by copyright. It is the physical use of that idea, such as a design or a written novel, which is covered under copyright law.[22] It is important to creators like writers and artists as well as those such as publishers that own rights, as it provides them with a legal right of ownership of the work that they produce.[23] Something also to take into consideration is that copyrights can last up to fifty years (in the United States, this number however can vary in other countries) after the death of the original copyright owner. It is important to note, that copyrights can be passed down to a family member, which in turn leaves a lasting legacy to pass down to different generations as a valuable (and memorable) estate in·your memory well after you are gone.[24]

Copyright protection is a basic pillar of any capitalist society, creating a legal framework that allows and encourages entrepreneurship by extending legal protection to industrious individuals and organisations for proprietary. It can be argued that copyright laws create and maintain the concept of branding, which has become an ever-present and vital component of success in virtually any market.[25] The Copyright Act, 1957 (Act No. 14 of 1957) governs the laws and applicable rules related to the subject of copyrights in India. Copyright Law in the country was governed by the Copyright Act of 1914, was essentially the extension of the British Copyright Act, 1911 to India, and borrowed extensively from the new Copyright Act of the United Kingdom of 1956.[26] A trademark registration is valid all over India. Even though the registration of a trademark is not compulsory, it has significant advantages.[27]

Trademark

Trademark protection ensures that the owners of marks have the exclusive right to use them to identify goods or services, or to authorise others to use them in return for payment. The period of protection varies, but a trademark can be renewed indefinitely upon payment of the corresponding fees. Trademarks may be one or a combination of words, letters and numerals. Almost all countries in the world register and protect trademarks. Each national or regional office maintains a Register of Trademarks containing full application information on all registrations and renewals, which facilitates examination, search and potential opposition by third parties.[28]

Trademark may be located on a package, a label, a voucher or on the product itself. Trademarks are used to claim exclusive properties of products or services. The usage of trademarks by its owner can cause legal issues if this usage makes them guilty of false advertising or if the trademark is offensive. A trademark is typically a name, word, phrase, logo, symbol, design, image, or a combination of these elements. Terms such as mark, brand and logo are sometimes used interchangeably with "trademark". Specialised types of trademark include certification marks, collective trademarks and defensive trademarks. Certification mark on a commercial product may indicate several things. A collective trademark is a trademark owned by an organisation, used by its members to identify themselves with a level of quality or accuracy, geographical origin, or other characteristics set by the organisation. Trademark dilution is a trademark law concept giving the owner of a famous trademark standing to forbid others from using that mark in a way that would lessen its uniqueness.[29]

Indian trademark law statutorily protects trademarks as per the Trademark Act, 1999 and also under the common law remedy of passing off.[30] The first trademark law in India was passed in the year 1940 and was known as the Trade Marks Act, 1940. This law was subsequently replaced by the Trade and Merchandise Act, 1958. Thereafter the Government of India amended this Act in order to bring the Indian trademark law in compliance with its TRIPS obligations. The new Act that was passed was the Trade Marks Act, 1999. This Act came into force in the year 2003. The Trade Marks Act, 1999 and the Trade Marks Rules, 2002, presently govern the trademark law in India.[31]

Industrial Designs

Industrial designs are what make an article attractive and appealing; hence, they add to the commercial value of a product and increase its marketability. Protecting industrial designs helps to promote economic development by encouraging creativity in the industrial and manufacturing sectors, as well as in traditional arts and crafts. In most countries, an industrial design must be registered in order to be protected under industrial design law.[32]

Industrial design studies function and form and the connection between product, user, and environment. Generally, industrial design professionals work in small scale design, rather than overall design of complex systems such as buildings or ships. Although the process of design may be considered 'creative,' many analytical processes also take place. In fact, many industrial designers often use various design methodologies in their creative process. Industrial design rights are intellectual property rights that make exclusive the visual design of objects that are not purely utilitarian. A design patent would also be considered under this category.[33] Industrial designers develop the concepts for manufactured products, such as cars, home appliances, and toys. They combine art, business, and engineering to make products that people use every day. Industrial designers focus on the user experience in creating style and function for a particular gadget or appliance.[34]

India's Design Act, 2000 was enacted to consolidate and amend the law relating to protection of design and to comply with the articles 25 and 26 of TRIPS agreement. The new act, (earlier Patent and Design Act, 1911 was repealed by this act) now defines "design" to mean only the features of shape, configuration, pattern, ornament, or composition of lines or colours applied to any article, whether in two- or three-dimensional, or in both forms, by any industrial process or means, whether manual or mechanical or chemical, separate or combined, which in the finished article appeal to and are judged solely by the eye; but does not include any mode or principle of construction.[35]

Geographical Indication

Geographical indication is a sign used on goods that have a specific geographical origin and possess qualities or a reputation due to that place of origin. Most commonly, a geographical indication consists of the name of the place of origin of the goods. Geographical indications are understood by consumers to denote the origin and quality of products. An appellation of origin is a special kind of geographical indication used on products that have a specific quality exclusively or essentially due to the geographical environment in which the products are produced.[36]

Geographical indication (GI) is a name or sign used on certain products which corresponds to a specific geographical location or origin (e.g. a town, region, or country). Geographical indications have long been associated with the concept of terror and with Europe as an entity, where there is a tradition of associating certain food products with particular regions. They are generally traditional products, produced by rural communities over generations that have gained a reputation on the markets for their specific qualities. Like trademarks, geographical indications are regulated locally by each country because conditions of registration such as differences in the generic use of terms vary from country to country.[37]

Geographical indication acts as a mechanism that helps producers differentiate their products from competing products in the market and enables producers to build a reputation and goodwill around their products that will fetch a premium price. A number of studies attest to the potential economic benefits of GI registration. The concept of geographical indication has its origin in 19th century Europe and has considerably evolved since then. The current international framework is laid down in Article 22 of the Trade Related Aspects of Intellectual Property Rights Agreement which mandates member countries to provide for the protection of all GIs, where the obligation is for members to provide the 'legal means for interested parties' to secure protection of their GIs.[38]

The Geographical Indications of Goods (Registration and Protection) Act, 1999 is a sui generis Act of the Parliament of India for protection of geographical indications in India. India, as a member of the World Trade Organisation (WTO), enacted the Act to comply with the Agreement on Trade-Related Aspects of Intellectual Property Rights. According to section 1 (3)(e) of the Act, Geographical indication has been defined as *"an indication which identifies such goods as agricultural goods, natural goods or manufactured goods as originating, or manufactured in the territory of a country, or a region or locality in that territory, where a given quality, reputation or other characteristic of such goods is essentially attributable to its geographical origin and in case where such goods are manufactured goods one of the activities of either the production or of processing or preparation of the goods concerned takes place in such territory, region or locality, as the case may be."*[39]

Trade Secrets

Trade secret is an invented formula, practice, process, design, instrument, pattern, commercial method, or compilation of information which is not generally known or reasonably ascertainable by others, and by which a business can obtain an economic advantage over competitors or customers. The precise language by which a trade secret is defined varies by jurisdiction. A company can protect its confidential information through non-compete and non-disclosure contracts with its employees. Secret formulae are often protected by restricting the key information to a few trusted individuals.[40]

Trade secret protection is very limited. A trade secret holder is only protected from unauthorised disclosure and use of the trade secret by others and from another person obtaining the trade secret by some improper means. There are several factors used to determine if subject matter qualifies as a trade secret. Among the factors considered are the extent of measures taken by the trade secret owner to guard the secrecy of the information and the ease or difficulty with which the information could be properly acquired or duplicated by others.[41]

Trade Dress

Trade dress is a legal term of art that generally refers to characteristics of the visual appearance of a product or its packaging (or even the design of a building) that signify the source of the product to consumers. Trade dress can be protected as getup under the law of passing off in the UK. Passing off is a common law remedy for protecting an unregistered trademark. Getup, packaging, business strategy, marketing techniques, advertisement themes etc. can also be protected under passing off.[42] It means the design and shape of the materials in which a product is packaged. Product configuration, the design and shape of the product itself, may also be considered a form of trade dress.[43]

The term "trade secret" generally refers to secret, commercially valuable information, including such subject matter as confidential formulae, techniques for manufacturing a product, and customer lists. Trade secret protection is largely a matter of state law.[44] Trade dress refers to characteristics of the visual or sensual appearance of a product that may also include its packaging which may be registered and protected from being used by competitors in relation to their business and services. The characteristic includes their shape (three-dimensional), packaging, colour, graphic design or even the smell of the product. The concept of trade dress was first brought in under the Trademarks Act, 1999 under the definition of 'mark' which replaced the previous Trade and Merchandise Marks Act, 1958. Indian Courts have been repeatedly recognising the concept of the trade dress even prior to 1999 or 2003 by under common law remedies.[45]

Conclusion

Intellectual property rights are like any other property right. They allow creators, or owners, of patents, trademarks or copyrighted works to benefit from their own work or investment in a creation. One can broadly classify the various forms of IPRs into two categories: (a) IPRs that stimulate inventive and creative activities (patents, utility models, industrial designs, copyright, plant breeders' rights and layout designs for integrated circuits) and (b) IPRs that offer information to consumers (trademarks and geographical indications). Patents provide incentives to individuals by offering them recognition for their creativity and material reward for their marketable inventions. These incentives encourage innovation, which assures that the quality of human life is continuously enhanced. Patents have emerged as a major area of business competence. It has become as important as understanding innovation, technology, marketing, finance, corporate governance, industrial economics and strategy.

Copyright and related rights protection is an essential component in fostering human creativity and innovation. Copyright is described under the umbrella term intellectual property along with rights and trade name. Copyright can to apply for any work, it must be an original idea or literature that is put to use. Copyright protection is a basic pillar of any capitalist society, creating a legal framework that allows and encourages entrepreneurship by extending legal protection to industrious individuals and organisations for proprietary. Trademark protection ensures that the owners of marks have the exclusive right to use them to identify goods or services, or to authorise others to use them in return for payment. Trademark may be located on a package, a label, a voucher or on the product itself. Industrial design studies function and form and the connection between product, user, and environment. Geographical indication is a sign used on goods that have a specific geographical origin and possess qualities or a reputation due to that place of origin. Trade secret is an invented formula, practice, process, design, instrument, pattern, commercial method, or compilation of information. Trade dress is a legal term of art that generally refers to characteristics of the visual appearance of a product or its packaging (or even the design of a building) that signify the source of the product to consumers.

References

1. *Rights* (2015), Retrieved from http://en.wikipedia.org/wiki/Rights
2. *Property rights* (2015), Retrieved from http://en.wikipedia.org/wiki/Property_rights_%28economics%29
3. *Intellectual property* (2015), Retrieved from http://en.wikipedia.org/wiki/Intellectual_property
4. *What is the Intellectual property right?* (2015), World trade organisation, Retrieved from https://www.wto.org/english/tratop_e/trips_e/intel1_e.htm
5. *What is Intellectual Property?* (2015), Retrieved from http://www.wipo.int/edocs/pubdocs/en/intproperty/450/wipo_pub_450.pdf
6. Mahima Puri and Anjali Varma (2005), *Intellectual property conventions and Indian* law, Retrieved from http://icrier.org/pdf/wp166.pdf
7. R Saha (2015), *Management of Intellectual Property Rights in India*, Retrieved from http://www.pfc.org.in/workshop/workshop.pdf
8. *What is Intellectual Property?* (2015), Retrieved from http://www.wipo.int/edocs/pubdocs/en/intproperty/450/wipo_pub_450.pdf
9. *The importance of protecting intellectual property* (2015), Retrieved from http://www.interparty.org/importance-of-protecting-intellectual-property.html
10. Rajkumar S. Adukia (2015), *Handbook on intellectual property rights in India,* Retrieved from http://www.caaa.in/Image/34_Hb_on_IPR.pdf
11. Why is IP important? (2014), *Global intellectual property centre*, Retrieved from http://www.theglobalipcenter.com/resources/why-is-ip-important/
12. *The Importance of Patents: It Pays to Know Patent Rules* (2015), Retrieved from http://web.mit.edu/e-club/hadzima/the-importance-of-patents.html
13. *What is Intellectual Property?* (2015), Retrieved from http://www.wipo.int/edocs/pubdocs/en/intproperty/450/wipo_pub_450.pdf
14. *Patent* (2015), Retrieved from http://en.wikipedia.org/wiki/Patent
15. *What is patent?* (2015), Retrieved from http://www.wipo.int/edocs/pubdocs/en/patents/450/wipo_pub_l450pa.pdf
16. *Why patent? The importance of patents for innovation* (2015), Retrieved from http://www.pacra.org.zm/index.php?option=com_ content&view=article&id=162:why-patent-the-importance-of-patents-for-innovation&catid=1:latest-news

17. *Significance of IP* (2015), Retrieved from http://www.giipinfo.com/significance_of_patents.aspx
18. Aayush Sharma (2014), *India: Section 3(D) of Indian Patents Act 1970: Significance and Interpretation*, Retrieved from http://www.mondaq.com/india/x/295378/Patent/SECTION+3D+OF+ INDIAN+ PATENTS+ACT+1970+SIGNIFICANCE
19. *Indian Patent Office* (2015), Retrieved from http://en.wikipedia.org/wiki/Indian_Patent_Office
20. *What is Intellectual Property?* (2015), Retrieved from http://www.wipo.int/edocs/pubdocs/en/intproperty/450/wipo_pub_450.pdf
21. *Copyright* (2015), Retrieved from http://en.wikipedia.org/wiki/Copyright
22. *Importance of copyrights* (2015), Retrieved from http://infosecawareness.in/children/importance-of-copyrights
23. *Why copyright is important* (2015), Retrieved from http://schools.cla.co.uk/how-copyright-affects-schools/why-copyright-is-important/
24. *Why Copyright protection is so important?* (2015), Retrieved from https://www.copyrightsworld.com/copyright/why-copyright-protection-is-so-important/
25. David Ingram (2015), *Why Are Copyright Laws Important?* Retrieved from http://info.legalzoom.com/copyright-laws-important-20146.html
26. *Indian copyright law* (2015), Retrieved from http://en.wikipedia.org/wiki/Copyright_law_of_India
27. See http://www.nextbigwhat.com/trademark-registration-in-india-the-entrepreneurs-guide-297/
28. *What is Intellectual Property?* (2015), Retrieved from http://www.wipo.int/edocs/pubdocs/en/intproperty/450/wipo_pub_450.pdf
29. *Trade mark* (2015), Retrieved from http://en.wikipedia.org/wiki/Trademark
30. *Indian trademark law* (2015), Retrieved from http://en.wikipedia.org/wiki/Indian_trademark_law
31. *Introduction to Trademarks, Embassy of USA- New Delhi,* Retrieved from http://newdelhi.usembassy.gov/iprtrademark.html
32. *What is Intellectual Property?* (2015), Retrieved from http://www.wipo.int/edocs/pubdocs/en/intproperty/450/wipo_pub_450.pdf
33. *Industrial design* (2015), Retrieved from http://en.wikipedia.org/wiki/Industrial_design
34. See http://www.bls.gov/ooh/arts-and-design/industrial-designers.htm
35. *Industrial design right* (2015), Retrieved from http://en.wikipedia.org/wiki/Industrial_design_right
36. *What is Intellectual Property?* (2015), Retrieved from http://www.wipo.int/edocs/pubdocs/en/intproperty/450/wipo_pub_450.pdf

37. *Geographical indication* (2015), Retrieved from http://en.wikipedia.org/wiki/Geographical_indication
38. *The Protection of Geographical Indications in India: Issues and Challenges* (2013), Retrieved from http://www.teriin.org/div/briefing_paper_GI.pdf
39. *Geographical Indications of Goods (Registration and Protection) Act, 1999*, Retrieved from http://en.wikipedia.org/wiki/Geographical_Indications_of_Goods_%28Registration_and_Protection%29_Act,_1999
40. *Trade secret* (2015), Retrieved from http://en.wikipedia.org/wiki/Trade_secret
41. See http://www.uspto.gov/web/offices/com/doc/ipnii/lawsec.pdf
42. *Trade dress* (2015), Retrieved from http://en.wikipedia.org/wiki/Trade_dress
43. See https://www.law.cornell.edu/wex/trade_dress
44. John R. Thomas (2014), *The Role of Trade Secrets in Innovation Policy,* Retrieved from http://fas.org/sgp/crs/secrecy/R41391.pdf
45. *Trade dress and Its Interpretation by Courts in India* (2015), Retrieved from http://www.hg.org/article.asp?id=7277

5

Labour Rights

"Freedom is a timeless value. The United Nations Charter calls for encouraging respect for fundamental freedoms. The Universal Declaration of Human Rights mentions freedom more than twenty times. All countries have committed to protecting individual freedoms on paper - but in practice, too many break their pledge."

-Ban Ki-moon

Introduction

In a significant move to curb the rampant spread of child labour across the country, the Government of India is set to ban the all forms of child labour under the age of 14 years, making the employment of children below 14 years a criminal offense.[1] The Union Cabinet of India approved the Child and Adolescent Labour (Prohibition) Act today putting a blanket ban on employing anybody below 18 years in hazardous occupation. Such hazardous occupations have also been re-classified in line with the increase in the minimum age of child labour from 14 to 18 years. However, it will allow employing children only between 14-18 years in non-hazardous industries like forest gathering, child care etc. Children between 14-18 years have been defined as "adolescents" in the amended Act. Employing a child below 14 years in any kind of occupation is set to become a cognisable offence, punishable with a maximum three years imprisonment or fine up to a maximum of Rs 50,000.[2]

Over the years the Government of India has multiplied its efforts to address the needs and rights of exploited children.[3] The largest and most structured intervention in the area of child labour in India is the National Child Labour Projects (NCLP).[4] The programme, addressing children rescued from hazardous labour and centrally managed by the Ministry of Labour includes the establishment of special schools to provide children with the skills they need to be mainstreamed into the formal system, vocational training, supplementary nutrition, health services etc.[5] In January 2005, the National Child Labour Projects scheme has been expanded to 250 districts in 21 different Indian states, covering 42 per cent of all districts of the country (2001 Census).[6] UNICEF uses the Article 32 of the Convention on Rights of the Child (CRC),which articulates child labour as *"any work that is likely to be hazardous or to interfere with the child's education, or to be harmful to the child's health or physical, spiritual, moral or social development"*, as the foundation of its work in India.[7]

Our Constitution makers were wise and sagacious to provide, that children should receive distributive justice in free India. The rights against exploitation were mentioned in the draft proposed by Dr B.R. Ambedkar, K.M. Munshi and K.T. Shah. While Dr Ambedkar's draft simply provided that subjecting a person to forced labour or involuntary servitude would be an offence, K.M. Munshi's draft article suggested for abolition of all forms of slavery, child labour, traffic in human beings and compulsory labour.[8] Constitution of India contains provisions for survival, development and protection of children; these are mainly included in Part III and Part IV of the Constitution, i.e., fundamental rights and directive principles of state policy. India follows pro-active policy towards tackling child labour problem.[9]

The Children (Pledging of Labour) Act, 1933

The Royal Commission on Labour was established in 1929 to inquire into various matters relating to labour in this country. The Report of the Commission was finalised in 1931. The Commission had examined the conditions of the child labour in different industries and had found that children had been obliged to work for any number of hours per day as required by their masters.[10] The Royal Commission of Labour found evidence in such widely separated areas as Amritsar, Ahmadabad and Madras of the practice of pledging child labour, that is, the taking of advances by parents or guardians on agreements, written or oral, pledging the labour of their children. The Commission considering that the state would be justified in adopting strong measures to eradicate the evil, and the Bill seeks to do so by imposing penalties on parents by agreements pledging the labour of children and on person knowingly employing children whose labour has been pledged.[11]

The Employment of Children Act, 1938[12]

The Employment of Children Act, 1938 had been in force till repealed and replaced by Child Labour (Prohibition and Regulation) Act, 1986. The main object of the Act was to prevent exploitation of child labour in workshops and other specified occupations and to regulate the employment of children in certain industrial employments. Children under the age of 15 years shall not be employed to work in occupations to which this Article applies which are scheduled as dangerous or unhealthy by the competent authority. The keys points of this Act are: (a) Prohibited the employment of children under 15 years in occupations connected with transport of goods, passengers, mail or railways; (b) Raised the minimum age for handling goods on docks from 12 to 14 years ; (c) Provided for the requirement of a certification of age.[13]

The Factories Act, 1948[14]

The Factories Act, 1948 prohibits employment of a child below 14 years in any factory. Section 67 of the Act, enacts an absolute prohibition of employment of a child in any factory. It means no child below the age of 14 years can be asked to work or if he himself wants to work can be permitted to work in any factory. The Act defines a 'young person' as one who is either a child or an adolescent. A child above the age of fifteen and below the age of eighteen cannot be employed to work for more than four and half hours and cannot be employed during the night. The Act is administered by the Ministry of Labour and Employment through its Directorate General Factory Advice Service and Labour Institutes (DGFASLI) and by the State Governments through their factory inspectorates. DGFASLI was set up with the objective of advising the Central and State Governments on administration of the Factories Act and coordinating the factory inspection services in the States.[15] It serves as a technical arm to assist the Ministry in formulating national policies on occupational safety and health in factories and docks. It also advises factories on various problems concerning safety, health, efficiency and well-being of the persons at work places.[16]

The Minimum Wages Act, 1948[17]

The Minimum Wages Act 1948 is an Act of Parliament concerning Indian labour law that sets the minimum wages that must be paid to skilled and unskilled labours. The Indian Constitution has defined a 'living wage' that is the level of income for a worker which will ensure a basic standard of living including good health, dignity, comfort, education and provide for any contingency. The Minimum Wages Act 1948 generally specifies minimum wage rates on a per day basis, and extends to the entire country and is revised within a period of not less than five years; however there is a provision to increase dearness allowance every two years.[18] Under the Minimum Wages Act, State and Central Governments have the power to fix and revise minimum wages. The act specifies that the "appropriate" government should fix the wages i.e. if the wages to be fixed are in relation to any authority of Central government or Railway administration then the Central government fixes it.[19] The intention of the Act is to fix minimum rates of wages in which the labour force is vulnerable to exploitation i.e. is not well organised and has no effective bargaining power.[20] It provides for an institutional mechanism and procedure for fixation, review, revision and enforcement of minimum rates of wages.[21]

The Plantation of Labour Act, 1951[22]

This Act extends to whole of India except the State of Jammu and Kashmir. It applies to plantations in Tea, Coffee, Rubber or Cinchona, etc in which 30 or more persons are employed. It prohibited the employment of children less than twelve years in plantation. The child worker (A person who has completed 15 years) can be allowed to work if employed only between 6 am. and 7 pm.[23] The total maximum working hours in a week for a child and an adolescent prescribed under the Act, are 40 hours. A child who has completed his 12 year and adolescent will not be allowed to work in any plantation unless he is certified to be fit by a duly appointed certifying surgeon and such a child or adolescent is required to carry with him while he is at work a token giving a reference of such certificate. There is also a provision for penalty for using false certificate of fitness under the Act.[24]

The Plantation Labour Act, 1951 provides for the welfare of plantation labour and regulates the conditions of work in plantations. The Act applies to any land used as plantations which measures five hectares or more in which 15 or more persons are working. However, the State Governments are free to declare any plantation land less than five hectares or less than 15 persons to be covered by the Act. It applies to all the plantation workers whose monthly wages does not exceed Rs 750 per month.[25] The Act is administered by the Ministry of Labour through its Industrial Relations Division. The Division is concerned with improving the institutional framework for dispute settlement and amending labour laws relating to industrial relations.[26]

The Mines Act, 1952[27]

The Mines Act, 1952 contains provisions for measures relating to the health, safety and welfare of workers in the coal, metalliferous and oil mines. The Act prescribes the duties of the owner to manage mines and mining operation and the health and safety in mines.[28] It also prescribes the number of working hours in mines, the minimum wage rates, and other related matters. The Central Government has set up 'Courts of Inquiry' in order to investigate into the accidents which result in the death of 10 or more miners.[29] This Act defines child as a person who has not completed his 15 years. The Act not only prohibits the employment of children in mines, but also prohibits the presence of children in any part of a mine which is below ground or in any open cast working in which any mining operation is being carried on. Even an adolescent is not allowed to work in any part of a mine which is below ground, unless he has completed his 16th year and has a medical certificate of fitness for work.[30]

The Merchant Shipping Act, 1958[31]

The Act prohibits the employment of children in any capacity, which is below 14 years of age. Employment of young person's less than 18 years of age as trimmers and strikers is also made conditional in any ship to the extent of production of medical fitness certificate from a competent authority. The Act has been constantly under revision and amendments to ratify the changes approved by the International Maritime Organisation, through its conventions and protocols, to which India is a Member. The Merchant Shipping Act as is existed today has 24 parts. The review committee appointed by the Government of India, in 1991 under the Chairmanship of DG(s) to study the provision of the Act in its entirety and give suggestions for amendments taking into consideration the International Convention which India has ratified but not statutorily enacted, has suggested comprehensive amendments to the Act including the amendment of the preamble of the Act.[32]

Child Labour (Prohibition and Regulation) Act, 1986[33]

The Child Labour (Prohibition and Regulation) Act, 1986 was enacted to prohibit the engagement of children below the age of fourteen years in factories, mines and hazardous employments and to regulate their conditions of work in certain other employments. According to the Act, no child shall be employed or permitted to work in any of the occupations set forth in Part A of the Schedule or in any workshop wherein any of the processes set forth in Part B of the Schedule is carried on, provided that nothing in this Act shall apply to any workshop wherein any process is carried on by the occupier with the aid of his family or to any school established by, or receiving assistance or recognition from the Government.

The Central Industrial Relation Machinery (CIRM) in the Ministry of Labour is responsible for enforcing this Act. CIRM is an attached office of the Ministry and is also known as the Chief Labour Commissioner (Central) Organisation. The CIRM is headed by the Chief Labour Commissioner (Central). In addition, a Central Advisory Board on Child Labour has also been constituted under the Ministry to review the implementation of the existing legislations and suggest measures for welfare of working children.[34]

According to Child Labour (Prohibition and Regulation) Act, 1986, The Central Government may, by notification in the Official Gazette, constitute an advisory committee to be called the Child Labour Technical Advisory Committee (hereafter in this section referred to as the Committee) to advise the Central Government for the purpose of addition of occupations and processes to the Schedule. Every child employed in an establishment shall be allowed in each week, a holiday of one whole day, which day shall be specified by the occupier in a notice permanently exhibited in a conspicuous place in the establishment and the day so specified shall not be altered by the occupier more than once in three months.

Every occupier in relation to an establishment in which a child was employed or permitted to work immediately before the date of commencement of this Act in relation to such establishment shall, within a period of thirty days from such commencement, send to the Inspector within whose local limits the establishment is situated, a written notice containing the following particulars, namely: (a) the name and situation of the establishment; (b) the name of the person in actual management of the establishment; (c) the address to which communications relating to the establishment should be sent; and

(d) the nature of the occupation or process carried on in the establishment.[35] Every occupier, in relation to an establishment, who employs, or permits to work, any child after the date of commencement of this Act in relation to such establishment, shall, within a period of thirty days from the date of such employment, send to the Inspector within whose local limits the establishment is situated.[36]

If any question arises between an Inspector and an occupier as to the age of any child who is employed or is permitted to work by him in an establishment, the question shall, in the absence of a certificate as to the age of such child granted by the prescribed medical authority, be referred by the Inspector for decision to the prescribed medical authority. There shall be maintained by every occupier in respect of children employed or permitted to work in any establishment, a register to be available for inspection by an Inspector at all times during working hours or when work is being carried on in any such establishment, showing—(a) the name and date of birth of every child so employed or permitted to work; (b) hours and periods of work of any such child and the intervals of rest to which he is entitled; (c) the nature of work of any such child; and (d) such other particulars as may be prescribed.[37]

The appropriate Government may, by notification in the Official Gazette, make rules for the health and safety of the children employed or permitted to work in any establishment or class of establishments. Whoever employs any child or permits any child to work in contravention of the provisions of section 3 shall be punishable with imprisonment for a term which shall not be less than three months but which may extend to one year or with fine which shall not be less than ten thousand rupees but which may extend to twenty thousand rupees or with both. Whoever, having been convicted of an offence under section 3, commits a like offence afterwards, he shall be punishable with imprisonment for a term which shall not be less than six months but which may extend to two years. Any person, police officer or Inspector may file a complaint of the commission of an offence under this Act in any court of competent jurisdiction.[38]

Every certificate as to the age of a child which has been granted by a prescribed medical authority shall, for the purposes of this Act, be conclusive evidence as to the age of the child to whom it relates. No court inferior to that of a Metropolitan Magistrate or a Magistrate of the first class shall try any offence under this Act. The appropriate Government may appoint Inspectors for the purposes of securing compliance with the provisions of this Act and any Inspector so appointed shall be deemed to be a public servant within the meaning of the Indian Penal Code (45 of 1860). The appropriate Government may, by notification in the Official Gazette and subject to the condition of previous publication, make rules for carrying into effect the provisions of this Act.[39]

If any difficulty arises in giving effect to the provisions of this Act, the Central Government may, by order published in the Official Gazette, make such provisions not inconsistent with the provisions of this Act as appear to it to be necessary or expedient for removal of the difficulty: Provided that no such order shall be made after the expiry of a period of three years from the date on which this Act receives the assent of the President. Every order made under this section shall, as soon as may be after it is made, be laid before the Houses of Parliament. The Employment of Children Act, 1938 (26 of 1938) is hereby repealed. Notwithstanding such repeal, anything done or any action taken or purported to have been done or taken under the Act so repealed shall, in so far as it is not inconsistent with the provisions of this Act, be deemed to have been done or taken under the corresponding provisions of this Act.[40]

The Child Labour (Prohibition and Regulation Amendment Bill, 2012 was introduced in Rajya Sabha on 4 December, 2012 further to amend the Child Labour (Prohibition and Regulation) Act, 1986. The amendment also seeks a blanket ban on employing children below 18 years in hazardous industries like mining. The Bill is referred to Standing Committee on Labour and Employment.[41]

National Commission on Labour[42]

National Commission on Labour is an Indian statutory body to recommend the changes in the labour laws. The first National Commission on Labour was set up on 24th December 1966 under the Chairmanship of Justice P. B. Gajendragadkar. The Commission submitted its report in August, 1969 after detailed examination of all aspects of labour problems, both in the organised and unorganised sectors. The second National Commission on Labour (NCL) was set up on 2002 under the chairmanship of Ravindra Varma.[43]

Central Board for Workers Education[44]

The Central Board for Workers Education (CBWE) is an autonomous body under the Ministry of Labour and Employment, Government of India. It is registered under the Societies Registration

Act, 1860. Started in 1958, the Workers Education Scheme in India has been playing a very significant role in our national development; creating an enlightened and disciplined work force and bringing about desirable behavioural changes in our workforce in the organised, unorganised and rural sectors. It gets grants-in-aid from the Ministry of Labour and Employment to operate its activities. The Scheme of Workers Education aims at achieving the objectives of creating and increasing awareness and educating the workforce for their effective participation in the socio-economic development of the country[45]. Workers Education covers a whole range of skills and knowledge, which contribute to the harmonious development of a worker's personality, his role in the society and the knowledge and attitudes required for such roles.[46]

Ministry of Women and Child Development[47]

The Ministry of Women and Child Development, a branch of the Government of India, is the apex body for formulation and administration of the rules and regulations and laws relating to women and child development in India. The current minister for the Ministry of Women and Child Development is Maneka Gandhi having held the portfolio since May, 2014. The Department of Women and Child Development was set up in the year 1985 as a part of the Ministry of Human Resource Development to give the much needed impetus to the holistic development of women and children. With effect from 30.01.2006, the Department has been upgraded to a Ministry.

As a nodal Ministry for the advancement of women and children, the Ministry formulates plans, policies and programmes; enacts/ amends legislation, guides and coordinates the efforts of both governmental and non-governmental organisations working in the field of Women and Child Development. For holistic development of the child, the Ministry has been implementing the world's largest and most unique and outreach programme of Integrated Child Development Services providing a package of services comprising supplementary nutrition, immunisation, health check-up and referral services, pre-school non-formal education.[48]

The National Commission for Women (NCW) was constituted on 31.1.1992 as an apex level statutory body under the National Commission for Women Act, 1990. The main task of the Commission is to study and monitor all matters relating to the Constitutional and legal safeguards provided for women and to review the existing legislations and suggest amendments, wherever necessary. The Ministry signed a Memorandum of Understanding (MOU) with UNDP in July 2004 for implementation of a project titled "Promoting Gender Equality". A Standing Committee under the chairpersonship of Joint Secretary (Women Welfare) was constituted to facilitate programme implementation.[49]

Integrated Child Development Services[50]

It is India's primary social welfare scheme to tackle malnutrition and health problems in children below six years of age and their mothers. The main beneficiaries of the programme were aimed to be the children below six years of age, pregnant and lactating mothers, and adolescent girls. The Integrated Child Development Services Scheme was conceived in 1975 with an integrated delivery package of early childhood services. Today this programme reaches out to 8.06 million expectant and nursing mothers and 39.35 million children under six years of age. The scheme aims to improve the nutritional and health status of vulnerable groups including pre-school children, pregnant women and nursing mothers. A key element of this programme is that all the services are provided less than one roof, the anganwadi centre. The Ministry of Women and Child Development is the nodal department for UNICEF, which has provided essentials supplies to the ICDS Scheme since 1975.[51]

The predefined objectives of ICDS are: (a) To raise the health and nutritional level of poor Indian children below six years of age: (b) To create a base for proper mental, physical and social development of children in India; (c) To reduce instances of mortality, malnutrition and school dropouts among Indian Children; (d) To coordinate activities of policy formulation and implementation among all departments of various ministries involved in the different government programmes and schemes aimed at child development across India; (e) To provide health and nutritional information and education to mothers of young children to enhance child rearing capabilities of mothers in country of India; (f) To provide nutritional food to the mothers of young children and also at the time of pregnancy period.[52]

The Integrated Child Development Services programme is potentially well-poised to address some of the underlying causes of persistent under nutrition. The programme adopts a multi-sectoral approach to child well-being, incorporating health, education and nutrition interventions, and is implemented through a network of anganwadi centers at the community level. The Department of Women and Child Development's (DWCD) emphasis on a "life-cycle approach" means that malnutrition is fought through interventions targeted at unmarried adolescent girls, pregnant women, mothers and children aged 0 to six years. Eight key services are provided, including supplementary feeding, immunisation, health checkups and referrals, health and nutrition education to adult women, micronutrient supplementation and preschool education for three to six year olds.

Total government expenditure on the programme has grown sharply over time. An average of 700 million rupees was spent per year on the program between 1975 and 1992, but this amount rose more than six-fold to average 4,542 million rupees per year between 1992 and 1997. For 1999-2000, the budgetary allocation for the programme was over 8,557 million rupees and more than US$400 million have been allocated under India's Tenth Five-Year Plan (2002-2007). The program has been supported by several donors, including UNICEF, SIDA, WFP, CARE and NORAD. The World Bank has supported efforts to improve nutrition in India, in general, since 1980 through six projects. With an overall investment of US$ 712.3 million in the sector, India accounts for the largest volume of Bank Group lending devoted specifically to nutrition programmes.[53]

ICDS policy stipulates that there should be one anganwadi center in place per 1000 population, with more intensive placement of one per 700 population in tribal areas, where poverty tends to be more prevalent. While this policy aims to promote an equitable distribution of centers, in reality, the coverage of villages by ICDS is much more pronounced in wealthier states. States with lower per capita Net State Domestic Product (NSDP) have a smaller percentage of villages covered by the ICDS programme than those with higher NSDP.[54] Effective targeting restricts nutrition interventions to those individuals or groups that are most vulnerable to malnutrition. In so doing, it maximises the social returns and minimises costs. However, the high generalised malnutrition prevalence in India and the administrative costs associated with excluding those who are relatively well-off means that rigorous targeting of ICDS benefits to particular socioeconomic groups is unlikely to prove a feasible strategy.

The ICDS scheme places special emphasis on the participation of children of lower castes. Some anganwadi centers have been constructed in close proximity to scheduled caste and schedule tribe colonies, and anganwadi workers are expected to take steps to encourage the recruitment of these children into the programme.[55] In Maharashtra, Madhya Pradesh and Chhattisgarh, the percentage of scheduled tribe children attending the AWC is higher than any other caste, while in Kerala, Rajasthan and Uttar Pradesh, a greater percentage of scheduled caste children than other children attend. Growth monitoring activities are hampered by poor access to appropriate equipment, such as weighing scales, growth cards and wall or book charts. Often the equipment is nominally present, but not of sufficient quantity or quality.[56]

Funding ICDS initially the scheme was 100 per cent funded by the centre except for nutrition supplements, which were funded by states and union territories. In response to resource constraints faced by many states, the central government increased fiscal support to cover half of the supplementary nutrition costs in 2006. For 2009-10, the central government has proposed that the sharing ratio be modified to 90:10 and 50:50 for general assistance and supplementary nutrition, respectively, for all states (except the North-eastern ones) and 90:10 for all components for North-Eastern states.[57] The programme adopts a multi-sectoral approach incorporating both health and education interventions. The Ministry of Women and Child Development (MoWCD) is responsible for coordinating ICDS and working with state governments to monitor and evaluate the scheme's performance.[58] In many states, panchayats have also been actively involved in the implementation and monitoring of ICDS since the 73rd Amendment Act was passed in 1992. Between 2000 and 2010 approximately Rs 35,000 crore has been allocated to ICDS by the union government. ICDS's status as a flagship programme is reflected in its place in successive union budgets: the programme secured between 75-85 per cent of all funds allocated to MoWCD. The success of ICDS rests largely on communities accepting the services provided. Community uptake of ICDS services can be improved through awareness drives to raise consciousness of the community on issues related to women and children.[59]

Gujarat high court has issued notice to the state government and the Centre over a PIL seeking implementation of Right to Education Act (RTE) and Early Childhood Care and Education policy by providing facilities to the anganwadi centres and adequate staff. Petitioner Mujahid Nafees has submitted before the court that the policies are for holistic development of children during pre-primary stage. The Integrated Child Development Services scheme run by the department of women and child development has been assigned with the responsibility for implementation. Training was imparted and pre-education kits were also distributed.[60] However, there is huge vacancy at all levels in this dispensation to carry out responsibilities fixed for implementation of the law. There is a provision for separate sanitation facility for children and ICDS workers, but only 33 per cent of anganwadi centres have toilet facility across the state. The PIL also claimed that none of the anganwadi centres enjoys electricity connection. There are some 9,000 vacancies of ICDS workers. Instead of 26 DPOs, there are only 11 DPOs posted across the state.[61]

Malnutrition among women and children remains abysmally high in Uttar Pradesh despite several thousand crores spent annually on supplementary nutrition programmes. According to data kept by the Union ministry of women and child development, Uttar Pradesh is among the worst performing states in the area of underweight and malnutrition among children between the age group of 0 to 6 years.[62] Ironically, the poor performance persists despite a consecutive annual fund infusion of nearly Rs 3,000 crore towards the Integrated Child Development Services scheme to which both the Centre and the state governments contribute.[63] According to the state's own records, 35.5 per cent of the total children who were identified as beneficiaries of the supplementary nutrition programme under ICDS were underweight, with 62,728 falling in the Grade III and IV - severely malnourished - categories. The UP figures are also considerably higher than the national average of 28.4 per cent. At present UP has more than two crore children identified as beneficiaries of the supplementary nutrition programme (SNP), while nearly 50 lakh pregnant and lactating mothers are covered under ICDS.[64]

National Child Labour Project[65]

For rehabilitation of child labour, Government had initiated the National Child Labour Project (NCLP) Scheme in 1988 to rehabilitate working children in 12 child labour endemic districts of the country. Its coverage has increased progressively to cover 271 districts in the country presently. As on date the Scheme is in operation in 266 districts. Under the NCLP Scheme, children are withdrawn from work and put into special schools, where they are provided with bridging education, vocational training, mid-day meal, stipend, healthcare facilities etc. and finally mainstreamed to the formal education system. The NCLP scheme is a Central Sector scheme.[66] Under the scheme, project societies are set up at the district level under the Chairpersonship of the Collector/ District Magistrate for overseeing the implementation of the project. The National Policy on Child Labour, prescribes the need to focus on general development programmes for the benefit of the families of child Labour.[67]

Mid Day Meal Scheme[68]

The Mid Day Meal Scheme is a programme of the Government of India designed to improve the nutritional status of school-age children nation wide. The programme supplies free lunches on working days for children in Primary and Upper Primary Classes in Government, Government Aided, Local Body, Education Guarantee Scheme, and Alternate Innovative Education Centres, Madarsa and Maqtabs supported under Sarva Shiksha Abhiyan, and National Child Labour Project schools run by the Ministry of Labour. The roots of the programme can be traced back to the Pre-Independence era, when a Mid Day Meal Programme was introduced in 1925 in Madras Corporation by the British administration.[69] Gujarat was the second state to introduce MDM scheme in 1984, but it was later discontinued. The central and state governments share the cost of the Midday Meal Scheme, with the centre providing 75 per cent and the states 25 per cent. The central government provides grains and financing for other food. Costs for facilities, transportation, and labour are shared by the federal and state governments.[70]

The MDMS was started with two major objectives: firstly to enhance the child's nutrition level secondly to provide the basic education. MDMS was introduced basically to improve the overall development of the primary school children's education. Therefore, it has varied objectives like: (a) To increase the nutritional level of the school going children; (b) To enhance the educational attainment of the children; (c) To retain the children in the school for a long period of time; and (d) To develop the process of socialisation, etc.[71] Apart from the education, the nutritional aspects of MDMS have several dimensions including elimination of classroom hunger, the growth of school children's health. It is argued that if the children come everyday to school they can eat nutritious meal regularly and therefore child starvation could be checked. This makes it possible not only to realise their intake of calories and proteins but also to provide nutritional supplements such as Iron and Iodine, which are required in many hilly regions.[72] The Supreme Court directed all the state governments to implement MDMS and to provide every child a cooked meal with a minimum content of 300 calorie and 8-12 grams protein every day of school for a minimum of 200 days in every government and government aided primary schools.[73]

The National Programme of Nutritional Support to Primary Education which is popularly known as the Mid-day Meal Scheme was launched by the Government of India in 1995 with the objective of giving a boost to universalisation of primary education by increasing enrolment, attendance and retention and simultaneously improving the nutritional status of students in primary classes. Accordingly, many of the states started distributing food grains (dry rations) @ 3 kg. / per month/ per child with 80 per cent attendance in class. The Cooked mid-day meal (CMDM) scheme was introduced in all Government and Government-assisted primary schools in the form of a country-wide "Day of action on mid-day meals" in April 2002 by a landmark direction of the Supreme Court.[74]

Government of India launched National Programme of Nutritional Support to Primary Education (Commonly known as Mid-Day Meal Scheme) on August 15, 1995 to provide mid-day meal to the children studying at primary stage. The Department of School Education and Literacy, Ministry of Human Resource Development has prescribed a comprehensive and elaborate mechanism for monitoring and supervision of the Mid Day Meal Scheme.[75] The Guidelines provide that, as far as possible, the responsibility of cooking/supply of cooked mid day meal should be assigned to local women's / mothers.[76] Self-Help Group or local Youth Club affiliated to the Nehru Yuva Kendras or a voluntary organisation or by personnel engaged directly by the SMDC/Gram Panchayat/Municipality-Involvement of Self Help Groups under the scheme is increasing gradually. Quality of MDM largely depends on the quality of food grains. FCI is held responsible for issue of food grains of best available quality, which will in any case be at least of Fair Average Quality (FAQ). FCI appoints a Nodal Officer for each State to take care of various problems in supply of food grains under the MDM Programme.[77]

Despite the broad-based efforts of the Central Government for more than a decade and a half and a few pioneering efforts earlier on, the problem of malnutrition, anemia, deficiency in vitamin A and Iodine is very common among children in India. Given the scope of MDM scheme in terms of the expenditures incurred and number of beneficiaries on one hand, and the abysmal health and demographic statistics on the other, it becomes imperative that an evaluation of the scheme be attempted to judge its efficacy. The obvious enormity of the administrative and logistical responsibilities of offering mid day meals in schools raises the issue of alternative forms of nutrition delivery to the children. Because the programme does not prescribe any cardinal minimum numbers for micronutrients, perhaps, the minimum micronutrient numbers based on the ICMR norms may act as guidelines for a separate programme that may take care of that need.[78]

In April 2001, People's Union for Civil Liberties (Rajasthan) initiated the right to food litigation. This public interest litigation has covered a large range of issues relating to right to food, but the best known intervention by the court is on midday meals. On November 28, 2001 the Supreme Court of India gave directive making it mandatory for the state governments to provide cooked meals instead of 'dry rations'. In one of its many directions in the litigation the Supreme Court directed the government to fully implement its scheme of providing cooked meals to all children in primary schools[79]. This landmark direction converted the mid-day meal scheme into a legal entitlement, the violation of which can be taken up in the court of law. In May 2004, a new coalition government was formed at the centre, which promised universal provision of cooked meals fully funded by the centre. This 'promise' made in the Common Minimum Programme was followed by enhanced financial support to the states for cooking and building sufficient infrastructure.[80] Given this additional support the scheme has expanded its reach to cover most children in primary schools in India. A model for public-private partnership also evolved in Hyderabad where Naandi Foundation manages a central kitchen to provide cooked meals to about two lakh children in Hyderabad[81].

Convention on the Rights of the Child[82]

1. *Article 1 (Definition of the child):* The Convention defines a 'child' as a person below the age of 18, unless the laws of a particular country set the legal age for adulthood younger. The Committee on the Rights of the Child, the monitoring body for the Convention, has encouraged States to review the age of majority if it is set below 18 and to increase the level of protection for all children under 18.

2. *Article 2 (Non-discrimination):* The Convention applies to all children, whatever their race, religion or abilities; whatever they

think or say, whatever type of family they come from. It doesn't matter where children live, what language they speak, what their parents do, whether they are boys or girls, what their culture is, whether they have a disability or whether they are rich or poor. No child should be treated unfairly on any basis.

3. *Article 3 (Best interests of the child):* The best interests of children must be the primary concern in making decisions that may affect them. All adults should do what is best for children. When adults make decisions, they should think about how their decisions will affect children. This particularly applies to budget, policy and law makers.

4. *Article 4 (Protection of rights):* Governments have a responsibility to take all available measures to make sure children's rights are respected, protected and fulfilled. When countries ratify the Convention, they agree to review their laws relating to children. This involves assessing their social services, legal, health and educational systems, as well as levels of funding for these services. Governments are then obliged to take all necessary steps to ensure that the minimum standards set by the Convention in these areas are being met. They must help families protect children's rights and create an environment where they can grow and reach their potential.

5. *Article 5 (Parental guidance):* Governments should respect the rights and responsibilities of families to direct and guide their children so that, as they grow, they learn to use their rights properly. Helping children to understand their rights does not mean pushing them to make choices with consequences that they are too young to handle. Article 5 encourages parents to deal with rights issues "in a manner consistent with the evolving capacities of the child". The Convention does not take responsibility for children away from their parents and give more authority to governments. It does place on governments the responsibility to protect and assist families in fulfilling their essential role as nurturers of children.

6. *Article 6 (Survival and development):* Children have the right to live. Governments should ensure that children survive and develop healthily.

7. *Article 7 (Registration, name, nationality, care):* All children have the right to a legally registered name, officially recognised by the government. Children have the right to a nationality (to belong to a country).Children also have the right to know and, as far as possible, to be cared for by their parents.

8. *Article 8 (Preservation of identity):* Children have the right to an identity - an official record of who they are. Governments should respect children's right to a name, a nationality and family ties.

9. *Article 9 (Separation from parents):* Children have the right to live with their parent(s), unless it is bad for them. Children whose parents do not live together have the right to stay in contact with both parents, unless this might hurt the child.

10. *Article 10 (Family reunification):* Families whose members live in different countries should be allowed to move between those countries so that parents and children can stay in contact, or get back together as a family.

11. *Article 11 (Kidnapping):* Governments should take steps to stop children being taken out of their own country illegally. This article is particularly concerned with parental abductions. The Convention's Optional Protocol on the sale of children, child prostitution and child pornography has a provision that concerns abduction for financial gain.

12. *Article 12 (Respect for the views of the child):* When adults are making decisions that affect children, children have the right to say what they think should happen and have their opinions taken into account. This does not mean that children can now tell their parents what to do. This Convention encourages adults to listen to the opinions of children and involve them in decision-making — not give children authority over adults. Article 12 does not interfere with parents' right and responsibility to express their views on matters affecting their children.

13. *Article 12 (Respect for the views of the child):* When adults are making decisions that affect children, children have the right to say what they think should happen and have their opinions taken into account. The right of all children to be heard and taken seriously constitutes one of the fundamental values of the Convention. The Committee on the Rights of the Child (the Committee) has identified Article 12 as one of the four general principles of the Convention, the others being the right to non-discrimination, the right to life and development, and the primary consideration of the child's best interests, which highlights the fact that this article establishes not only a right in itself, but should also be considered in the interpretation and implementation of all other rights.

14. *Article 13 (Freedom of expression):* Children have the right to get and share information, as long as the information is not damaging to them or others. In exercising the right to freedom of expression,

children have the responsibility to also respect the rights, freedoms and reputations of others. The freedom of expression includes the right to share information in any way they choose, including by talking, drawing or writing, conscience and religion): Children have the right to think and believe what they want and to practice their religion, as long as they are not stopping other people from enjoying their rights. Parents should help guide their children in these matters. The Convention respects the rights and duties of parents in providing religious and moral guidance to their children. Religious groups around the world have expressed support for the Convention, which indicates that it in no way prevents parents from bringing their children up within a religious tradition.

15. *Article 15 (Freedom of association):* Children have the right to meet together and to join groups and organisations, as long as it does not stop other people from enjoying their rights. In exercising their rights, children have the responsibility to respect the rights, freedoms and reputations of others.

16. *Article 16 (Right to privacy):* Children have a right to privacy. The law should protect them from attacks against their way of life, their good name, their families and their homes.

17. *Article 17 (Access to information; mass media):* Children have the right to get information that is important to their health and well-being. Governments should encourage mass media – radio, television, newspapers and Internet content sources – to provide information that children can understand and to not promote materials that could harm children.

18. *Article 18 (Parental responsibilities; state assistance):* Both parents share responsibility for bringing up their children, and should always consider what is best for each child. Governments must respect the responsibility of parents for providing appropriate guidance to their children – the Convention does not take responsibility for children away from their parents and give more authority to governments. It places a responsibility on governments to provide support services to parents, especially if both parents work outside the home.

19. *Article 19 (Protection from all forms of violence):* Children have the right to be protected from being hurt and mistreated, physically or mentally. Governments should ensure that children are properly cared for and protect them from violence, abuse and neglect by their parents, or anyone else who looks after them.

20. *Article 20 (Children deprived of family environment):* Children who cannot be looked after by their own family have a right to special care and must be looked after properly, by people who respect their ethnic group, religion, culture and language.

21. *Article 21 (Adoption):* Children have the right to care and protection if they are adopted or in foster care. The first concern must be what is best for them. The same rules should apply whether they are adopted in the country where they were born, or if they are taken to live in another country.

22. *Article 22 (Refugee children):* Children have the right to special protection and help if they are refugees (if they have been forced to leave their home and live in another country), as well as all the rights in this Convention.

23. *Article 23 (Children with disabilities):* Children who have any kind of disability have the right to special care and support, as well as all the rights in the Convention, so that they can live full and independent lives.

24. *Article 24 (Health and health services):* Children have the right to good quality healthcare - the best healthcare possible - to safe drinking water, nutritious food, a clean and safe environment, and information to help them stay healthy. Rich countries should help poorer countries achieve this.

25. *Article 25 (Review of treatment in care):* Children who are looked after by their local authorities, rather than their parents, have the right to have these living arrangements looked at regularly to see if they are the most appropriate. Their care and treatment should always be based on "the best interests of the child".

26. *Article 26 (Social security):* Children either through their guardians or directly have the right to help from the government if they are poor or in need.

27. *Article 27 (Adequate standard of living):* Children have the right to a standard of living that is good enough to meet their physical and mental needs. Governments should help families and guardians who cannot afford to provide this, particularly with regard to food, clothing and housing.

28. *Article 28 (Right to education):* All children have the right to a primary education, which should be free. Wealthy countries should help poorer countries achieve this right. Discipline in schools should respect children's dignity. For children to benefit from education, schools must be run in an orderly way - without the use of violence.

Any form of school discipline should take into account the child's human dignity.

29. *Article 29 (Goals of education):* Children's education should develop each child's personality, talents and abilities to the fullest. It should encourage children to respect others, human rights and their own and other cultures. It should also help them learn to live peacefully, protect the environment and respect other people. Children have a particular responsibility to respect the rights their parents, and education should aim to develop respect for the values and culture of their parents.

30. *Article 30 (Children of minorities/indigenous groups):* Minority or indigenous children have the right to learn about and practice their own culture, language and religion. The right to practice one's own culture, language and religion applies to everyone; the Convention here highlights this right in instances where the practices are not shared by the majority of people in the country.

31. *Article 31 (Leisure, play and culture):* Children have the right to relax and play, and to join in a wide range of cultural, artistic and other recreational activities.

32. *Article 32 (Child labour):* The government should protect children from work that is dangerous or might harm their health or their education. While the Convention protects children from harmful and exploitative work, there is nothing in it that prohibits parents from expecting their children to help out at home in ways that are safe and appropriate to their age.

33. *Article 33 (Drug abuse):* Governments should use all means possible to protect children from the use of harmful drugs and from being used in the drug trade.

34. *Article 34 (Sexual exploitation):* Governments should protect children from all forms of sexual exploitation and abuse. This provision in the Convention is augmented by the Optional Protocol on the sale of children, child prostitution and child pornography.

35. *Article 35 (Abduction, sale and trafficking):* The government should take all measures possible to make sure that children are not abducted, sold or trafficked. This provision in the Convention is augmented by the Optional Protocol on the sale of children, child prostitution and child pornography.

36. *Article 36 (Other forms of exploitation):* Children should be protected from any activity that takes advantage of them or could harm their welfare and development.

37. *Article 37 (Detention and punishment):* No one is allowed to punish children in a cruel or harmful way. Children who break the law should not be treated cruelly. They should not be put in prison with adults, should be able to keep in contact with their families, and should not be sentenced to death or life imprisonment without possibility of release.

38. *Article 38 (War and armed conflicts):* Governments must do everything they can to protect and care for children affected by war. Children under 15 should not be forced or recruited to take part in a war or join the armed forces. The Convention's Optional Protocol on the involvement of children in armed conflict further develops this right, raising the age for direct participation in armed conflict to 18 and establishing a ban on compulsory recruitment for children under 18.

39. *Article 39 (Rehabilitation of child victims):* Children who have been neglected, abused or exploited should receive special help to physically and psychologically recover and reintegrate into society. Particular attention should be paid to restoring the health, self-respect and dignity of the child.

40. *Article 40 (Juvenile justice):* Children who are accused of breaking the law have the right to legal help and fair treatment in a justice system that respects their rights. Governments are required to set a minimum age below which children cannot be held criminally responsible and to provide minimum guarantees for the fairness and quick resolution of judicial or alternative proceedings.

41. *Article 41 (Respect for superior national standards):* If the laws of a country provide better protection of children's rights than the articles in this Convention, those laws should apply.

42. *Article 42 (Knowledge of rights):* Governments should make the Convention known to adults and children. Adults should help children learn about their rights, too.

43. *Articles 43-54 (implementation measures):* These articles discuss how governments and international organisations like UNICEF should work to ensure children are protected in their rights.[83]

Conclusion

Over the years the Government of India has multiplied its efforts to address the needs and rights of exploited children. The largest and most structured intervention in the area of child labour in India is the National Child Labour Projects. For rehabilitation of child labour,

Government had initiated the National Child Labour Project (NCLP) Scheme in 1988 to rehabilitate working children in 12 child labour endemic districts of the country. National Commission on Labour is an Indian statutory body to recommend the changes in the labour laws. The Central Board for Workers Education is an autonomous body under the Ministry of Labour and Employment, Government of India.

The Ministry of Women and Child Development, a branch of the Government of India, is the apex body for formulation and administration of the rules and regulations and laws relating to women and child development in India. The Integrated Child Development Services Scheme was conceived in 1975 with an integrated delivery package of early childhood services. Today this programme reaches out to 8.06 million expectant and nursing mothers and 39.35 million children under six years of age. The Mid Day Meal Scheme is a programme of the Government of India designed to improve the nutritional status of school-age children nation wide. The MDMS was started with two major objectives: firstly to enhance the child's nutrition level secondly to provide the basic education.

References

1. Child labour in India, Retrieved from http://hindustanchildlabour.weebly.com/
2. India moves to band all forms of child labour, Retrieved from http://bba.org.in/?q=content/india-moves-ban-all-forms-child-labour
3. Care and concerns (2015), Retrieved from http://careandconcerns2003.blogspot.in/
4. Care and Concerns: Stop child labour, Retrieved from http://www.wattpad.com/story/32732137-care-%26-concerns-stop-child-labour
5. UNICEF, Retrieved from http://unicef.in/
6. India: Third and Fourth Combined Periodic Report on the Convention on the Rights of the Child, Retrieved from http://wcd.nic.in/crc3n4/crc3n4_1r.pdf
7. Care and concerns; lets spread smile together (2015), Retrieved from https://careandconcerns2003.wordpress.com/
8. See http://shodhganga.inflibnet.ac.in:8080/jspui/bitstream/10603/8530/16/16_chapter%208.pdf
9. See http://elearning.sol.du.ac.in/mod/book/tool/print/index.php?id=903
10. See http://shodhganga.inflibnet.ac.in:8080/jspui/bitstream/10603/8530/16/16_chapter%208.pdf

11. See http://www.mu.ac.in/myweb_test/M.A.%28Part-I%29%20History%20Paper%20-%20II%20%28Option%20-%20E%29%20Indian%20National%20Movement% 20%281857A.D.% 20to%201947%20 A.D.%29%20Eng.pdf
12. See http://www.doccentre.net/docsweb/LABOURLAWS/bare-acts/employing_children_act.htm
13. Employment of Children Act, 1938, see http://www.ilo.org/dyn/natlex/docs/WEBTEXT/47334/65072/E38BGD01.htm
14. See http://mpsdma.nic.in/Website_Material/Factories_Act.pdf
15. See https://www.ilo.org/dyn/natlex/docs/WEBTEXT/32063/64873/E87IND01.htm
16. The Factories Act, 1948, Retrieved from http://en.wikipedia.org/wiki/Factories_Act_1948
17. See http://www.ilo.org/dyn/travail/docs/623/Minimum% 20Wages%20Act%201948.pdf
18. See http://dc-siwan.bih.nic.in/minimum_wages_act_1948.pdf
19. See http://www.hrdiap.gov.in/group12012/minimum%20wages%20act.pdf
20. See http://vikaspedia.in/social-welfare/unorganised-sector-1/the-minimum-wages-_central_-rules1950
21. Minimum Wages Act 1948, Retrieved from http://en.wikipedia.org/wiki/Minimum_Wages_Act_1948
22. See http://www.teaboard.gov.in/pdf/policy/Plantations% 20Labour%20Act_amended.pdf
23. See http://labourbureau.nic.in/Report_Plant_Act_2008.pdf
24. See http://www.doccentre.net/docsweb/LABOURLAWS/bare-acts/plantation_act.htm
25. http://www.ilo.org/dyn/legosh/en/f?p= LEGPOL:503:10271455808762:::503:P503_REFERENCE_ID:131783
26. http://artassam.nic.in/Labour%20&%20Employment%20Deptt/PLANTATIONS%20LABOUR%20ACT,%201951.pdf
27. See http://mineral.up.nic.in/ma_1952.pdf
28. See http://www.prsindia.org/uploads/media/minesamendment.pdf
29. Amendments to the Mines Act, 1952 (35 of 1952), Retrieved from http://pib.nic.in/newsite/erelease.aspx?relid=68802
30. See http://labour.nic.in/upload/uploadfiles/files/Divisions/LC&ILAS/P_K_Sarkar.pdf
31. http://labour.gov.in/upload/uploadfiles/files/ActsandRules/Service_and_Employment/TheMerchantShippingAct1958.pdf
32. See http://dpal.kar.nic.in/Central%20Acts&Ordinance%20PDF/Act%2040%20of%202007%20PR-98.pdf

33. http://bba.org.in/sites/default/files/Child%20Labour%20_ Prohibition %20_%20Regulation_%20Act,%201986.pdf
34. See http://labour.nic.in/upload/uploadfiles/files/Divisions/childlabour/act.pdf
35. See http://www.tnchildlabour.tn.gov.in/prohibition.htm
36. Child Labour (Prohibition and Regulation) Act, 1986, Retrieved from http://business.gov.in/legal_aspects/child_labour.php
37. See http://164.100.47.134/lsscommittee/Labour/15_Labour_40.pdf
38. See http://www.ncpcr.gov.in/view_file.php?fid=413
39. See http://clc.gov.in/Acts/shtm/chla.php
40. http://www.prsindia.org/uploads/media/Child%20Labour/Child%2 0Labour%20%28Prohibition%20and%20Regulation%29%20%28A%29%20Bill, %202012.pdf
41. See http://www.cry.org/resources/pdf/Child-Labour-Act-1986.pdf
42. National Commission on Labour, Retrieved from http://en.wikipedia.org/wiki/National_Commission_on_Labour
43. See http://www.cbwe.gov.in/recommendations/national-commission-on-labour—recommendations.aspx
44. See http://www.cbwe.gov.in/about-us.aspx
45. Official website of Central Board for Workers Education.
46. See http://www.cbwe.gov.in/
47. Ministry of Women and Child Development, Retrieved from http://en.wikipedia.org/wiki/Ministry_of_Women_and_Child_ Development_ %28India%29
48. See http://wcd.nic.in/
49. See http://www.childlineindia.org.in/ministry-of-women-and-child-development.htm
50. Integrated Child Development Services, Retrieved from http://en.wikipedia.org/wiki/Integrated_Child_Development_Services
51. Integrated Child Development Services (ICDS) Scheme, Retrieved from http://wcd.nic.in/icds.htm
52. See http://www.childlineindia.org.in/Integrated-Child-Development-Scheme-ICDS.htm
53. See http://cdf.ifmr.ac.in/wp-content/uploads/2011/03/ICDS-Scheme-Brief.pdf
54. See http://unicef.in/Uploads/Publications/Resources/pub_doc61.pdf
55. See https://data.gov.in/keywords/integrated-child-development-scheme-icds
56. See http://siteresources.worldbank.org/SOUTHASIAEXT/Resources/223546-1147272668285/undernourished_chapter_2.pdf
57. See http://motherchildnutrition.org/india/program-outline.html
58. Integrated Child Development Services (2015), Retrieved from https://data.gov.in/keywords/integrated-child-development-services

59. See http://planningcommission.nic.in/reports/peoreport/peo/peo_icds.pdf
60. A Gupta (2013), Integrated Child Development Services, Retrieved from http://www.iapsmupuk.org/journal/index.php/IJCH/article/view/382
61. U Kapil (2002), Integrated Child Development Services, Retrieved from http://www.ncbi.nlm.nih.gov/pubmed/12173700
62. See http://deogarh.nic.in/otheroffices/nclp/nclp/nclp_dgh.pdf
63. http://socialwelfare.icdsbih.gov.in/Schemes_Programmes/Schemes_Programmes.php?grpID=4&SubGroupID=1
64. India - Integrated Child Development Services, Retrieved from http://www.unicef.org/earlychildhood/files/india_icds.pdf
65. See http://labour.nic.in/content/division/nclp.php
66. See http://articles.economictimes.indiatimes.com/2014-07-14/news/51485014_1_child-labour-nclp-working-children
67. See http://www.childlineindia.org.in/national-child-labour-project.htm
68. Mid Day Meal Scheme (2015), Retrieved from http://en.wikipedia.org/wiki/Midday_Meal_Scheme
69. Mid day meal (2015), Retrieved from http://mdm.nic.in/
70. See http://www.archive.india.gov.in/sectors/education/index.php?id=7
71. See http://mhrd.gov.in/mid-day-meal
72. See http://econ.berkeley.edu/sites/default/files/Bonds.pdf
73. See http://www.childlineindia.org.in/mid-day-meal-scheme.htm
74. An evaluation of mid day meal, Retrieved from http://www.iimahd.ernet.in/~satish/MDMJISPEPaper%282%29.pdf
75. Uma, Mid-Day Meal Scheme and Primary Education in India: Quality Issues, International Journal of Scientific and Research Publications, Volume 3, Issue 11, November 2013, Retrieved from http://www.ijsrp.org/research-paper-1113/ijsrp-p2360.pdf
76. See http://trgmdm.nic.in/mdm_training/StaticPages/MonthlyDataEntry.pdf
77. See http://cdf.ifmr.ac.in/wp-content/uploads/2011/03/MDM-Scheme-Brief.pdf
78. See http://trgmdm.nic.in/mdm_training/StaticPages/AnnualDataEntry.pdf
79. See http://www.aea-southasia.org/uploads/9.pdf
80. See http://www.mssrf.org/sites/default/files/School-Feeding-Programmes-in-India.pdf
81. See http://www.educationforallinindia.com/best-practices-mid-day-meal-skmalik.pdf
82. See http://www.unicef.org/crc/files/Rights_overview.pdf
83. See https://www.unicef.org.au/Discover/What-we-do/Convention-on-the-Rights-of-the-Child/childfriendlycrc.aspx

6

Women Rights

"You can search throughout the entire universe for someone who is more deserving of your love and affection than you are yourself, and that person is not to be found anywhere. You yourself, as much as anybody in the entire universe deserve your love and affection."

- Buddha

Introduction

Women's rights are the rights and entitlements claimed for women and girls of many societies worldwide. Although males seem to have dominated in many ancient cultures, there are some exceptions. The rights of women and men to have equal pay and equal benefits for equal work were openly denied by the British Hong Kong Government up to the early 1970s. During the 19th century some women began to ask for, demand, and then agitate and demonstrate for the right to vote, the right to participate in their government and its law making. During the 19th century some women in the United States and Britain began to challenge laws that denied them the right to their property once they married. In the subsequent decades women's rights again became an important issue in the English speaking world. The International Council of Women was the first women's organisation to work across national boundaries for the common cause of advocating human rights for women. The Universal Declaration of Human Rights, adopted in 1948, enshrines "the equal rights of men and women", and addressed both the equality and equity issues.[1]

Feminism began in the western world in the late 19th century and has gone through three waves. First-wave feminism was oriented around the station of middle- or upper-class white women and involved suffrage and political equality. The feminist movement can be traced back to the 14th century when Christine de Pizan, a French poet, became one of the first female artists to make a living through writing. The Women's movement effected change in Western society, including women's suffrage, the right to initiate divorce proceedings and "no fault" divorce, the right of women to make individual decisions regarding pregnancy (including access to contraceptives and abortion), and the right to own property. The feminist movement's agenda includes acting as a counter to the putatively patriarchal strands in the dominant culture. The increased entry of women into the workplace beginning in the 20th century has affected gender roles and the division of labour within households.[2]

A woman is a female human. The term *woman* is usually reserved for an adult, with the term girl being the usual term for a female child or adolescent. Womanhood is the period in a female's life after she has passed through childhood and adolescence, generally around the age 18. There are various words used to refer to the quality of being a woman. In many prehistoric cultures, women assumed a particular cultural role. In hunter-gatherer societies, women were generally the gatherers of plant foods, small animal foods and fish, while men hunted meat from large animals.

The UN Declaration on the Elimination of Violence against Women defines "violence against women" as "any act of gender-based violence that results in, or is likely to result in, physical, sexual or mental harm or suffering to women, including threats of such acts, coercion or arbitrary deprivation of liberty, whether occurring in public or in private life and identifies three forms of such violence: that which occurs *in the family*, that which occurs *within the general community*, and that which is perpetrated or condoned *by the State*. It also states that "*violence against women is a manifestation of historically unequal power relations between men and women.*"[3]

Importance of Women Rights

Women are the integral part of our society and can not be neglected due to their nearly 50 per cent shares in the population of the nation[4]. The role of women in society has been greatly overseen in the last few decades but now are coming to a more perspective to people. In the early days women were seen as wives who were intended to cook, clean, and take care of the kids.[5] Women in India constitute nearly 50 per cent of its population. According to 1991 census, there were 40.6 crores of women as against 43.7 crores of men. Roughly, there are 929 women for every 1000 men.

After Independence the Constitution of India gave equal rights to men and women in all walks of life. But even today one cannot say that all women in India enjoy equal rights with men in all matters. There are many reasons for this (1) the customs and traditions prevalent for centuries, (2) The high percentage of illiteracy among women, (3) Ignorance of their rights, (4) Patriarchal Society, (5) Economic system, (6) Acceptance of the theory of Karma or fatalism, (7) Unchecked male domination in all walks of life.[6] Understanding India has often been difficult for those who look for archetypes in each country. India's sheer size, variety and apparent contradictions confound many observers. The persistence of poverty, illiteracy, malnutrition and the low rank in human development index makes it look somewhat similar to other poor and developing countries.[7]

The right to equality and non-discrimination on the basis of gender is increasingly recognised as being at the core of human rights, including workers' rights. Demographic and labour market trends indicate that greater attention should be devoted to older women workers. With unemployment and under-employment still the most serious economic problem in many countries and women still more vulnerable than men, the challenge remains to enlarge the world of work and to provide greater opportunities for productive and remunerative employment. The elimination of gender discrimination in the world of work is not only the right thing to do; it is also the smart thing to do.[8]

The primary pathways through which gender systems affect growth are by influencing the productivity of labour and the allocative efficiency of the economy. In terms of productivity, for example, if the access of women farmers to productive inputs and human capital were on a par with men's access, total agricultural output could increase by an estimated six to 20 per cent. Identification of women as being a reliable, productive and cheap labour force makes them the preferred workforce for textiles and electronic transnational corporations. Perception of women as 'good with money,' including being better at paying back loans, has led them to be targeted in microfinance programme. Justice institutions, from the police to the courts, continue to deny women's right to justice. Women and girls remain unable to access justice, given that in many countries there are still laws that discriminate against women in relation to the family, property, citizenship and employment.[9]

Economic Rights

Women's economic empowerment requires bold and sustained action to advance women's opportunities and rights and to ensure that women can participate and be heard.[10] Investing in women's economic empowerment sets a direct path towards gender equality, poverty eradication and inclusive economic growth. Women make enormous contributions to economies, whether in businesses, on farms, as entrepreneurs or employees, or by doing unpaid care work at home.[11] Economic empowerment is the capacity of women and men to participate in, contribute to and benefit from growth processes in ways which recognise the value of their contributions, respect their dignity and make it possible to negotiate a fairer distribution of the benefits of growth. The economic empowerment of women is a prerequisite for sustainable development, pro-poor growth and the achievement of all the Millennium Development Goals. Increasing the role of women in the economy is part of the solution to the financial and economic crises and critical for economic resilience and growth. Some issues relating to women's economic empowerment are particularly challenging or sensitive.[12]

Female entrepreneurs encompass approximately one-third of all entrepreneurs worldwide. A recent international study found that women from low to middle income countries (such as Russia and the Philippines) are more likely to enter early stage entrepreneurship when compared to those of higher income countries (such as Belgium, Sweden and Australia). Even though female entrepreneurship and the formation of women business networks are steadily rising, there are a number of challenges and obstacles that female entrepreneur's face.[13] Women's entrepreneurship is both about women's position in society and the role of entrepreneurship in the same society. Women are faced with specific obstacles (such as family responsibilities) that have to be overcome in order to give them access to the same opportunities as men.[14]

Women's economic and social empowerment is an accepted part of development programming. Understanding the risks and benefits of economic empowerment programming is crucial in designing programmes that maximise benefits and minimise harm. There are numerous programs around the world to that aim to increase women's empowerment and decrease violence against women; yet relatively few have documented their actual effectiveness. Men typically have more education and more income generating opportunities than women. The evidence suggests that when women upset this gender status quo they are at a higher risk for violence. Women's empowerment was measured through household decision-making (woman, man or joint), negotiation, attitudes towards violence and women's rights, and incidence of intimate partner violence.[15]

Women have the potential to change their own economic status, as well as that of the communities and countries in which they live. Unequal opportunities between women and men continue to hamper women's ability to lift them from poverty and gain more options to improve their lives. Women's economic empowerment i.e. their capacity to bring about economic change for themselves is increasingly viewed as the most important contributing factor to achieving equality between women and men. Economic development efforts to combat poverty can only succeed if women are part of the solution.[16] The Government of India set aside some reasonable amount of money which women who have business ideas can borrow in order to start businesses. Women are encouraged to start small business in order to have their own source of income thus they become independent. Most women are given a chance of finishing their education to the degree level. They are discouraged from getting married and raising a family when they are young. There are various scholarships that benefits women in India to achieve their career by going back to school or various training institutions where they can further their education.[17]

Political Rights

Women in India participate in voting, run for public offices and political parties at lower levels more than men. Political activism and voting are the strongest areas of women's political participation. The Constitution of India establishes a parliamentary system of government, and guarantees its citizens the right to be elected, freedom of speech, freedom to assemble and form associations, and vote. To remedy low participation of women electors, India in 1994 established quotas in constitutional amendments (73rd and 74th) to reserve 33 per cent of seats in local governments for women. Local governing bodies in India are called Panchayati Raj Institutions and one-third of seats and leadership positions must be reserved for women. Seats reserved for women are rotated for assurance that each seat has an equal chance of being reserved. The Women's Reservation Bill (108th amendment) has been introduced in the national parliament to reserve 33 per cent of Lok Sabha and Vidhan Sabha seats for women.[18]

Political participation is the hallmark of a democratic setup. Nature, success and effectiveness of democracy largely depend on the extent to which equal, effective and actual participation is provided by the system to all its citizens. Political participation appears to be a complex phenomenon, a dependent variable that hinges upon many sectors such as the psychological, socio-economic and political, which provide orientation to individuals either positively or negatively.[19] The 15th Lok Sabha in India (2009) comprised 61 women members, one only 11.2 per cent of the total Lok Sabha membership. While it has increased from 9.02 per cent in 1999, it is almost half of the world average of 22.2 per cent. The Rajya Sabha does not fare much better, with 27 women members comprising 11.5 per cent of the total membership in 2013. Women in India are much better represented in the Panchayati Raj Institutions as compared to the Parliament. As per the Ministry of Panchayati Raj, in 2008 the Gram Panchayats had 37.8 per cent women members, the Intermediate Panchayats 37 per cent women members and the District Panchayats 35.3 per cent women members. The total representation of women in all three tiers of the Panchayat amounted to 36.87 per cent.[20]

Social Rights

In the 1970s and 1980s, civil and political rights were frequently referred to as "first generation rights" while economic and social rights were referred to as "second generation rights," implying a hierarchy in the development of human rights within the UN system. Women's rights have been an important focus for women's organising since the beginning of feminist movements.[21] Investing in women is said to be a key to development. Educate her, buy her a cow or goat, or help her start a business and great things will follow: sustained increases in income, greater empowerment and social inclusion, health and education for the children, and (especially in war-affected regions) mental health and happiness.[22]

The principle of gender equality is enshrined in the Indian Constitution in its Preamble, Fundamental Rights, Fundamental Duties and Directive Principles. The Constitution not only grants equality to women, but also empowers the State to adopt measures of positive discrimination in favour of women. Women's equality in power sharing and active participation in decision-making, including decision-making in political process at all levels will be ensured for the achievement of the goals of empowerment. All measures will be taken to guarantee women equal access to and full participation in decision-making bodies at every level, including the legislative, executive, judicial, corporate, statutory bodies, as also the advisory Commissions, Committees, Boards, Trusts etc.

The important role played by women in electronics, information technology and food processing and agro industry and textiles has been crucial to the development of these sectors. India has also ratified various international conventions and human rights instruments committing to secure equal rights of women. Key among them is the ratification of the Convention on Elimination of All Forms of Discrimination against Women in 1993.[23]

Legal Rights

Violence against Women is prevalent in every country in the world and is one of the leading causes of morbidity for women.[24] Securing women's legal rights, especially to land and other property, and ensuring that women's voices and priorities are heard and acted on are vital components of empowerment - securing women's land rights has a direct impact on their ability to access finance.[25] Equal access to education for women and girls will be ensured. Special measures will be taken to eliminate discrimination, universalise education, eradicate illiteracy, create a gender-sensitive educational system, increase enrolment and retention rates of girls and improve the quality of education to facilitate life-long learning as well as development of occupation/vocation/technical skills by women. Reducing the gender gap in secondary and higher education would be a focus area.

Legal empowerment is a powerful tool that the Asian Development Bank can use in working to reduce poverty. In developing nations, women and disadvantaged groups are frequently the most oppressed and poorly educated. Legal empowerment initiatives aim to give women and disadvantaged group's confidence, information, training, and assistance. Legal empowerment work relies upon developing complex and mutually reinforcing working relationships between varying parties. If the work is to evolve, it is essential that legal empowerment practitioners work in a transparent manner, meeting regularly with government counterparts to share information, and encourage public officials and agencies to develop a sense of ownership in the work.

To ensure that citizens can access justice, the system must be readily accessible and usable. Legal information must be publicly and readily available. It must be published in plain, easily understood language. Steps must also be taken to ensure that illiterate members of society can access information on their rights and how to access justice. Lack of economic independence places broad constraints on citizens' access to justice and critical resources, and participation in administrative and other public decision-making processes. In Bangladesh, Indonesia, Pakistan, and other developing Asian countries, the informal justice system has far greater relevance to the economic means and other circumstances of disadvantaged groups.[26]

Legal empowerment is a powerful tool for reducing poverty. It gives people the knowledge, skills, and confidence to participate in development projects.[27] The foremost being equal access to education and other opportunities for skill development. The Government has been making efforts for creating a congenial work environment for women workers. For this purpose, a separate 'Cell for Women Labour' has been set up in the Ministry to focus attention on the condition of working women and bring about an improvement therein.[28]

National Commission for Women

The National Commission for Women (NCW) is a statutory body of the Government of India, generally concerned with advising the government on all policy matters affecting women. It was established in January 1992 under the provisions of the Indian Constitution, as defined in the 1990 National Commission for Women Act. The objective of the NCW is to represent the rights of women in India and to provide a voice for their issues and concerns.[29]

Indian Constitution and Women Rights

Women in India now participate fully in areas such as education, sports, politics, media, art and culture, service sectors, science and technology, etc. The Constitution of India guarantees to all Indian women equality (Article 14), no discrimination by the State (Article 15(1)), equality of opportunity (Article 16), and equal pay for equal work (Article 39(d)). In addition, it allows special provisions to be made by the State in favour of women and children (Article 15(3)), renounces practices derogatory to the dignity of women (Article 51(A) (e)), and also allows for provisions to be made by the State for securing just and humane conditions of work and for maternity relief (Article 42).[30]

Women's Rights as Human Rights

"Women's Rights Are Human Rights" is a term used in the women's rights movement and is the name of a speech given by Hillary Rodham Clinton, at the time the First Lady of the United States, on September 5, 1995, at the United Nations Fourth World Conference on Women in Beijing. Clinton declared that *"that it is no longer acceptable to discuss women's rights as separate from human rights"*. Delegates from over 180 countries heard her say: *"If there is one message that echoes forth from this conference, let it be that human rights are women's rights and women's rights are human rights, once and for all."*[31]

Human rights reflect the moral conscience of the world and the highest common aspiration that everyone should live in liberty, free from want and fear. So, human rights can be seen as a global vision backed by state obligations. Human rights for women, as for all individuals, are protected in the tenets of international law and international conferences provide the opportunity for governments to make, or repeat, declarations of commitment. Human rights are not just about liberty and freedoms but also about equality, equity and justice and another milestone advance were made when the World Summit for Social Development recognised 'that the enjoyment of human rights was a fundamental basis for social development.'[32]

Human rights and fundamental freedoms are the birthright of all human beings; their protection and promotion is the first responsibility of Governments. The Platform for Action reaffirms that all human rights - civil, cultural, economic political and social, including the right to development are universal, indivisible, interdependent and interrelated, as expressed in the Vienna Declaration and Programme of Action adopted by the World Conference on Human Rights.[33] Gender equality is at the very heart of human rights and United Nations values. A fundamental principle of the United Nations Charter adopted by world leaders in 1945 is equal rights of men and women, and protecting and promoting women's human rights is the responsibility of all States. Discrimination based on sex is prohibited under almost every human rights treaty - including the International Covenant on

Civil and Political Rights and the International Covenant on Economic, Social and Cultural Rights, which under their common Article 3 provide for the rights to equality between men and women in the enjoyment of all rights.

Considered the international bill of rights for women, the Convention defines what constitutes discrimination against women and sets an agenda for national action to end such discrimination. It was adopted by the United Nations in 1979 and came into force on 3rd September 1981. In 1994, the United Nations resolved to appoint a Special Rapporteur - an independent expert — on the causes and consequences of violence against women. The Special Rapporteur investigates and monitors violence against women, and recommends and promotes solutions for its elimination. In 2010, the Human Rights Council established a Working Group on the issue of discrimination against women in law and in practice to promote the elimination of laws that discriminate against women and/or have a discriminatory impact on them.[34]

In 1993, 45 years after the Universal Declaration of Human Rights was adopted, and eight years after CEDAW entered into force, the UN World Conference on Human Rights in Vienna confirmed that women's rights were human rights. In 1994, the International Conference on Population and Development in Cairo (ICPD) articulated and affirmed the relationship between advancement and fulfillment of rights and gender equality and equity. In 1995, the Fourth World Conference on Women in Beijing generated global commitments to advance a wider range of women's rights. The inclusion of gender equality and women's empowerment as one of the eight Millennium Development Goals was a reminder that many of those promises have yet to be kept.[35]

Challenges before Women

Women in India face a lot of social inequalities ranging from gender specific abortions, mistreatment by their spouses, to eve teasing. Unlike in western cultures, Indians have a strong inclination for sons over daughters. Pregnancies are planned using differential contraception. An estimated ten million female foetuses have been aborted illegitimately in India. Eve teasing is a euphemism for sexual harassment of females by males in public areas. It is becoming increasingly difficult to prove such crimes because offenders have found clever ways of harassing women.[36] The violation of women's fundamental rights through physical, mental, emotional, and sexual violence against women has become almost commonplace in the Indian context. Violence against women has taken particularly acute forms in circumstances where populations are already marginalised, such as in areas affected by armed conflict, areas undergoing mass displacement.[37]

Conclusion

Women are the integral part of our society and can not be neglected due to their nearly 50 per cent shares in the population of the nation. The right to equality and non-discrimination on the basis of gender is increasingly recognised as being at the core of human rights, including workers' rights. Demographic and labour market trends indicate that greater attention should be devoted to older women workers. Women's economic empowerment requires bold and sustained action to advance women's opportunities and rights and to ensure that women can participate and be heard. Women's economic and social empowerment is an accepted part of development programming. Women in India participate in voting, run for public offices and political parties at lower levels more than men. Political activism and voting are the strongest areas of women's political participation. The Constitution of India establishes a parliamentary system of government, and guarantees its citizens the right to be elected, freedom of speech, freedom to assemble and form associations, and vote.

The principle of gender equality is enshrined in the Indian Constitution in its Preamble, Fundamental Rights, Fundamental Duties and Directive Principles. Legal empowerment is a powerful tool that the Asian Development Bank can use in working to reduce poverty. In developing nations, women and disadvantaged groups are frequently the most oppressed and poorly educated. Legal empowerment is a powerful tool for reducing poverty. It gives people the knowledge, skills, and confidence to participate in development projects. The National Commission for Women (NCW) is a statutory body of the Government of India, generally concerned with advising the government on all policy matters affecting women.

References

1. *Women's rights* (2015), Retrieved from http://en.wikipedia.org/wiki/Women%27s_rights
2. *Feminist women* (2015), Retrieved from http://en.wikipedia.org/wiki/Feminist_movement

3. *Female* (2015), Retrieved from http://en.wikipedia.org/wiki/Woman
4. See http://www.hamariweb.com/articles/article.aspx?id=4852
5. *Role of women in society*, Retrieved from http://www.megaessays.com/viewpaper/100876.html
6. *Essay on the role of women in India*, Retrieved from http://www.preservearticles.com/201104105204/the-role-of-women-in-india.html
7. *Role of India in the global economy* (2006), Retrieved from http://articles.economictimes.indiatimes.com/2006-10-28/news/27444338_1_gdp-power-parity-gross-national-income
8. Lin Lean Lim, *Women and the Global Economy*, Retrieved from http://www.un.org/womenwatch/daw/csw/beirutglo.htm
9. Dr. Sarah Bradshaw (2013), *Women's role in economic development: Overcoming the constraints*, Retrieved from http://unsdsn.org/wp-content/uploads/2014/02/130520-Women-Economic-Development-Paper-for-HLP.pdf
10. *Women's economic empowerment, UNDP,* Retrieved from http://www.undp.org/content/undp/en/home/ourwork/povertyreduction/focus_areas/focus_gender_and_poverty/women_s_economicempowerment.html
11. See more at: http://www.unwomen.org/en/what-we-do/economic-empowerment#sthash.JYXzO012.dpuf
12. *Women's Economic Empowerment: Issues paper* (2011), Retrieved from http://www.oecd.org/social/gender-development/47561694.pdf
13. *Female entrepreneur* (2015), Retrieved from http://en.wikipedia.org/wiki/Female_entrepreneur
14. *Women entrepreneurship: Issues and policies* (2004), Retrieved from http://www.oecd.org/cfe/smes/31919215.pdf
15. *Getting down to business: Women's economic and social empowerment in Burundi,* Retrieved from https://www.rescue.org/sites/default/files/resource-file/Burundi%20EASE%20Imact%20Eval%20Formatted%20Final.pdf
16. *Economic empowerment,* Retrieved from http://www.icrw.org/what-we-do/economic-empowerment
17. *Status of Women in India*, Retrieved from http://www.womenempowermentinindia.com/status-of-women-in-india/
18. *Women's political participation in India* (2015), Retrieved from http://en.wikipedia.org/wiki/Women%27s_political_participation_in_India
19. *Political Participation and Women in India*, chapter III, Retrieved from http://shodhganga.inflibnet.ac.in/bitstream/10603/189/3/12_chapter2.pdf
20. Apoorva Rathod, *Women's Political Participation and Representation in India*, Retrieved from http://www.delhipolicygroup.com/uploads/publication_file/1066_Women_in_Politics_final.pdf

21. Diane Elson / Jasmine Gideon, *Organising for Women's Economic and Social Rights: How useful is the International Covenant an Economic, Social and Cultural Rights?*, Organising for Women's Economic and Social Rights.
22. Christopher Blattman, Eric Green, Jeannie Annan, Julian Jamison (2013), *Building Women's Economic and Social Empowerment Through Enterprise: An Experimental Assessment of the Women's Income Generating Support (WINGS) Program in Uganda*, Retrieved from https://www.poverty-action.org/sites/default/files/wings_full_policy_report_0.pdf
23. *National policy for the empowerment of women* (2001), Retrieved from http://wcd.nic.in/empwomen.htm
24. See http://www.unwomensouthasia.org/assets/VAWIP-Report.pdf
25. *Women's economic empowerment, UNDP,* Retrieved from http://www.undp.org/content/undp/en/home/ourwork/povertyreduction/focus_areas/focus_gender_and_poverty/women_s_economicempowerment.html
26. *National policy for the empowerment of women* (2001), Retrieved from http://wcd.nic.in/empwomen.htm
27. See http://www.unwomensouthasia.org/assets/VAWIP-Report.pdf
28. *Legal Empowerment for Women and Disadvantaged Groups,* Retrieved from https://asiafoundation.org/resources/pdfs/LegalEmpowerment.pdf
29. *National Commission for Women* (2015), Retrieved from http://en.wikipedia.org/wiki/National_Commission_for_Women
30. *Women in India* (2015), Retrieved from http://en.wikipedia.org/wiki/Women_in_India
31. *Women's Rights Are Human Rights,* Retrieved from http://en.wikipedia.org/wiki/Women%27s_Rights_Are_Human_Rights
32. *Women rights are human rights,* Retrieved from http://www.womenaid.org/press/info/humanrights/hum.html
33. See http://www.un.org/womenwatch/directory/human_rights_of_women_3009.htm
34. See http://www.ohchr.org/EN/Issues/Women/WRGS/Pages/WRGSIndex.aspx
35. *The human rights of women,* Retrieved from http://www.unfpa.org/resources/human-rights-women
36. *Women Rights in India*, Retrieved from http://www.womenempowermentinindia.com/women-rights-in-india/
37. *Women's justice,* Retrieved from http://www.hrln.org/hrln/womens-justice-.html
38. *National policy for the empowerment of women* (2001), Retrieved from http://wcd.nic.in/empwomen.htm
39. See http://www.unwomensouthasia.org/assets/VAWIP-Report.pdf

7

LGBT Rights

"While physics and mathematics may tell us how the universe began, they are not much use in predicting human behaviour because there are far too many equations to solve. I'm no better than anyone else at understanding what makes people tick, particularly women."

-Stephen Hawking

Introduction

The legal status of people in same-sex relationships depends very much on where they live. At one end of the spectrum there are those countries that punish homosexuality with the death penalty - Iran, Mauritania, Saudi Arabia, Sudan and Yemen - as well as in parts of Nigeria and Somalia. At the other end, there are those countries where gay couples have the same marriage rights as heterosexual couples. Some states have conflicting laws on same-sex relationships, simultaneously having laws that punish and protect, while other countries have different laws in different regions.[1]

From its beginning with riots against police oppression of gays in New York City more than 40 years ago, the fight for gay rights continues today on new fronts.[2] The homosexual movement is organising and strategising to achieve their latest goal in the schools. Gay history is an important psychological tool that homosexual movement uses to convince schoolchildren that homosexual behaviour is a normal and positive influence in society. Gay history push has been slowly but steadily progressing. Since the 1990s individual "gay activist" teachers have woven homosexual themes into their classes, including history lessons. In 2011, California passed Senate Bill 48, the Orwellian-labeled "FAIR Education Act." It requires that the "historical contributions" of "lesbian, gay, bisexual, and transgender Americans" be included in courses, instructional material, and textbooks in California Public Schools.[3]

The American Psychological Association defines *sexual orientation* as *"an enduring pattern of emotional, romantic, and/or sexual attractions to men, women, or both sexes,"* ranging *"along a continuum, from exclusive attraction to the other sex to exclusive attraction to the same sex."* Gender identity refers to a person's internal sense of being male, female or something else; gender expression refers to the way a person communicates gender identity to others through behaviour, clothing, hairstyles, voice or body characteristics.[4] Societal attitudes towards homosexuality vary greatly in different cultures and different historical periods, as do attitudes toward sexual desire, activity and relationships in general. All cultures have their own values regarding appropriate and inappropriate sexuality; some sanction same-sex love and sexuality, while others disapprove of such activities,[5] poignantly; homosexuality would seem to be the one topic that unites the leaders of the world's faiths, an issue over which Franklin Graham and Malaysia's Mahathir Mohamed could break bread. Even the Dalai Lama views it as "sexual misconduct."[6]

How are LGBT?

LGBT is an initialism that stands for lesbian, gay, bisexual, and transgender. The initialism has become mainstream as a self-designation and has been adopted by the majority of sexuality and gender identity-based community centers and media in the United States and some other English-speaking countries.[7] Being LGBT is not just about physical attraction, but rather, encompasses the same needs all people have, to love another person and be loved in return.[8] They also stand for *"love, grace, beauty, and truth."* Beauty is the spot-on synonym for bisexual. Often the most misunderstood part of the LGBT acronym, bisexuality is typically defined as sexual attraction toward both males and females. Truth becomes the definition of transgender when a person stops pretending to be someone they are no.[9]

Gay is a term that primarily refers to a homosexual person or the trait of being homosexual. The term was originally used to refer to feelings of being carefree, happy, or bright and showy.[10] Lesbian is a female homosexual: a female who experiences romantic love or sexual attraction to other females. Female homosexual behaviour may be present in every culture, although the concept of a lesbian as a woman who pairs exclusively with other women is not. Attitudes about female homosexual behaviour are dependent upon women's roles in each society, and each culture's definition of sex.[11] Today many countries have made lesbian relationships legal and even there takes place lesbian marriages in western countries. Today lesbianism is no more considered a taboo in modern societies, but only a slightly deviated way of thinking.[12]

Bisexuality is romantic attraction, sexual attraction or sexual behaviour toward both males and females. The term *bisexuality* is mainly used in the context of human attraction to denote romantic or sexual feelings toward both men and women. The American Psychological Association states that *"sexual orientation falls along a continuum. In other words, someone does not have to be exclusively homosexual or heterosexual, but can feel varying degrees of both. Sexual orientation develops across a person's lifetime–different people realise at different points in their lives that they are heterosexual, bisexual or homosexual."*[13]

Transgender is the state of one's gender identity or gender expression not matching one's assigned sex. It is independent of sexual orientation; transgender people may identify as heterosexual, homosexual, bisexual, etc; some may consider conventional sexual orientation labels inadequate or inapplicable to them. While people self-identify as transgender, the transgender identity umbrella includes sometimes-overlapping categories. These include transsexual; transvestite or cross-dresser; genderqueer; androgyne; and bigender. Transsexual people identify as a member of the sex opposite to that assigned at birth, and desire to live and be accepted as such.[14]

History of LGBT

Hinduism is one of the world's oldest religions, and Hindus constitute a sixth of the world's population today. *"Same sex desire and even sexual activity have been represented and discussed in Indian literature for two millennia, often in a nonjudgmental and even celebratory manner,"* according to Hindu scholar Ruth Vanita. When Europeans arrived in India, they were shocked by Hinduism, which they termed idolatrous, and by the range of sexual practices, including same-sex relations, which they labeled licentious. Described as neither male nor female, but rather as a third-gender, *hijras* are traditionally depicted as a powerful force within Hinduism.[15] The earliest documents concerning same-sex relationships come from Ancient Greece. Such relationships did not replace marriage between man and woman, but occurred before and beside it.

The first historical mention of the performance of same-sex marriages occurred during the early Roman Empire according to controversial historian John Boswell. The first Roman emperor to have married a man was Nero, who is reported to have married two other males on different occasions. His first marriage was with one of his freedmen, Pythagoras, with whom Nero took the role of the bride.[16]

Reasons of LGBT

Lesbianism can be caused by both mental and physical reasons. Many a times a person develops lesbian traits at the early childhood itself. Certain physical conditions back lesbian mentality. Today, lesbianism is no more concerned a mental disorder. There are two common models of lesbianism. If a girl experiences the company of other girl or girl more than that with a boy, she may possibly become a lesbian. On the other hand, if a girl, by whatever reasons, happened to hate a boy or boys, she may become a lesbian.[17]

The 2008, discovery by Australian researchers of a genetic variation in transgender women, their receptor gene for the sex hormone testosterone was longer, making it less efficient at communicating signals set off speculation that insufficient uptake of male hormones in utero contributed to a more feminized brain.[18] There has been a lot of research into what causes someone to be transgender. As the Crossport Gender Support Group explains, Theories of both psychological and biological causality have been forwarded and it is quite likely there are different causes for different individuals. Lately, strong research suggests that an incorrect amount of miss-timed secretion of male hormone during stages of fetal development may create a transgendered individual - whether male or female. Biologically, nature will produce a female unless male androgens are supplied at the right times and in the right amounts. There are physiological and mental gray areas between male and female absolutes. Additionally, there are some theories arguing a genetic model of causality.[19]

There may be some reasons of bisexuality: The first cause could be the same issues that contribute to forming a homosexual orientation, such as neglectful same-sex parenting, peer rejection and sexual abuse. Second, one may participate in bisexuality because they were introduced to that kind of behaviour. Sometimes when parents don't provide any healthy guidelines or morals to follow, when there are opportunities for bisexuality, they may experiment with sex with both genders. Third, an individual may be drawn to bisexuality because they are narcissistic; they want both sexes to find them appealing.[20]

Same-Sex Marriage

Same-sex marriage is marriage between two people of the same sex. Legal recognition of same-sex marriage or the possibility to perform a same-sex marriage is sometimes referred to as marriage equality, particularly by supporters. Introduction of same-sex marriage laws has varied by jurisdiction, being variously accomplished through a legislative change to marriage laws, a court ruling based on constitutional guarantees of equality, or by direct popular vote. Same-sex marriages can be performed in a secular civil ceremony or in a religious setting. In 2010, a Columbia University Mailman School of Public Health study examining the effects of institutional discrimination on the psychiatric health of lesbian, gay and bisexual (LGB) individuals found an increase in psychiatric disorders, including a more than doubling of anxiety disorders, among the LGB population living in states that instituted bans on same-sex marriage.[21]

Same-sex couples want to marry for all the same reasons as their opposite-sex counterparts. These reasons include: for legal security, to publicly celebrate their commitment, to provide greater legal protection for their children, or simply because they are in love. Married partners have immediate access to all relationship entitlements, protections and responsibilities. A marriage certificate also allows married partners to easily prove their legal rights if challenged, for example, in emergency situations. Another practical benefit of marriage is that it is a widely recognized legal relationship. Allowing same-sex couples to be included in such a universal and valued institution as marriage will provide them and their families with real social and cultural benefits. Exclusion of same-sex attracted people from marriage also sends out the message that discrimination on the grounds of sexual orientation is acceptable.[22]

On 15th July 2010, the Argentine Senate approved a bill extending marriage rights to same-sex couples. Belgium became the second country in the world to legally recognise same-sex marriages when a bill passed by the Belgian Federal Parliament took effect on 1st June 2003. Brazil's Supreme Court ruled in May 2011 that same-sex couples are legally entitled to legal recognition of cohabitation. Legal recognition of same-sex marriage in Canada followed a series of constitutional challenges based on the equality provisions of the Canadian Charter of Rights and Freedoms. On 7th June 2012, the Folketing (Danish parliament) approved new laws regarding same-sex civil and religious marriage. Registered partnerships have been legal in Finland since in 2002. The Netherlands was the first country to extend marriage laws to include same-sex couples, following the recommendation of a special commission appointed to investigate the issue in 1995.

Same-sex marriage became legal in Norway on 1st January 2009 when a gender neutral marriage bill was enacted after being passed by the Norwegian legislature in June 2008. Portugal created de facto unions similar to common-law marriage for cohabiting opposite-sex partners in 1999, and extended these unions to same-sex couples in 2001. Spain was the third country in the world to legalise same-sex marriage, which has been legal since 3rd July 2005, and was supported by the majority of the Spanish people. Same-sex marriage in Sweden has been legal since 1st May 2009, following the adoption of a new, gender-neutral law on marriage by the Swedish parliament on 1st April 2009, making Sweden the seventh country in the world to open marriage to same-sex couples nationwide.

On 26th June 2013, the Supreme Court ruled it unconstitutional for the federal government of the United States to deny federal benefits of marriage to married same-sex couples, if it is recognised or performed in a state that allows same-sex marriage. Uruguay's Chamber of Deputies passed a bill on 12 December 2012, to extend marriage rights to same-sex couples. Australian federal law currently bans recognition of same-sex marriages. Registered partnerships are available in New South Wales, Tasmania, Queensland and Victoria. Colombia has no laws providing for same-sex marriage. Since 1st August 2001, Germany has registered partnerships for same-sex couples, providing most but not all rights of marriage. Same-sex marriage is not explicitly prohibited under Indian law and at least one couple has had their marriage recognised by the courts. Ireland made civil partnerships for same-sex couples legal in January 2011. Same-sex marriage is not legal in Japan. Malta has recognised same-sex unions since April 2014, following the enactment of the Civil Unions Bill, first introduced in September 2013.

In November 2008, Nepal's highest court issued final judgment on matters related to LGBT rights, which included permitting same-sex couples to marry. A same-sex marriage bill is pending in Parliament after the Green Liberal Party of Switzerland, in December 2013, opposed a Christian Democratic People's Party of Switzerland's initiative banning same-sex marriage. In Vietnam, currently only a marriage between a man and a woman is recognised. Vietnam's Ministry of Justice began seeking advice on legalising same-sex marriage from other governmental and non-governmental organisations in April and May 2012."[23]

LGBT in India

Lesbian, gay, bisexual and transgender rights in India have historically and culturally been accepted under the *Hijra* concept. Homosexual intercourse was made a criminal offence under Section 377 of the Indian Penal Code, 1860. This made it an offence for a person to voluntarily have carnal intercourse against the order of nature. On 23rd February 2012, the Ministry of Home Affairs expressed its opposition to the decriminalisation of homosexual activity, stating that in India, homosexuality is seen as being immoral. On 11th December 2013, the Supreme Court set aside the 2009 Delhi High Court order decriminalising consensual homosexual activity within its jurisdiction. On January 28, 2014 Supreme Court dismissed the Review Petition filed by Central Government, NGO Naz Foundation and several others, against its December 11 verdict on Section 377 of IPC.[24]

Chapter XVI, Section 377 of the Indian Penal Code dating back to 1860, introduced during the British rule of India, criminalises sexual activities against the order of nature, arguably including homosexual acts. The 11th December 2013 judgment of the Supreme Court, upholding Section 377 was met with support from religious leaders. In its judgment the Supreme Court bench of Justices G. S. Singhvi and S. J. Mukhopadhaya stated *"In view of the above discussion, we hold that Section 377 IPC does not suffer from the vice of unconstitutionality and the declaration made by the Division Bench of the High Court is legally unsustainable."* The bench also noted that the Parliament should debate and decide on the matter. A bench of justices upheld the constitutional validity of Section 377 of Indian Penal Code that makes anal sex a punishable offense.[25]

Gay rights activists argue that section 377 violates articles 14, 15, 19 and 21 of the Indian constitution, which guarantee equality, freedom of expression and personal liberty to all its citizens. Upholding it will deny basic human rights to sexual minorities in the country. Further, they say, it will inhibit discussion on an issue already considered controversial and taboo, especially as discussion on sex and sexuality in any form is rare. There have been arguments that upholding section 377 will lead to further alienation of LGBT persons and groups, and cause a severe setback to HIV/AIDS prevention efforts, especially among men who have sex with men (MSM).[26] Whether the Delhi High Court had overstepped its mandate four years back is a matter of debate. Its historic judgment in 2009, which decriminalised homosexuality in the country, was something of a watershed moment for gay rights in India. Many more young people had come out of the closet. Harish Iyer, a Mumbai-based equal-rights activist, says there was a more than 100 per cent increase in people wanting to come out of the closet after 2009.[27]

Human Rights Violation

Human rights are moral principles or norms that describe certain standards of human behaviour, and are regularly protected as legal rights in municipal and international law. The doctrine of human rights has been highly influential within international law, global and regional institutions. The philosophy of human rights attempts to examine the underlying basis of the concept of human rights and critically looks at its content and justification. Human rights can be classified and organised in a number of different ways. At an international level the most common categorisation of human rights has been to split them into civil and political rights, and economic, social and cultural rights. The foundation of the United Nations and the provisions of the United Nations Charter provided a basis for a comprehensive system of international law and practice for the protection of human rights. The Universal Declaration of Human Rights was adopted by the United Nations General Assembly in 1948, partly in response to the atrocities of World War II. In 1966, the International Covenant on Civil and Political Rights (ICCPR) and the International Covenant on Economic, Social and Cultural Rights (ICESCR) were adopted by the United Nations, between them making the rights contained in the UDHR binding on all states that have signed this treaty, creating human-rights law.[28]

Laws affecting lesbian, gay, bisexual, and transgender people vary greatly by country or territory everything from legal recognition of same-sex marriage or other types of partnerships, to the death penalty as punishment for same-sex romantic/sexual activity or identity. LGBT rights are considered human rights and civil rights. Anti-LGBT laws include, but are not limited to, the following: sodomy laws penalising consensual same-sex sexual activity with fines, jail terms, or the death penalty; anti-lesbianism laws; and higher ages of consent for same-sex activity. Sodomy law is a law that defines certain sexual acts as crimes. The precise sexual acts meant by the term sodomy are rarely spelled out in the law, but are typically understood by courts to include any sexual act deemed to be unnatural or immoral.[29]

People around the world face violence and inequality and sometimes torture, even execution because of who they love, how they look, or who they are. Sexual orientation and gender identity are integral aspects of ourselves and should never lead to discrimination or abuse. Human Rights Watch works for lesbian, gay, bisexual, and transgender people's rights, with activists representing a multiplicity of identities and issues.[30]

Challenges before LGBT

During the discovery of ones sexual orientation, LGBT youth are likely have an increased risk of mental health disparities, one of the most prominent mental health problems being depression and suicidal ideation. Other issues, such as being victimised at school, and being threatened physically and verbally, relates to the development of post-traumatic stress symptoms. Research has shown that LGBT adolescents, in addition to mental health problems, encounter increased risks of developing heavy substance abuse problems due to the different harassments that they are subjected to. Harassment and violence is considered, along with discrimination, direct and overt oppression towards the LGBT population.[31]

For transgender people, making the difficult decision to transition from being publicly a man or woman to the gender one really identifies with can be a traumatic experience. According to the lesbian, gay, bisexual and transgender charity Stonewall Scotland, transgender issues still cause a lot of anxiety among employers. The biggest issue in many offices is use of the toilet. Employers who ban their transitioning staff from using the female toilet may face legal action.

Being transgender, an umbrella term used to describe a whole range of people whose gender identity differs in some way from what they were assigned at birth, has no impact on a person's work output and a progressive equality policy can enhance a company's reputation and improve employees' performance and productivity.[32]

Much of the discrimination transgender people face mirrors that experienced by lesbian, gay and bisexual people, but is often more severe. Much of the discrimination faced by transgender people comes from the same place as does anti-gay discrimination. Transgender people commonly face a wide variety of discriminatory barriers to full equality. Transgender people sometimes face difficulties meeting their basic needs (getting a job, housing, or healthcare) or in having their gender identity respected (like in the simple act of going to a public rest room).[33] Discrimination in India's healthcare system against transgender people remains rife despite new laws earlier in 2014 aimed at ensuring them equal treatment. Stress caused by the fear of being treated unfairly, worries about abuse and administrative hurdles are preventing many of the country's two million transgender people from seeking medical care.[34]

Hijra suffering from knee pain also complained of rashes on her tongue but had not revealed her HIV status. With regard to the treatment many *hijras* prefer allopathic doctors in private clinics. In the data from civil society, doctors also have shared their positive experiences of treating the *hijras* who come to them and who pay their fees without fail. Some of them adopt home remedies for minor illnesses like cold, stomach pain, acidity, flu etc.[35]

Conclusion

LGBT is an initialism that stands for lesbian, gay, bisexual, and transgender. Gay is a term that primarily refers to a homosexual person or the trait of being homosexual. Lesbian is a female homosexual. Bisexuality is romantic attraction, sexual attraction or sexual behaviour toward both males and females. Transgender is the state of one's gender identity or gender expression not matching one's assigned sex. Lesbianism can be caused by both mental and physical reasons. Lesbian, gay, bisexual and transgender rights in India have historically and culturally been accepted under the *Hijra* concept. Homosexual intercourse was made a criminal offence under Section 377 of the Indian Penal Code, 1860. Gay rights activists argue that section 377 violates articles 14, 15, 19 and 21 of the Indian constitution, which guarantee equality, freedom of expression and personal liberty to all its citizens.

References

1. Where is it illegal to be gay? See http://www.bbc.com/news/world-25927595
2. See http://usnews.nbcnews.com/_news/2013/03/23/17418872-gay-rights-timeline-key-dates-in-the-fight-for-equality
3. LGBT movement organising to mandate "gay history" in schools across America, see http://www.massresistance.org/docs/gen2/14b/GLSEN-Conference-040514/gay-history/index.html
4. See http://www.apa.org/topics/lgbt/transgender.aspx
5. LGBT rights opposition, Retrieved from http://en.wikipedia.org/wiki/LGBT_rights_opposition
6. See http://www.slate.com/articles/life/faithbased/2003/11/a_ common_missed_conception.html
7. KGBT, Retrieved from http://en.wikipedia.org/wiki/LGBT
8. See http://www.belongto.org/service.aspx?contentid=2160
9. See http://world.time.com/2013/12/12/indias-gay-rights-movement-rises-up-after-supreme-court-criminalises-homosexuality/
10. Gay, Retrieved from http://en.wikipedia.org/wiki/Gay
11. Lesbian, See http://en.wikipedia.org/wiki/Lesbian
12. See http://www.prokerala.com/relationships/sexuality/lesbianism-causes-treatments.php
13. Bisexuality (2015), Retrieved from http://en.wikipedia.org/wiki/Bisexuality
14. Transgender (2014), Retrieved from http://en.wikipedia.org/wiki/Transgender
15. Stances of Faiths on LGBT Issues: Hinduism, Retrieved from http://www.hrc.org/resources/entry/stances-of-faiths-on-lgbt-issues-hinduism
16. Same sex marriage (2015), Retrieved from http://en.wikipedia.org/wiki/Same-sex_marriage
17. Lesbianism - Is it a Right Practice? Retrieved from http://www.prokerala.com/relationships/sexuality/lesbianism-causes-treatments.php
18. Sabrina Rubin Erdely (2014), The science of transgender, Retrieved from http://www.rollingstone.com/culture/news/the-science-of-transgender-20140730
19. Ellen Friedrichs, What causes a transgender identity, Retrieved from http://gayteens.about.com/od/transgenderteenissues/f/transgender_causes.htm
20. What causes of bisexuality? Retrieved from http://www.exodusglobalalliance.org/whatcausesbisexualityp392.php

21. Same sex marriage (2015), Retrieved from http://en.wikipedia.org/wiki/Same-sex_marriage
22. 12 reasons why marriage equality matters, Retrieved from http://www.australianmarriageequality.org/12-reasons-why-marriage-equality-matters/
23. Same sex marriage (2015), Retrieved from http://en.wikipedia.org/wiki/Same-sex_marriage
24. LGBT in India (2015), Retrieved from http://en.wikipedia.org/wiki/LGBT_rights_in_India
25. Section 377 of the Indian Penal Code, Retrieved from http://en.wikipedia.org/wiki/Section_377_of_the_Indian_Penal_Code
26. See http://www.dnaindia.com/india/report-section-377-and-lgbt-rights-heres-what-you-need-to-know-1933370
27. http://world.time.com/2013/12/12/indias-gay-rights-movement-rises-up-after-supreme-court-criminalises-homosexuality/
28. Human rights (2014), Retrieved from http://en.wikipedia.org/wiki/Human_rights
29. LGBT Rights by country or territory (2015), Retrieved from http://en.wikipedia.org/wiki/LGBT_rights_by_country_or_territory
30. LGBT Rights, Retrieved from http://www.hrw.org/topic/lgbt-rights
31. Edward M. Johns, The Challenges and Approaches to Working with Lesbian, Gay, Bisexual, and Transgender Youth, Retrieved from http://hilo.hawaii.edu/academics/hohonu/documents/Vol07x05The Challenges andApproachestoWorking....pdf
32. Transgender issues in the workplace, Retrieved from http://www.theguardian.com/careers/transgender-issues-in-the-workplace
33. Discrimination against transgender people, Retrieved from https://www.aclu.org/lgbt-rights/discrimination-against-transgender-people
34. Indian transgender healthcare challenges, Retrieved from http://www.aljazeera.com/indepth/features/2014/06/healthcare-distant-india-transgenders-201461882414495902.html
35. Anitha Chettiar, Problems Faced by Hijras (Male to Female Transgenders) in Mumbai with Reference to Their Health and Harassment by the Police, *International Journal of Social Science and Humanity*, Vol. 5, No. 9, Sep-tember 2015, Retrieved from http://www.ijssh.org/papers/551-W10007. pdf
36. http://www.brainyquote.com/quotes/keywords/human.html#AcLeDlkFalwK9b4S.99

8

Disability Rights

"Just as treasures are uncovered from the earth, so virtue appears from good deeds, and wisdom appears from a pure and peaceful mind. To walk safely through the maze of human life, one needs the light of wisdom and the guidance of virtue."

- Buddha

Introduction

The World Health Organisation has published the International Classification of Functioning, Disability and Health (ICF) in 2001. The ICF provides a standard language for classifying changes in body function and structure, activity, participation levels, and environmental factors that influence health. This helps to assess the health, functioning, activities, and factors in the environment that either help or create barriers for people to fully participate in society.[1] Assistive Technology is a generic term for devices and modifications (for a person or within a society) that help overcome or remove a disability. The first recorded example of the use of a prosthesis dates to at least 1800 BC. The Paralympic Games are held after the (summer and winter) Olympics. The Paralympic Games include athletes with a wide range of physical disabilities.[2]

Around 15 per cent of the world's population, or estimated one billion people, live with disabilities, according to World Health Organisation. They are the world's largest minority. Eighty per cent of persons with disabilities live in developing countries, according to the UN Development Programme. Disability rates are significantly higher among groups with lower educational attainment in the countries of the Organisation for Economic Co-operation and Development (OECD), says the OECD Secretariat. The World Bank estimates that 20 per cent of the world's poorest people have some kind of disability, and tend to be regarded in their own communities as the most disadvantaged. According to UNICEF, 30 per cent of street youths have some kind of disability.

An estimated 386 million of the world's working-age people have some kind of disability, says the International Labour Organisation (ILO). Unemployment among the persons with disabilities is as high as 80 per cent in some countries. Ninety per cent of children with disabilities in developing countries do not attend school, says UNESCO. Mortality for children with disabilities may be as high as 80 per cent in countries where under-five mortality as a whole has decreased below 20 per cent, says the United Kingdom's Department for International Development.[3]

Who are Disable?

Disabilities are an umbrella term, covering impairments, activity limitations, and participation restrictions. Disability is not just a health problem. It is a complex phenomenon, reflecting the interaction between features of a person's body and features of the society in which he or she lives[4]. The term disability broadly describes impairment in a person's ability to function, caused by changes in various subsystems of the body, or to mental health. An individual may also qualify as disabled if they have had an impairment in the past or is seen as disabled based on a personal or group standard or norm. A disability may be present from birth, or occur during a person's lifetime.

The United Nations Declaration on the Rights of Disabled Persons of 1975 provides that: *the term 'disabled person' means any person unable to ensure by himself or herself wholly or partly, the necessities of a normal individual and/or social life, as a result of deficiency, either congenital or not in his or her physical or mental capabilities.'* According to World Health Organisation disability is a *'restriction or lack (resulting from impairment) of ability to perform an activity in the manner or within the range considered normal for a human being.'*

Types of Disability

Disability can be classified in various ways:

1. *Physical disabilities:* A physical disability is one that affects a person's mobility or dexterity. A person with a physical disability

may need to use some sort of equipment for assistance with mobility. It also includes people who have lost limbs or who, because of the shape of their body, require slight adaptations to be made to enable them to participate fully in society.

2. *Intellectual or Learning Disabilities:* People with an intellectual, learning, or cognitive disability have a reduced capacity to learn tasks or process information. A learning disability may make it difficult for a person to take in information and communicate what they know.

3. *Psychiatric disabilities:* A psychiatric disability (or mental illness) can develop at any age and is often not apparent to other people. Psychiatric disabilities are often the most misunderstood disabilities in the community, and peoples' attitudes may be based on prejudice and myth (e.g. schizophrenics are potentially violent).

4. *Neurological disabilities:* A neurological disability is associated with damage to the nervous system that results in the loss of some physical or mental functions. A neurological disability may affect a person's capacity to move or manipulate things or the way they act or express their feelings.[5]

5. *Visual Disability:* Visual impairment is when a person has sight loss that cannot be fully corrected using glasses or contact lenses. It's estimated that as many as two million people in the UK may be living with this sort of sight problem. Of these, around 365,000 are registered as blind or partially sighted. Visual impairment is usually classified as either 'sight impaired' or 'severely sight impaired'.[6]

6. *Hearing Disability:* It is a partial or total inability to hear. In children it may affect the development of language and can cause work related difficulties for adults. There are a number of measures that can prevent hearing loss and include avoidance of loud noise, chemical agents, and physical trauma. The terms hearing impairment or hard of hearing are usually reserved for people who have relative insensitivity to sound in the speech frequencies.[7]

Physical impairments vary greatly

1. *Cerebral Palsy* (CP): CP is defined as damage to the motor areas of the brain prior to brain maturity (in most cases, this occurs before, during or shortly after birth).

2. *Spinal Cord Injury*: Spinal cord injury can result in paralysis or paresis (weakening). The extent of paralysis/paresis and the parts of the body affected are determined by how high or low on the spine the damage occurs and the type of damage to the cord.

3. *Head Injury and Stroke*: The term "head injury" is used to describe a huge array of injuries, including concussion, brain stem injury, closed head injury, cerebral hemorrhage, depressed skull fracture, foreign object (e.g., bullet), anoxia, and post-operative infections.

4. *Arthritis*: Arthritis is defined as pain in joints, usually reducing range of motion and causing weakness. Rheumatoid arthritis is a chronic syndrome.

5. *ALS (Lou Gehrig's disease)*: ALS is a fatal degenerative disease of the central nervous system characterised by slowly progressive paralysis of the voluntary muscles.

6. *Multiple Sclerosis* (MS): MS is defined as a progressive disease of the central nervous system characterised by the destruction of the insulating material covering nerve fibers.

7. *Muscular Dystrophy* (MD): MD is a hereditary, progressive condition resulting in muscular weakness and loss of control, contractions and difficulty in walking and breathing.[8]

Disable People in India

The *World report on disability* is the first document to give an extensive global picture of the situation of people with disabilities, their needs, and the barriers they face to participating fully in their societies. Published in 2011 by the World Health Organisation and the World Bank, the report assembles scientific information on disability, with relevance to the fields of public health, human rights and development.[9]

Census 2001 in India has revealed that over 21 million people in India as suffering from one or the other kind of disability. This is equivalent to 2.1 per cent of the population. Among the total disabled in the country, 12.6 million are males and 9.3 million are females. Among the five types of disabilities on which data has been collected, disability in seeing at 48.5 per cent emerges as the top category. Others in sequence are: In movement (27.9 per cent), Mental (10.3 per cent), speech (7.5 per cent), and hearing (5.8 per cent). The disabled by sex follow a similar pattern except for that the proportion of disabled females is higher in the category in seeing and in hearing. Across the country, the highest number of disabled has been reported from the state of Uttar Pradesh (3.6 million). Significant numbers of disabled have also been reported from the state like Bihar (1.9 million), West Bengal (1.8 million), Tamil Nadu and Maharashtra (1.6 million each). Tamil Nadu is the only state, which has a higher number of disabled females than males. Among the states, Arunachal Pradesh has the highest proportion of disabled males (66.6 per cent) and lowest proportion of female disabled.[10]

The country's disabled population has increased by 22.4 per cent between 2001 and 2011. The number of disabled, which was 2.19 crore in 2001, rose in 2011 to 2.68 crore, 1.5 crore males and 1.18 crore females. Rural areas have more disabled people than urban areas. In Maharashtra, Andhra Pradesh, Odisha, Jammu and Kashmir and Sikkim, the disabled account for 2.5 per cent of the total population, while Tamil Nadu and Assam are among those where the disabled population is less than 1.75 per cent of the total population, says the 2011 Census on the disabled. The growth rate of disabled population is more in urban areas and among urban females. The decadal growth in urban areas is 48.2 per cent and 55 per cent among urban females. Among scheduled castes it is 2.45 per cent. Most of the disabled are those with movement disability. According to the Census, 20.3 per cent of the disabled are movement disabled followed by hearing impaired (18.9 per cent) and visually impaired (18.8 per cent). Nearly 5.6 per cent of the disabled population is mentally challenged, a classification introduced in the 2011 census.[11]

Legal Perspectives

At present there are following laws in our country to safeguard the rights of disabled persons: (a) *The Mental Health Act, 1987*- This is an act to consolidate and amend the law relating to the treatment and care of mentally ill persons, to make better provision with respect to their property and affairs, and for matters connected therewith or incidental thereto; (b) *The Rehabilitation Council Act of India (RCI, 1992)*- The Act was created to provide for the constitution of the Rehabilitation Council of India for regarding training of the Rehabilitation Professional and maintaining of a Central Rehabilitation Register and related issues; (c) *The Persons with Disabilities (Equal Opportunities, Full Participation and Protection of Rights) Act, 1995*- The Act is guided by the philosophy of empowering persons with disabilities and their associates. The endeavour of the Act has been to introduce an instrument for promoting equality and participation of persons with disability on the one hand and eliminating discriminations of all kinds, on the other; and (d) *The National Trust (For welfare of persons with Autism, Cerebral Palsy, Metal Retardation and Multiple Disabilities) Act, 1999*- The trust aims to provide total care to persons with mental retardation and cerebral palsy and also manage the properties bequeathed to the Trust. The Trust also supports programmes that promotes independence and address the concerns of those special persons who do not have family support. The Thrust will be empowered to receive grants.

Until 1995 there was no law that even defined discrimination against people with disabilities. It is only with the 'Persons with Disabilities Act,' passed in 1995 that discrimination specifically against persons with disabilities came under the purview of the law. Implementation of the Act requires a multi-sectoral collaborative approach by the appropriate governments, including various Central Ministries/Departments, States/Union Territories, local bodies. Chapter VI of The Disability Act 1995 is entitled 'Employment'. Clause 41 categorically mandates incentives to employers, both in public and private sectors, who ensure that at least five per cent of their work force is composed of persons with disabilities.

1. *Education:* The appropriate Governments and the local authorities shall – (i) ensure that every child with a disability has access to free education in an appropriate environment till he attains the age of eighteen years; (ii) promote setting up of special schools in Government and private sector for those in need of special education, in such a manner that children with disabilities living in any part of the country have access to such schools.

2. *Employment:* Every appropriate Government shall appoint in every establishment such percentage of vacancies not less than three per cent for persons or class of persons with disability of which one per cent each shall be reserved for persons suffering from – (i) Blindness or Low Vision, (ii) Hearing Impairment, and (iii) Locomotor Disabilities and Cerebral Plasy.

3. *Affirmative Action:* Aids and appliances shall be made available to people with disabilities. Allotment of land shall be made at concessional rates to the people with disabilities for: House, Business, Special recreational centers, Special schools, Research schools, and Factories by entrepreneurs with disability.

4. *Non-discrimination:* Public building, rail compartments, buses, ships and aircrafts will be designed to give easy access to disabled people. In all public places and in waiting rooms, toilets shall be wheel chair accessible. Braille and sound symbols are also to be provided in lifts.

5. *Grievance Redressed:* In case of violation of rights as prescribed in the act people with disabilities may move an application to (i) Chief Commissioner for Persons with Disabilities in the Centre, and (ii) Commissioner for Persons with Disabilities in the States.

6. *Social Security:* Financial assistance to non-government organisation for rehabilitation of persons with disabilities. Insurance coverage will be providing for the benefit of the government employees with disabilities. Unemployment allowance to people with disabilities registered with the special employment exchange for more than a year and who could not be placed in any gainful occupation.

The Ministry of Social Justice and Empowerment of the Government of India has been holding national consultative meetings on proposed amendments to the Persons with Disabilities Equal Opportunities, Protection of Rights and Full Participation Act (PWD Act). Meetings have been held in Delhi, Guwahati and most recently in Kolkata on March 13, 2010. The Persons with Disabilities Equal Opportunities, Protection of Rights and Full Participation Act, (PWD Act) of 1995 had heralded a new dawn in the lives of disabled people in India. For the first time in the history of independent India, a separate law had been formulated which talked about the multiple needs of disabled people. To the delight of disability groups, India ratified the UN Convention on the Rights of Persons with Disabilities (Disability Convention) in October 2007. The Convention recognises that persons with disability are right-holders instead of passive recipients of government schemes. In contrast, the PWD Act has a different foundation.[12]

The light at the end of the tunnel for India's 100 million people with disabilities appears to be getting closer as the Ministry of Social Justice and Empowerment made public the latest version of the Rights of Persons with Disabilities Bill. This Bill who seeks to replace the Persons with Disabilities (Equal Opportunities, Protection of Rights and Full Participation) Act, 1995, attempts to bring India in line with the 21 century understanding of the rights of persons with disabilities as captured in the UN Convention on the Rights of Persons with Disabilities ratified by India. This version of the Bill is the last in a series of versions that were made public by the Ministry over the last two years. There are some major differences between this version and earlier versions and the changes proposed are a mixed bag - some progressive and some regressive ones. Given below are some of the more significant changes in the new version.[13]

The Constitution of India ensures equality, freedom, justice and dignity of all individuals and implicitly mandates an inclusive society for all including persons with disabilities. In the recent years, there have been vast positive changes in the perception of the society towards persons with disabilities. It has been realised that a majority of persons with disabilities can lead a better quality of life if they have equal opportunities and effective access to rehabilitation measures. The preamble, the directive principles of state policy and the fundamental rights enshrined in the fundamental rights enshrined in the Constitution, envisaged a very positive role for the state towards its disadvantaged citizens.

Under rights to equality the constitution of India guarantees to all citizens equality before law and equal protection of law and it prohibits discrimination on grounds of religious, race, caste, sex, place of birth of any of them. Article 41 declares that, the state shall within the limits of its economic capacity and development make effective provision for securing the right to work, to education and to public assistance in case of unemployment, old age sickness and disablement. Article 46 lays down an obligation on the state 'to promote with special care the educational and economic interests of the weaker sections of the people, and protect them from social injustice and all forms of exploitation.

Human Rights Violation

Employment remained a challenge for persons with disabilities in many countries, a United Nations expert told the Commission for Social Development, as some delegations described national achievements in that field.[14] As would be expected, people with visual impairments have the greatest problem with information displayed on the screen. However, mandatory use of a mouse or other pointing device requiring eye-hand coordination is also a problem. Special programmes exist to provide individuals with the ability to magnify the screen image.[15]

On December 13, 2006, the United Nations formally agreed on the Convention on the Rights of Persons with Disabilities, the first human rights treaty of the 21st century, to protect and enhance the rights and opportunities of the world's estimated 650 million disabled people. As of April 2011, 99 of the 147 signatories had ratified the Convention. In 1976, the United Nations launched its International Year for Disabled Persons (1981), later renamed the International

Year of Disabled Persons.[16] A major outcome of the International Year of Disabled Persons was the formulation of the World Programme of Action Concerning Disabled Persons adopted by the UN General Assembly in December 1982. This also is recognised by the Preamble (f) of the Convention on the Rights of Persons with Disabilities.[17]

To provide a time frame during which Governments and organisations could implement the activities recommended in the World Programme of Action, the General Assembly proclaimed 1983-1992 the United Nations Decade of Disabled Persons. On the 2012 International Day of People with Disability, the United Kingdom government introduced mandatory work for disabled people who received welfare benefits in order to "Improve disabled peoples chances of getting work by mandatory employment."[18]

The Convention on the Rights of Persons with Disabilities is an international human rights treaty of the United Nations intended to protect the rights and dignity of persons with disabilities. The Convention has served as the major catalyst in the global movement from viewing persons with disabilities as objects of charity, medical treatment and social protection towards viewing them as full and equal members of society, with human rights. The text was adopted by the United Nations General Assembly on 13 December 2006, and opened for signature on 30 March 2007. The Convention is monitored by the Committee on the Rights of Persons with Disabilities.[19] The Convention follows the civil law tradition, with a preamble, in which the principle that "all human rights are universal, indivisible, interdependent and interrelated" of Vienna Declaration and Programme of Action is cited, followed by 50 articles. Unlike many UN covenants and conventions, it is not formally divided into parts.

There are eight guiding principles that underlie the Convention: (a) Respect for inherent dignity, individual autonomy including the freedom to make one's own choices, and independence of persons; (b) Non-discrimination; (c) Full and effective participation and inclusion in society; (d) Respect for difference and acceptance of persons with disabilities as part of human diversity and humanity; (e) Equality of opportunity; (f) Accessibility; (g) Equality between men and women; (h) Respect for the evolving capacities of children with disabilities and respect for the right of children with disabilities to preserve their identities.[20]

The Optional Protocol to the Convention on the Rights of Persons with Disabilities is a side-agreement to the Convention which allows its parties to recognise the competence of the Committee on the Rights of Persons with Disabilities to consider complaints from individuals. The Optional Protocol entered into force with the Convention on 3rd May 2008. As of September 2012, it has 92 signatories and 78 parties.[21] The Optional Protocol to the Convention on the Rights of Persons with Disabilities is a side-agreement to the Convention on the Rights of Persons with Disabilities.

Convention on the Rights of Persons with Disabilities and Optional Protocol[22]

Article	*Explanation*
1 Purpose	The purpose of the present Convention is to promote, protect and ensure the full and equal enjoyment of all human rights and fundamental freedoms by all persons with disabilities, and to promote respect for their inherent dignity. Persons with disabilities include those who have long-term physical, mental, intellectual or sensory impairments which in interaction with various barriers may hinder their full and effective participation in society on an equal basis with others.
2 Definitions	For the purposes of the present Convention: "Communication" includes languages, display of text, Braille, tactile communication, large print, accessible multimedia as well as written, audio, plain-language, human-reader and augmentative and alternative modes, means and formats of communication, including accessible information and communication technology; "Language" includes spoken and signed languages and other forms of non-spoken languages. "Discrimination on the basis of disability" means any distinction, exclusion or restriction on the basis of disability which has the purpose or effect of impairing or nullifying the recognition, enjoyment or exercise, on an equal basis with others, of all human rights and fundamental

(Contd.)

(Contd. Table)

Article	*Explanation*
	freedoms in the political, economic, social, cultural, civil or any other field. It includes all forms of discrimination, including denial of reasonable accommodation; "Reasonable accommodation" means necessary and appropriate modification and adjustments not imposing a disproportionate or undue burden, where needed in a particular case, to ensure to persons with disabilities the enjoyment or exercise on an equal basis with others of all human rights and fundamental freedoms; "Universal design" means the design of products, environments, programmes and services to be usable by all people, to the greatest extent possible, without the need for adaptation or specialised design. "Universal design" shall not exclude assistive devices for particular groups of persons with disabilities where this is needed.
3 General principles	The principles of the present Convention shall be: (*a*) Respect for inherent dignity, individual autonomy including the freedom to make one's own choices, and independence of persons; (*b*) Non-discrimination; (*c*) Full and effective participation and inclusion in society; (*d*) Respect for difference and acceptance of persons with disabilities as part of human diversity and humanity; (*e*) Equality of opportunity; (*f*) Accessibility; (*g*) Equality between men and women; (*h*) Respect for the evolving capacities of children with disabilities and respect for the right of children with disabilities to preserve their identities.
4 General obligations	States Parties undertake to ensure and promote the full realisation of all human rights and fundamental freedoms for all persons with disabilities without discrimination of any kind on the basis of disability. With regard to economic, social and cultural rights, each State Party undertakes to take measures to the maximum of its available resources and, where

(Contd.)

(Contd. Table)

Article	*Explanation*
	needed, within the framework of international cooperation, with a view to achieving progressively the full realisation of these rights, without prejudice to those obligations contained in the present Convention that are immediately applicable according to international law. In the development and implementation of legislation and policies to implement the present Convention, and in other decision-making processes concerning issues relating to persons with disabilities, States Parties shall closely consult with and actively involve persons with disabilities, including children with disabilities, through their representative organisations. The provisions of the present Convention shall extend to all parts of federal States without any limitations or exceptions.
5 Equality and non-discrimination	States Parties recognise that all persons are equal before and under the law and are entitled without any discrimination to the equal protection and equal benefit of the law. States Parties shall prohibit all discrimination on the basis of disability and guarantee to persons with disabilities equal and effective legal protection against discrimination on all grounds. In order to promote equality and eliminate discrimination, States Parties shall take all appropriate steps to ensure that reasonable accommodation is provided. Specific measures which are necessary to accelerate or achieve de facto equality of persons with disabilities shall not be considered discrimination under the terms of the present Convention.
6 Women with disabilities	States Parties recognise that women and girls with disabilities are subject to multiple discrimination, and in this regard shall take measures to ensure the full and equal enjoyment by them of all human rights

(Contd.)

(Contd. Table)

Article	*Explanation*
	and fundamental freedoms. States Parties shall take all appropriate measures to ensure the full development, advancement and empowerment of women, for the purpose of guaranteeing them the exercise and enjoyment of the human rights and fundamental freedoms set out in the present Convention.
7 Children with disabilities	States Parties shall take all necessary measures to ensure the full enjoyment by children with disabilities of all human rights and fundamental freedoms on an equal basis with other children. In all actions concerning children with disabilities, the best interests of the child shall be a primary consideration. States Parties shall ensure that children with disabilities have the right to express their views freely on all matters affecting them, their views being given due weight in accordance with their age and maturity, on an equal basis with other children, and to be provided with disability and age-appropriate assistance to realise that right.
8 Awareness -raising	States Parties undertake to adopt immediate, effective and appropriate measures: (*a*) To raise awareness throughout society, including at the family level, regarding persons with disabilities, and to foster respect for the rights and dignity of persons with disabilities; (*b*) To combat stereotypes, prejudices and harmful practices relating to persons with disabilities, including those based on sex and age, in all areas of life; (*c*) To promote awareness of the capabilities and contributions of persons with disabilities. Measures to this end include: (*a*) Initiating and maintaining effective public awareness campaigns designed: (i) To nurture receptiveness to the rights of persons with disabilities; (ii) To promote positive perceptions and greater social awareness

(Contd.)

(Contd. Table)

Article	*Explanation*
	towards persons with disabilities; (iii) To promote recognition of the skills, merits and abilities of persons with disabilities, and of their contributions to the workplace and the labour market; (*b*) Fostering at all levels of the education system, including in all children from an early age, an attitude of respect for the rights of persons with disabilities; (*c*) Encouraging all organs of the media to portray persons with disabilities in a manner consistent with the purpose of the present Convention; (d) Promoting awareness-training programmes regarding persons with disabilities and the rights of persons with disabilities.
9 Accessibility	To enable persons with disabilities to live independently and participate fully in all aspects of life, States Parties shall take appropriate measures to ensure to persons with disabilities access, on an equal basis with others, to the physical environment, to transportation, to information and communications, including information and communications technologies and systems, and to other facilities and services open or provided to the public, both in urban and in rural areas. These measures, which shall include the identification and elimination of obstacles and barriers to accessibility, shall apply to, inter alia: (*a*) Buildings, roads, transportation and other indoor and outdoor facilities, including schools, housing, medical facilities and workplaces; (*b*) Information, communications and other services, including electronic services and emergency services.States Parties shall also take appropriate measures: (*a*) To develop, promulgate and monitor the implementation of minimum standards and guidelines for the accessibility of facilities and services open or provided to the public; (*b*) To ensure that private entities that offer facilities and services which are open or provided to the public

(Contd.)

(Contd. Table)

Article	*Explanation*
	take into account all aspects of accessibility for persons with disabilities; (*c*) To provide training for stakeholders on accessibility issues facing persons with disabilities; (*d*) To provide in buildings and other facilities open to the public signage in Braille and in easy to read and understand forms; (*e*) To provide forms of live assistance and intermediaries, including guides, readers and professional sign language interpreters, to facilitate accessibility to buildings and other facilities open to the public; (*f*) To promote other appropriate forms of assistance and support to persons with disabilities to ensure their access to information; (*g*) To promote access for persons with disabilities to new information and communications technologies and systems, including the Internet; (*h*) To promote the design, development, production and distribution of accessible information and communications technologies and systems at an early stage, so that these technologies and systems become accessible at minimum cost.
10 Right to life	States Parties reaffirm that every human being has the inherent right to life and shall take all necessary measures to ensure its effective enjoyment by persons with disabilities on an equal basis with others.
11 Situations of risk and humanitarian emergencies	States Parties shall take, in accordance with their obligations under international law, including international humanitarian law and international human rights law, all necessary measures to ensure the protection and safety of persons with disabilities in situations of risk, including situations of armed conflict, humanitarian emergencies and the occurrence of natural disasters.
12 Equal recognition before the law	States Parties reaffirm that persons with disabilities have the right to recognition everywhere as persons before the law. States Parties shall recognise that persons with disabilities enjoy legal capacity on an

(Contd.)

(Contd. Table)

Article	*Explanation*
	equal basis with others in all aspects of life. States Parties shall take appropriate measures to provide access by persons with disabilities to the support they may require in exercising their legal capacity. States Parties shall ensure that all measures that relate to the exercise of legal capacity provide for appropriate and effective safeguards to prevent abuse in accordance with international human rights law. Such safeguards shall ensure that measures relating to the exercise of legal capacity respect the rights, will and preferences of the person, are free of conflict of interest and undue influence, are proportional and tailored to the person's circumstances, apply for the shortest time possible and are subject to regular review by a competent, independent and impartial authority or judicial body. The safeguards shall be proportional to the degree to which such measures affect the person's rights and interests. Subject to the provisions of this article, States Parties shall take all appropriate and effective measures to ensure the equal right of persons with disabilities to own or inherit property, to control their own financial affairs and to have equal access to bank loans, mortgages and other forms of financial credit, and shall ensure that persons with disabilities are not arbitrarily deprived of their property.
13 Access to justice	States Parties shall ensure effective access to justice for persons with disabilities on an equal basis with others, including through the provision of procedural and age-appropriate accommodations, in order to facilitate their effective role as direct and indirect participants, including as witnesses, in all legal proceedings, including at investigative and other preliminary stages. In order to help to ensure effective access to justice for persons with disabilities,

(Contd.)

(Contd. Table)

Article	*Explanation*
	States Parties shall promote appropriate training for those working in the field of administration of justice, including police and prison staff.
14 Liberty and security of person	States Parties shall ensure that persons with disabilities, on an equal basis with others: (*a*) Enjoy the right to liberty and security of person; (*b*) Are not deprived of their liberty unlawfully or arbitrarily, and that any deprivation of liberty is in conformity with the law, and that the existence of a disability shall in no case justify a deprivation of liberty. States Parties shall ensure that if persons with disabilities are deprived of their liberty through any process, they are, on an equal basis with others, entitled to guarantees in accordance with international human rights law and shall be treated in compliance with the objectives and principles of the present Convention, including by provision of reasonable accommodation.
15 Freedom from torture or cruel, inhuman or degrading treatment or punishment	No one shall be subjected to torture or to cruel, inhuman or degrading treatment or punishment. In particular, no one shall be subjected without his or her free consent to medical or scientific experimentation. States Parties shall take all effective legislative, administrative, judicial or other measures to prevent persons with disabilities, on an equal basis with others, from being subjected to torture or cruel, inhuman or degrading treatment or punishment.
16 Freedom from exploitation, violence and abuse	States Parties shall take all appropriate legislative, administrative, social, educational and other measures to protect persons with disabilities, both within and outside the home, from all forms of exploitation, violence and abuse, including their gender-based aspects. States Parties shall also take all appropriate measures to prevent all forms of exploitation, violence and abuse by ensuring, inter alia,

(Contd.)

(Contd. Table)

Article	*Explanation*
	appropriate forms of gender- and age-sensitive assistance and support for persons with disabilities and their families and caregivers, including through the provision of information and education on how to avoid, recognise and report instances of exploitation, violence and abuse. States Parties shall ensure that protection services are age-, gender- and disability-sensitive. In order to prevent the occurrence of all forms of exploitation, violence and abuse, States Parties shall ensure that all facilities and programmes designed to serve persons with disabilities are effectively monitored by independent authorities. States Parties shall take all appropriate measures to promote the physical, cognitive and psychological recovery, rehabilitation and social reintegration of persons with disabilities who become victims of any form of exploitation, violence or abuse, including through the provision of protection services. Such recovery and reintegration shall take place in an environment that fosters the health, welfare, self-respect, dignity and autonomy of the person and takes into account gender- and age-specific needs. States Parties shall put in place effective legislation and policies, including women- and child-focused legislation and policies, to ensure that instances of exploitation, violence and abuse against persons with disabilities are identified, investigated and, where appropriate, prosecuted.
17 Protecting the integrity of the person	Every person with disabilities has a right to respect for his or her physical and mental integrity on an equal basis with others.
18 Liberty of	States Parties shall recognise the rights of persons with disabilities to liberty of movement, to freedom

(Contd.)

(Contd. Table)

Article	*Explanation*
movement and nationality	to choose their residence and to a nationality, on an equal basis with others, including by ensuring that persons with disabilities: (a) Have the right to acquire and change a nationality and are not deprived of their nationality arbitrarily or on the basis of disability; (b) Are not deprived, on the basis of disability, of their ability to obtain, possess and utilise documentation of their nationality or other documentation of identification, or to utilise relevant processes such as immigration proceedings, that may be needed to facilitate exercise of the right to liberty of movement; (c) Are free to leave any country, including their own; (d) Are not deprived, arbitrarily or on the basis of disability, of the right to enter their own country. Children with disabilities shall be registered immediately after birth and shall have the right from birth to a name, the right to acquire a nationality and, as far as possible, the right to know and be cared for by their parents.
19 Living independently and being included in the community	States Parties to the present Convention recognise the equal right of all persons with disabilities to live in the community, with choices equal to others, and shall take effective and appropriate measures to facilitate full enjoyment by persons with disabilities of this right and their full inclusion and participation in the community, including by ensuring that: (a) Persons with disabilities have the opportunity to choose their place of residence and where and with whom they live on an equal basis with others and are not obliged to live in a particular living arrangement; (b) Persons with disabilities have access to a range of in-home, residential and other community support services, including personal assistance necessary to support living and inclusion in the community, and to prevent isolation or

(Contd.)

(Contd. Table)

Article	*Explanation*
	segregation from the community; (c) Community services and facilities for the general population are available on an equal basis to persons with disabilities and are responsive to their needs.
20 Personal mobility	States Parties shall take effective measures to ensure personal mobility with the greatest possible independence for persons with disabilities, including by: (a) Facilitating the personal mobility of persons with disabilities in the manner and at the time of their choice, and at affordable cost; (b) Facilitating access by persons with disabilities to quality mobility aids, devices, assistive technologies and forms of live assistance and intermediaries, including by making them available at affordable cost; (c) Providing training in mobility skills to persons with disabilities and to specialist staff working with persons with disabilities; (d) Encouraging entities that produce mobility aids, devices and assistive technologies to take into account all aspects of mobility for persons with disabilities.
21 Freedom of expression and opinion, and access to information	States Parties shall take all appropriate measures to ensure that persons with disabilities can exercise the right to freedom of expression and opinion, including the freedom to seek, receive and impart information and ideas on an equal basis with others and through all forms of communication of their choice, as defined in Article 2 of the present Convention, including by: (a) Providing information intended for the general public to persons with disabilities in accessible formats and technologies appropriate to different kinds of disabilities in a timely manner and without additional cost; (b) Accepting and facilitating the use of sign languages, Braille, augmentative and alternative communication, and all other accessible means, modes and formats of communication of their

(Contd.)

(Contd. Table)

Article	*Explanation*
	choice by persons with disabilities in official interactions; (c) Urging private entities that provide services to the general public, including through the Internet, to provide information and services in accessible and usable formats for persons with disabilities; (d) Encouraging the mass media, including providers of information through the Internet, to make their services accessible to persons with disabilities; (e) Recognising and promoting the use of sign languages.
22 Respect for privacy	No person with disabilities, regardless of place of residence or living arrangements, shall be subjected to arbitrary or unlawful interference with his or her privacy, family, home or correspondence or other types of communication or to unlawful attacks on his or her honour and reputation. Persons with disabilities have the right to the protection of the law against such interference or attacks. States Parties shall protect the privacy of personal, health and rehabilitation information of persons with disabilities on an equal basis with others.
23 Respect for home and the family	States Parties shall take effective and appropriate measures to eliminate discrimination against persons with disabilities in all matters relating to marriage, family, parenthood and relationships, on an equal basis with others, so as to ensure that: (*a*) The right of all persons with disabilities who are of marriageable age to marry and to found a family on the basis of free and full consent of the intending spouses is recognised; (*b*) The rights of persons with disabilities to decide freely and responsibly on the number and spacing of their children and to have access to age-appropriate information, reproductive and family planning education are recognised, and the means necessary to enable them to exercise these

(Contd.)

(Contd. Table)

Article	*Explanation*
	rights are provided; (c) Persons with disabilities, including children, retain their fertility on an equal basis with others. States Parties shall ensure the rights and responsibilities of persons with disabilities, with regard to guardianship, wardship, trusteeship, adoption of children or similar institutions, where these concepts exist in national legislation; in all cases the best interests of the child shall be paramount. States Parties shall render appropriate assistance to persons with disabilities in the performance of their child-rearing responsibilities. States Parties shall ensure that children with disabilities have equal rights with respect to family life. With a view to realising these rights, and to prevent concealment, abandonment, neglect and segregation of children with disabilities, States Parties shall undertake to provide early and comprehensive information, services and support to children with disabilities and their families. States Parties shall ensure that a child shall not be separated from his or her parents against their will, except when competent authorities subject to judicial review determine, in accordance with applicable law and procedures, that such separation is necessary for the best interests of the child. In no case shall a child be separated from parents on the basis of a disability of either the child or one or both of the parents. States Parties shall, where the immediate family is unable to care for a child with disabilities, undertake every effort to provide alternative care within the wider family, and failing that, within the community in a family setting.
24 Education	States Parties recognise the right of persons with disabilities to education. In realising this right, States Parties shall ensure that: (a) Persons with disabilities are not excluded from the general education system

(Contd.)

(Contd. Table)

Article	*Explanation*
	on the basis of disability, and that children with disabilities are not excluded from free and compulsory primary education, or from secondary education, on the basis of disability; (b) Persons with disabilities can access an inclusive, quality and free primary education and secondary education on an equal basis with others in the communities in which they live; (c) Reasonable accommodation of the individual's requirements is provided; (d) Persons with disabilities receive the support required, within the general education system, to facilitate their effective education; (e) Effective individualised support measures are provided in environments that maximise academic and social development, consistent with the goal of full inclusion.States Parties shall enable persons with disabilities to learn life and social development skills to facilitate their full and equal participation in education and as members of the community. To this end, States Parties shall take appropriate measures, including: (a) Facilitating the learning of Braille, alternative script, augmentative and alternative modes, means and formats of communication and orientation and mobility skills, and facilitating peer support and mentoring; (b) Facilitating the learning of sign language and the promotion of the linguistic identity of the deaf community; (c) Ensuring that the education of persons, and in particular children, who are blind, deaf or deaf blind, is delivered in the most appropriate languages and modes and means of communication for the individual and in environments which maximise academic and social development.In order to help ensure the realisation of this right, States Parties shall take appropriate measures to employ teachers, including teachers with disabilities, who are qualified in sign language and/

(Contd.)

(Contd. Table)

Article	*Explanation*
	or Braille, and to train professionals and staff who work at all levels of education. Such training shall incorporate disability awareness and the use of appropriate augmentative and alternative modes, means and formats of communication, educational techniques and materials to support persons with disabilities. States Parties shall ensure that persons with disabilities are able to access general tertiary education, vocational training, adult education and lifelong learning without discrimination and on an equal basis with others. To this end, States Parties shall ensure that reasonable accommodation is provided to persons with disabilities.
25 Health	States Parties recognise that persons with disabilities have the right to the enjoyment of the highest attainable standard of health without discrimination on the basis of disability. States Parties shall take all appropriate measures to ensure access for persons with disabilities to health services that are gender-sensitive, including health-related rehabilitation. In particular, States Parties shall: (a) Provide persons with disabilities with the same range, quality and standard of free or affordable healthcare and programmes as provided to other persons, including in the area of sexual and reproductive health and population-based public health programmes; (b) Provide those health services needed by persons with disabilities specifically because of their disabilities, including early identification and intervention as appropriate, and services designed to minimise and prevent further disabilities, including among children and older persons. (c) Provide these health services as close as possible to people's own communities, including in rural areas; (d) Require health professionals to provide care of the same quality to

(Contd.)

(Contd. Table)

Article	*Explanation*
	persons with disabilities as to others, including on the basis of free and informed consent by, inter alia, raising awareness of the human rights, dignity, autonomy and needs of persons with disabilities through training and the promulgation of ethical standards for public and private healthcare; (e) Prohibit discrimination against persons with disabilities in the provision of health insurance, and life insurance where such insurance is permitted by national law, which shall be provided in a fair and reasonable manner; (f) Prevent discriminatory denial of healthcare or health services or food and fluids on the basis of disability.
26 Habilitation and rehabilitation	States Parties shall take effective and appropriate measures, including through peer support, to enable persons with disabilities to attain and maintain maximum independence, full physical, mental, social and vocational ability, and full inclusion and participation in all aspects of life. To that end, States Parties shall organise, strengthen and extend comprehensive habilitation and rehabilitation services and programmes, particularly in the areas of health, employment, education and social services, in such a way that these services and programmes: (a) Begin at the earliest possible stage, and are based on the multidisciplinary assessment of individual needs and strengths; (b) Support participation and inclusion in the community and all aspects of society, are voluntary, and are available to persons with disabilities as close as possible to their own communities, including in rural areas. States Parties shall promote the development of initial and continuing training for professionals and staff working in habilitation and rehabilitation services. States Parties shall promote the availability,

(Contd.)

(Contd. Table)

Article	*Explanation*
	knowledge and use of assistive devices and technologies, designed for persons with disabilities, as they relate to habilitation and rehabilitation.
27 Work and employment	States Parties recognise the right of persons with disabilities to work, on an equal basis with others; this includes the right to the opportunity to gain a living by work freely chosen or accepted in a labour market and work environment that is open, inclusive and accessible to persons with disabilities. States Parties shall safeguard and promote the realisation of the right to work, including for those who acquire a disability during the course of employment, by taking appropriate steps, including through legislation, to, inter alia: (a) Prohibit discrimination on the basis of disability with regard to all matters concerning all forms of employment, including conditions of recruitment, hiring and employment, continuance of employment, career advancement and safe and healthy working conditions; (b) Protect the rights of persons with disabilities, on an equal basis with others, to just and favourable conditions of work, including equal opportunities and equal remuneration for work of equal value, safe and healthy working conditions, including protection from harassment, and the redress of grievances; (c) Ensure that persons with disabilities are able to exercise their labour and trade union rights on an equal basis with others; (d) Enable persons with disabilities to have effective access to general technical and vocational guidance programmes, placement services and vocational and continuing training; (e) Promote employment opportunities and career advancement for persons with disabilities in the labour market, as well as assistance in finding, obtaining, maintaining and returning to employment; (f) Promote opportunities for self-employment,

(Contd.)

(Contd. Table)

Article	*Explanation*
	entrepreneurship, the development of cooperatives and starting one's own business; (g) Employ persons with disabilities in the public sector; (h) Promote the employment of persons with disabilities in the private sector through appropriate policies and measures, which may include affirmative action programmes, incentives and other measures; (i) Ensure that reasonable accommodation is provided to persons with disabilities in the workplace; (j) Promote the acquisition by persons with disabilities of work experience in the open labour market; (k) Promote vocational and professional rehabilitation, job retention and return-to-work programmes for persons with disabilities. States Parties shall ensure that persons with disabilities are not held in slavery or in servitude, and are protected, on an equal basis with others, from forced or compulsory labour.
28 Adequate standard of living and social protection	States Parties recognise the right of persons with disabilities to an adequate standard of living for themselves and their families, including adequate food, clothing and housing, and to the continuous improvement of living conditions, and shall take appropriate steps to safeguard and promote the realisation of this right without discrimination on the basis of disability. States Parties recognise the right of persons with disabilities to social protection and to the enjoyment of that right without discrimination on the basis of disability, and shall take appropriate steps to safeguard and promote the realisation of this right, including measures: (a) To ensure equal access by persons with disabilities to clean water services, and to ensure access to appropriate and affordable services, devices and other assistance for disability-related needs; (b) To ensure access by persons with disabilities, in particular

(Contd.)

(Contd. Table)

Article	*Explanation*
	women and girls with disabilities and older persons with disabilities, to social protection programmes and poverty reduction programmes; (c) To ensure access by persons with disabilities and their families living in situations of poverty to assistance from the State with disability-related expenses, including adequate training, counselling, financial assistance and respite care; (d) To ensure access by persons with disabilities to public housing programmes; (e) To ensure equal access by persons with disabilities to retirement benefits and programmes.
29 Participation in political and public life	States Parties shall guarantee to persons with disabilities political rights and the opportunity to enjoy them on an equal basis with others, and shall undertake: (a) To ensure that persons with disabilities can effectively and fully participate in political and public life on an equal basis with others, directly or through freely chosen representatives, including the right and opportunity for persons with disabilities to vote and be elected, inter alia, by: (i) Ensuring that voting procedures, facilities and materials are appropriate, accessible and easy to understand and use; (ii) Protecting the right of persons with disabilities to vote by secret ballot in elections and public referendums without intimidation, and to stand for elections, to effectively hold office and perform all public functions at all levels of government, facilitating the use of assistive and new technologies where appropriate; (iii) Guaranteeing the free expression of the will of persons with disabilities as electors and to this end, where necessary, at their request, allowing assistance in voting by a person of their own choice.To promote actively an environment in which persons with disabilities can effectively and fully participate in the conduct of

(Contd.)

(Contd. Table)

Article	*Explanation*
	public affairs, without discrimination and on an equal basis with others, and encourage their participation in public affairs, including: (a) Participation in non-governmental organisations and associations concerned with the public and political life of the country, and in the activities and administration of political parties; (b) Forming and joining organisations of persons with disabilities to represent persons with disabilities at international, national, regional and local levels.
30 Participation in cultural life, recreation, leisure and sport	States Parties recognise the right of persons with disabilities to take part on an equal basis with others in cultural life, and shall take all appropriate measures to ensure that persons with disabilities: (a) Enjoy access to cultural materials in accessible formats; (b) Enjoy access to television programmes, films, theatre and other cultural activities, in accessible formats; (c) Enjoy access to places for cultural performances or services, such as theatres, museums, cinemas, libraries and tourism services, and, as far as possible, enjoy access to monuments and sites of national cultural importance. States Parties shall take appropriate measures to enable persons with disabilities to have the opportunity to develop and utilise their creative, artistic and intellectual potential, not only for their own benefit, but also for the enrichment of society. States Parties shall take all appropriate steps, in accordance with international law, to ensure that laws protecting intellectual property rights do not constitute an unreasonable or discriminatory barrier to access by persons with disabilities to cultural materials. Persons with disabilities shall be entitled, on an equal basis with others, to recognition and support of their specific cultural and linguistic identity, including

(Contd.)

(Contd. Table)

Article	*Explanation*
	sign languages and deaf culture. With a view to enabling persons with disabilities to participate on an equal basis with others in recreational, leisure and sporting activities, States Parties shall take appropriate measures: (a) To encourage and promote the participation, to the fullest extent possible, of persons with disabilities in mainstream sporting activities at all levels; (b) To ensure that persons with disabilities have an opportunity to organise, develop and participate in disability-specific sporting and recreational activities and, to this end, encourage the provision, on an equal basis with others, of appropriate instruction, training and resources; (c) To ensure that persons with disabilities have access to sporting, recreational and tourism venues; (d) To ensure that children with disabilities have equal access with other children to participation in play, recreation and leisure and sporting activities, including those activities in the school system; (e) To ensure that persons with disabilities have access to services from those involved in the organisation of recreational, tourism, leisure and sporting activities.
31 Statistics and data collection	States Parties undertake to collect appropriate information, including statistical and research data, to enable them to formulate and implement policies to give effect to the present Convention. The process of collecting and maintaining this information shall: (a) Comply with legally established safeguards, including legislation on data protection, to ensure confidentiality and respect for the privacy of persons with disabilities; (b) Comply with internationally accepted norms to protect human rights and fundamental freedoms and ethical principles in the collection and use of statistics. The information collected in accordance with this article shall be

(Contd.)

(Contd. Table)

Article	*Explanation*
	disaggregated, as appropriate, and used to help assess the implementation of States Parties' obligations under the present Convention and to identify and address the barriers faced by persons with disabilities in exercising their rights. States Parties shall assume responsibility for the dissemination of these statistics and ensure their accessibility to persons with disabilities and others.
32 International cooperation	States Parties recognise the importance of international cooperation and its promotion, in support of national efforts for the realisation of the purpose and objectives of the present Convention, and will undertake appropriate and effective measures in this regard, between and among States and, as appropriate, in partnership with relevant international and regional organisations and civil society, in particular organisations of persons with disabilities. Such measures could include, inter alia: (a) Ensuring that international cooperation, including international development programmes, is inclusive of and accessible to persons with disabilities; (b) Facilitating and supporting capacity-building, including through the exchange and sharing of information, experiences, training programmes and best practices; Facilitating cooperation in research and access to scientific and technical knowledge; Providing, as appropriate, technical and economic assistance, including by facilitating access to and sharing of accessible and assistive technologies, and through the transfer of technologies. The provisions of this article are without prejudice to the obligations of each State Party to fulfill its obligations under the present Convention.
33 National	States Parties, in accordance with their system of organisation, shall designate one or more focal points

(Contd.)

(Contd. Table)

Article	*Explanation*
implementation and monitoring	within government for matters relating to the implementation of the present Convention, and shall give due consideration to the establishment or designation of a coordination mechanism within government to facilitate related action in different sectors and at different levels. States Parties shall, in accordance with their legal and administrative systems, maintain, strengthen, designate or establish within the State Party, a framework, including one or more independent mechanisms, as appropriate, to promote, protect and monitor implementation of the present Convention. When designating or establishing such a mechanism, States Parties shall take into account the principles relating to the status and functioning of national institutions for protection and promotion of human rights. Civil society, in particular persons with disabilities and their representative organisations shall be involved and participate fully in the monitoring process.
34 Committee on the Rights of Persons with Disabilities	There shall be established a Committee on the Rights of Persons with Disabilities, which shall carry out the functions hereinafter provided. The Committee shall consist, at the time of entry into force of the present Convention, of twelve experts. After an additional sixty ratifications or accessions to the Convention, the membership of the Committee shall increase by six members, attaining a maximum number of eighteen members. The members of the Committee shall serve in their personal capacity and shall be of high moral standing and recognised competence and experience in the field covered by the present Convention. When nominating their candidates, States Parties are invited to give due consideration to the provision set out in Article 4, paragraph 3, of the present Convention. The

(Contd.)

(Contd. Table)

Article	*Explanation*
	members of the Committee shall be elected by States Parties, consideration being given to equitable geographical distribution, representation of the different forms of civilisation and of the principal legal systems, balanced gender representation and participation of experts with disabilities. The members of the Committee shall be elected by secret ballot from a list of persons nominated by the States Parties from among their nationals at meetings of the Conference of States Parties. At those meetings, for which two-thirds of States Parties shall constitute a quorum, the persons elected to the Committee shall be those who obtain the largest number of votes and an absolute majority of the votes of the representatives of States Parties present and voting.The initial election shall be held no later than six months after the date of entry into force of the present Convention. At least four months before the date of each election, the Secretary-General of the United Nations shall address a letter to the States Parties inviting them to submit the nominations within two months. The Secretary-General shall subsequently prepare a list in alphabetical order of all persons thus nominated, indicating the State Parties which have nominated them, and shall submit it to the States Parties to the present Convention. The members of the Committee shall be elected for a term of four years. They shall be eligible for re-election once. However, the term of six of the members elected at the first election shall expire at the end of two years; immediately after the first election, the names of these six members shall be chosen by lot by the chairperson of the meeting referred to in paragraph 5 of this article. The election of the six additional members of the Committee shall be held on the occasion of regular elections, in

(Contd.)

(Contd. Table)

Article	*Explanation*
	accordance with the relevant provisions of this article. If a member of the Committee dies or resigns or declares that for any other cause she or he can no longer perform her or his duties, the State Party which nominated the member shall appoint another expert possessing the qualifications and meeting the requirements set out in the relevant provisions of this article, to serve for the remainder of the term.The Committee shall establish its own rules of procedure. The Secretary-General of the United Nations shall provide the necessary staff and facilities for the effective performance of the functions of the Committee under the present Convention, and shall convene its initial meeting. With the approval of the General Assembly of the United Nations, the members of the Committee established under the present Convention shall receive emoluments from United Nations resources on such terms and conditions as the Assembly may decide, having regard to the importance of the Committee's responsibilities. The members of the Committee shall be entitled to the facilities, privileges and immunities of experts on mission for the United Nations as laid down in the relevant sections of the Convention on the Privileges and Immunities of the United Nations.
35 Reports by States Parties	Each State Party shall submit to the Committee, through the Secretary- General of the United Nations, a comprehensive report on measures taken to give effect to its obligations under the present Convention and on the progress made in that regard, within two years after the entry into force of the present Convention for the State Party concerned. Thereafter, States Parties shall submit subsequent reports at least every four years and further whenever the Committee so requests.The Committee shall decide any

(Contd.)

(Contd. Table)

Article	*Explanation*
	guidelines applicable to the content of the reports. A State Party which has submitted a comprehensive initial report to the Committee need not, in its subsequent reports, repeat information previously provided. When preparing reports to the Committee, States Parties are invited to consider doing so in an open and transparent process and to give due consideration to the provision set out in Article 4, paragraph 3, of the present Convention. Reports may indicate factors and difficulties affecting the degree of fulfillment of obligations under the present Convention.
36 Consideration of reports	Each report shall be considered by the Committee, which shall make such suggestions and general recommendations on the report as it may consider appropriate and shall forward these to the State Party concerned. The State Party may respond with any information it chooses to the Committee.The Committee may request further information from States Parties relevant to the implementation of the present Convention. If a State Party is significantly overdue in the submission of a report, the Committee may notify the State Party concerned of the need to examine the implementation of the present Convention in that State Party, on the basis of reliable information available to the Committee, if the relevant report is not submitted within three months following the notification. The Committee shall invite the State Party concerned to participate in such examination. Should the State Party respond by submitting the relevant report, the provisions of paragraph 1 of this article will apply. The Secretary-General of the United Nations shall make available the reports to all States Parties. States Parties shall make their reports widely available to the public in

(Contd.)

(Contd. Table)

Article	*Explanation*
	their own countries and facilitate access to the suggestions and general recommendations relating to these reports. The Committee shall transmit, as it may consider appropriate, to the specialised agencies, funds and programmes of the United Nations, and other competent bodies, reports from States Parties in order to address a request or indication of a need for technical advice or assistance contained therein, along with the Committee's observations and recommendations, if any, on these requests or indications.
37 Cooperation between States Parties and the Committee	Each State Party shall cooperate with the Committee and assist its members in the fulfillment of their mandate. In its relationship with States Parties, the Committee shall give due consideration to ways and means of enhancing national capacities for the implementation of the present Convention, including through international cooperation.
38 Relationship of the Committee with other bodies	In order to foster the effective implementation of the present Convention and to encourage international cooperation in the field covered by the present Convention: (a) The specialised agencies and other United Nations organs shall be entitled to be represented at the consideration of the implementation of such provisions of the present Convention as fall within the scope of their mandate. The Committee may invite the specialised agencies and other competent bodies as it may consider appropriate to provide expert advice on the implementation of the Convention in areas falling within the scope of their respective mandates. The Committee may invite specialised agencies and other United Nations organs to submit reports on the implementation of the Convention in areas falling within the scope of their activities. The Committee,

(Contd.)

(Contd. Table)

Article	*Explanation*
	as it discharges its mandate, shall consult, as appropriate, other relevant bodies instituted by international human rights treaties, with a view to ensuring the consistency of their respective reporting guidelines, suggestions and general recommendations, and avoiding duplication and overlap in the performance of their functions.
39 Report of the Committee	The Committee shall report every two years to the General Assembly and to the Economic and Social Council on its activities, and may make suggestions and general recommendations based on the examination of reports and information received from the States Parties. Such suggestions and general recommendations shall be included in the report of the Committee together with comments, if any, from States Parties.
40 Conference of States Parties	The States Parties shall meet regularly in a Conference of States Parties in order to consider any matter with regard to the implementation of the present Convention. No later than six months after the entry into force of the present Convention, the Conference of States Parties shall be convened by the Secretary-General of the United Nations. The subsequent meetings shall be convened by the Secretary-General biennially or upon the decision of the Conference of States Parties.
41 Depositary	The Secretary-General of the United Nations shall be the depositary of the present Convention.
42 Signature	The present Convention shall be open for signature by all States and by regional integration organisations at United Nations Headquarters in New York as of 30 March 2007.
43 Consent to be bound	The present Convention shall be subject to ratification by signatory States and to formal confirmation by signatory regional integration

(Contd.)

(Contd. Table)

Article	*Explanation*
	organisations. It shall be open for accession by any State or regional integration organisation which has not signed the Convention.
44 Regional integration organisations	"Regional integration organisation" shall mean an organisation constituted by sovereign States of a given region, to which its member States have transferred competence in respect of matters governed by the present Convention. Such organisations shall declare, in their instruments of formal confirmation or accession, the extent of their competence with respect to matters governed by the present Convention. Subsequently, they shall inform the depositary of any substantial modification in the extent of their competence. References to "States Parties" in the present Convention shall apply to such organisations within the limits of their competence. For the purposes of Article 45, paragraph 1, and Article 47, paragraphs 2 and 3, of the present Convention, any instrument deposited by a regional integration organisation shall not be counted. Regional integration organisations, in matters within their competence, may exercise their right to vote in the Conference of States Parties, with a number of votes equal to the number of their member States that are Parties to the present Convention. Such an organisation shall not exercise its right to vote if any of its member States exercises its right, and vice-versa.
45 Entry into force	The present Convention shall enter into force on the thirtieth day after the deposit of the twentieth instrument of ratification or accession. For each State or regional integration organisation ratifying, formally confirming or acceding to the present Convention after the deposit of the twentieth such instrument, the Convention shall enter into force on

(Contd.)

(Contd. Table)

Article	*Explanation*
	the thirtieth day after the deposit of its own such instrument.
46 Reservations	Reservations incompatible with the object and purpose of the present Convention shall not be permitted. Reservations may be withdrawn at any time.
47 Amendments	Any State Party may propose an amendment to the present Convention and submit it to the Secretary-General of the United Nations. The Secretary-General shall communicate any proposed amendments to States Parties, with a request to be notified whether they favour a conference of States Parties for the purpose of considering and deciding upon the proposals. In the event that, within four months from the date of such communication, at least one-third of the States Parties favour such a conference, the Secretary-General shall convene the conference under the auspices of the United Nations. Any amendment adopted by a majority of two-thirds of the States Parties present and voting shall be submitted by the Secretary-General to the General Assembly of the United Nations for approval and thereafter to all States Parties for acceptance. An amendment adopted and approved in accordance with paragraph 1 of this article shall enter into force on the thirtieth day after the number of instruments of acceptance deposited reaches two-thirds of the number of States Parties at the date of adoption of the amendment. Thereafter, the amendment shall enter into force for any State Party on the thirtieth day following the deposit of its own instrument of acceptance. An amendment shall be binding only on those States Parties which have accepted it. If so decided by the Conference of States Parties by consensus, an amendment adopted and approved in accordance with

(Contd.)

(Contd. Table)

Article	*Explanation*
	paragraph 1 of this article which relates exclusively to Articles 34, 38, 39 and 40 shall enter into force for all States Parties on the thirtieth day after the number of instruments of acceptance deposited reaches two-thirds of the number of States Parties at the date of adoption of the amendment.
48 Denunciation	A State Party may denounce the present Convention by written notification to the Secretary-General of the United Nations. The denunciation shall become effective one year after the date of receipt of the notification by the Secretary-General.
49 Accessible format	The text of the present Convention shall be made available in accessible formats.
50 Authentic texts	The Arabic, Chinese, English, French, Russian and Spanish texts of the present Convention shall be equally authentic. IN WITNESS THEREOF the undersigned plenipotentiaries, being duly authorised thereto by their respective Governments, have signed the present Convention.

Source: http://www.un.org/disabilities/documents/convention/convoptprot-e.pdf

The Committee on the Rights of Persons with Disabilities is a body of human rights experts tasked with monitoring the implementation of the Convention. It initially consisted of 12 independent human rights experts, with half elected for a two-year term and half elected for four-years.[23] The Committee on the Rights of Persons with Disabilities (CRPD) is a United Nations body of 18 experts that meets two times a year in Geneva. The Committee is one of nine UN human rights treaty bodies, each responsible for overseeing the implementation of a particular treaty. All states parties are required to submit regular reports to the Committee outlining the legislative, judicial, policy and other measures they have taken to implement the rights affirmed in the Convention. The Office of the High Commissioner for Human Rights assists the work of the Committee.[24]

Protection of Persons with Mental Illness

The Principles for the Protection of Persons with Mental Illness and the Improvement of Mental Health Care were adopted by the United Nations General Assembly in 1991. They provide agreed but non-legally-binding basic standards that mental health systems should meet and rights that people diagnosed with mental disorder should have.[25]

International Disability and Development Consortium

It is a global consortium of disability and development related organisations. The aim of IDDC is to promote inclusive development internationally, with a special focus on promoting human rights for all disabled people living in economically poor communities in lower and middle-income countries. IDDC's work is primarily led by task groups where members collaborate to exchange views and ideas, and agree upon common strategies and positions. These task groups are thus fundamental to the implementation of the IDDC objectives.[26]

Handicap International

Handicap International is a non-governmental organisation created in 1982 to provide help in refugee camps in Cambodia and Thailand. Headquartered in France and Belgium, it has since opened branches in six other countries: Switzerland, Luxembourg, United Kingdom, Germany, Canada and the United States. Handicap International is one of the six founding members of the International Campaign to Ban Landmines which received the Nobel Peace Prize in 1997. Handicap International has been a vocal advocate of the Convention on Cluster Munitions (CCM), an international treaty banning the use, transfer and stockpile of these weapons adopted on 30 May 2008 in Dublin, Ireland[27].

Disability Discrimination Act 1995

The Disability Discrimination Act 1995 is an Act of the Parliament of the United Kingdom which has now been repealed and replaced by the Equality Act 2010, except in Northern Ireland where the Act still applies. In addition to imposing obligations on employers, the Act placed duties on service providers and required reasonable adjustments to be made when providing access to goods, facilities, services and premises. The DDA 1995 departed from the fundamental principles of older UK discrimination law (the Sex

Discrimination Act 1975 and the Race Relations Act 1976). These Acts, also repealed and replaced by the Equality Act 2010, made direct discrimination and indirect discrimination unlawful. However, these concepts are insufficient to deal with the issues of disability discrimination.[28]

Conclusion

Disabilities are an umbrella term, covering impairments, activity limitations, and participation restrictions. Disability is not just a health problem. The term disability broadly describes impairment in a person's ability to function, caused by changes in various subsystems of the body, or to mental health. The *World report on disability* is the first document to give an extensive global picture of the situation of people with disabilities, their needs, and the barriers they face to participating fully in their societies. The Ministry of Social Justice and Empowerment of the Government of India has been holding national consultative meetings on proposed amendments to the Persons with Disabilities Equal Opportunities, Protection of Rights and Full Participation Act (PWD Act). The Constitution of India ensures equality, freedom, justice and dignity of all individuals and implicitly mandates an inclusive society for all including persons with disabilities.

Census 2001 in India has revealed that over 21 million people in India as suffering from one or the other kind of disability. This is equivalent to 2.1 per cent of the population. Among the total disabled in the country, 12.6 million are males and 9.3 million are females. Among the five types of disabilities on which data has been collected, disability in seeing at 48.5 per cent emerges as the top category. Others in sequence are: In movement (27.9 per cent), Mental (10.3 per cent), speech (7.5 per cent), and hearing (5.8 per cent). Government of India was implemented various acts, i.e. The Mental Health Act, 1987; The Rehabilitation Council Act of India, 1992; The Persons with Disabilities (Equal Opportunities, Full Participation and Protection of Rights) Act, 1995; The National Trust (For welfare of persons with Autism, Cerebral Palsy, Metal Retardation and Multiple Disabilities) Act, 1999, for empowerment of disable persons.

References

1. Types of disabilities, Retrieved from http://www.cdc.gov/ncbddd/disabilityandhealth/types.html
2. Disability (2015), Retrieved from http://en.wikipedia.org/wiki/Disability

3. See http://www.un.org/disabilities/default.asp?id=18
4. Disabilities, World Health Organisation (2015), Retrieved from http://www.who.int/topics/disabilities/en/
5. From official website of National Educational Association of Disabled Students, Retrieved from http://www.neads.ca/en/about/projects/inclusion/guide/pwd_01.php
6. Visual impairment, Retrieved from http://www.nhs.uk/conditions/Visual-impairment/Pages/Introduction.aspx
7. Hearing disability (2015), Retrieved from
8. What Problems Do People with Disabilities Have? and Why? Retrieved from http://trace.wisc.edu/docs/software_guidelines/software.pcs/disabil.htm
9. World report on disability (2015), Retrieved from http://en.wikipedia.org/wiki/World_report_on_disability
10. Disabled people, Retrieved from http://censusindia.gov.in/Census_And_You/disabled_population.aspx
11. *The Times of India* (Dec 29, 2013), Disabled population up by 22.4 per cent in 2001-11, Retrieved from http://timesofindia.indiatimes.com/india/Disabled-population-up-by-22-4-in-2001-11/articleshow/28072371.cms
12. Swagata Raha, India needs new legislation on Disability Rights, Retrieved from http://infochangeindia.org/disabilities/analysis/india-needs-new-legislation-on-disability-rights.html
13. *The Hindu* (Sep 23, 2012), The Disabilities Bill is a mixed bag, Retrieved from http://www.thehindu.com/news/national/the-disabilities-bill-is-a-mixed-bag/article3927212.ece
14. See http://www.un.org/press/en/2014/soc4812.doc.htm
15. See http://trace.wisc.edu/docs/software_guidelines/software.pcs/disabil.htm
16. Disability (2015), Retrieved from http://en.wikipedia.org/wiki/Disability
17. International Year of Disabled Persons (2015), Retrieved from http://en.wikipedia.org/wiki/International_Year_of_Disabled_Persons
18. United Nations International Day of Persons with Disabilities (2015), Retrieved from http://en.wikipedia.org/wiki/United_Nations%27_International_Day_of_Persons_with_Disabilities
19. Convention on the Rights of Persons with Disabilities (2015), Retrieved from http://en.wikipedia.org/wiki/Convention_on_the_ Rights_of_Persons_with_Disabilities
20. Convention on the Rights of Persons with Disabilities (2015), Retrieved from http://en.wikipedia.org/wiki/Convention_on_the_ Rights_of_Persons_with_Disabilities

21. Convention on the Rights of Persons with Disabilities (2015), Retrieved from http://en.wikipedia.org/wiki/Convention_on_the_ Rights_of_Persons_ with_Disabilities
22. Convention on the Rights of Persons with Disabilities and Optional Protocol, Retrieved from http://www.un.org/disabilities/documents/convention/ convoptprot-e.pdf
23. Convention on the Rights of Persons with Disabilities (2015), Retrieved from http://en.wikipedia.org/wiki/Convention_on_the_Rights_of_ Persons_with_Disabilities
24. Committee on the Rights of Persons with Disabilities (2015), Retrieved from http://en.wikipedia.org/wiki/Committee_on_the_Rights_ of_Persons_with_Disabilities
25. Principles for the Protection of Persons with Mental Illness (2015), Retrieved from http://en.wikipedia.org/wiki/Principles_for_the_Protection_of_ Persons_with_Mental_Illness
26. International Disability and Development Consortium (2015), Retrieved from http://en.wikipedia.org/wiki/International_Disability_and_ Development_Consortium
27. Handicap International (2015), Retrieved from http://en.wikipedia.org/ wiki/Handicap_International
28. Disability Discrimination Act 1995 (2015), Retrieved from http:// en.wikipedia.org/wiki/Disability_Discrimination_Act_1995
29. Read more at http://www.brainyquote.com/quotes/keywords/ human.html#AcLeDlkFalwK9b4S.99

9

Orphan Rights

"Truth is, I'll never know all there is to know about you just as you will never know all there is to know about me. Humans are by nature too complicated to be understood fully. So, we can choose either to approach our fellow human beings with suspicion or to approach them with an open mind, a dash of optimism and a great deal of candour."

-Tom Hanks

Introduction

Today, 153 million children worldwide are orphans. There are serious consequences for the rights and development of such children. An orphan is a child who has one or two deceased parents. Of the 132 million orphans who live in developing countries, an estimated 13 million have lost both parents. One of the major causes of children being orphaned is the HIV/AIDS epidemic. In 2008, about 430,000 children became infected with the HIV virus. In most cases, the virus is transmitted from mother to child. If the HIV/AIDS epidemic could be contained, the number of orphans worldwide would diminish. Prevention and screening campaigns are needed to reach this goal, as well as guaranteed access to treatment.[1]

The global HIV/AIDS pandemic has been changing human lives and the shape of societies for more than 15 years in the heavily infected countries of Sub-Saharan Africa, Asia, Latin America and the Caribbean. The human and social costs these estimates represent are staggering. The growing demand for care and support of orphans and vulnerable children at the community level has strained traditional coping mechanisms to a crisis stage in the most heavily affected countries. Although African and Asian countries have responded with comprehensive policies and plans of action for these children (Malawi, Zimbabwe, Thailand), most countries have national plans still in development. Some countries, such as Malawi, have established a policy framework specifically to protect orphans, guide the way services are provided for them and define respective government and NGO areas of responsibility.[2]

As the HIV epidemic continues to unfold across southern Africa, countries are still struggling to find effective means to address many of its negative impacts at individual, family and community levels. One of the most complicated challenges is how to support the growing number of orphans and other children made vulnerable, or made more vulnerable, by the direct and indirect effects of HIV on their households.[3] During the past decade an illness that made itself known among homosexual men and users of intravenous drugs in developed countries has become a pandemic affecting millions of individuals, their families, and communities around the world. As the HIV and AIDS epidemic becomes increasingly complex and as the personal and social consequences rise, the ways societies respond to ensure children's right to education must become more contextualised, integrated, nuanced and dynamic.[4] The HIV epidemic has revealed a broad range of vulnerabilities faced by children and their families.[5]

Who is Orphan?

From Wikipedia, Orphan is a child whose parents are dead or have abandoned them permanently. In common usage, only a child who has lost both parents is called an orphan. When referring to animals, only the mother's condition is usually relevant. In the common use, an orphan does not have any surviving parent to care for him or her. However, the United Nations Children's Fund (UNICEF), Joint United Nations Programme on HIV and AIDS (UNAIDS), and other groups label any child that has lost one parent as an orphan. Famous orphans include world leaders such as Nelson Mandela and Andrew Jackson; the Hebrew prophet Moses and the Muslim prophet Muhammad; writers such as Edgar Allan Poe, and Leo Tolstoy.[6]

Reasons of Orphan

One of the major causes of children being orphaned is the HIV/ AIDS epidemic. Children can also lose parent due to natural disasters, famine, and war. The latter factor also contributes to the displacement of children across borders. Extreme poverty, illness, abuse and incest can also tear nuclear families apart and, in the end, lead to abandonment.[7] Wars and great epidemics, such as AIDS, have created many orphans. HIV/AIDS not only orphans children but also makes children more vulnerable in a number of ways. First and foremost, in many countries HIV/AIDS has reversed improvements in child morbidity and mortality rates achieved during the last several decades. The epidemic influences child survival both directly through mother-to-child transmission and indirectly through diverting resources and attention away from children to the care and treatment of a sick parent.[8]

Millions of children around the world have been orphaned by the AIDS crisis. Aside from the emotional and psychological effects that losing a parent can have, there is clear evidence that orphaned children are dropping out of school at a higher rate than non-orphaned children.[9]

Orphan Children in India

About 20 million children, about four per cent of the total population of India i.e. more than the total population of greater Delhi, are orphans. Of those 20 million, only 0.3 per cent of the children were orphaned by the death of their parents. The rest 99.7 per cent of them are abandoned children. It was states such like Uttar Pradesh, Bihar and West Bengal, which had the highest number of orphan children as compared to the northern and southern states of India. Poverty has been a significant contributor in high orphan children figures in these states. Many of the children who are trafficked are those whose parents have died or they have been abandoned.[10]

India has the second highest number of AIDS cases in the world (3.86 million); only South Africa has more. This number represents 10 per cent of the global burden and 68 per cent of the total burden for South Asia. The prevalence in the 15–49 age group is 0.8 per cent. AIDS is no longer restricted to high-risk populations; instead, it is spreading rapidly in the general population. The needs of orphans and vulnerable children (including street children), the children of sex workers and rag pickers, and those infected and affected by AIDS in India are vast. Community-based care for children affected by AIDS is relatively new. The Ministry of Social Justice and Empowerment funds some interventions that include street children and runs programmes for children in difficult circumstances. There are many problems to address. Discrimination is still very widespread.[11]

Government of India policy recognises the central importance of civil society groups, NGOs and the private sector, in coordination with government structures, to serve children affected by AIDS. USAID/India has been a catalyst, advocate, and supporter of the Government of India's vision and policies. They have provided innovative OVC programme funding to strengthen NGOs, work directly with National AIDS Control Organisation (NACO), and forge new public-private partnerships.[12] Childhood orphanhood is considered a major risk factor for poverty in adulthood, through, among other channels, shortfalls in human capital investments in children.[13]

Legal Perspectives

The mandate of the U.S. President's Emergency Plan is to bring compassionate relief and support to countries, communities, families, and children affected by the HIV/AIDS epidemic. The Emergency Plan uses a three-pronged strategy of prevention, treatment, and care interventions to accomplish this goal, and OVC programmes are among the HIV/AIDS care interventions it supports. The U.S. Government country teams make programming decisions for PEPFAR, and thus for OVC programmes, which receive approval in Washington through the Country Operational Plan and Reporting Systems (COPRS) reporting process. The U.S. Emergency Plan Five Year Global HIV/AIDS Strategy identifies several goals for developing OVC programs: to rapidly scale up compassionate care for OVCs; to build capacity for long-term sustainability of care; to advance policy initiatives with direct outcomes that support care for OVCs; and to collect strategic information to monitor and evaluate progress and ensure compliance with Emergency Plan policies and strategies.[14]

Human Rights Violation

An Orphan is any person who is below the age of 18, who has lost one or both parents due to death. A vulnerable child is any person who is below the age of 18, who has one or both parents who have deserted or neglected him/her to the extent that he/she has no means of survival and as such is exposed to dangers of abuse, exploitation and/or criminalisation and is, therefore, in need of care and protection. Vulnerable children include orphans, children living on the streets, children with challenging behaviour, children in need of legal and other forms of protection, children who have been or are physically, psychologically, emotionally, or sexually abused.[15] Children who are orphaned are more likely to suffer from detrimental health and nutritional outcomes; orphaned children are more likely to be stunted compared to non-orphans. In addition to orphanhood, children can be affected by HIV in a number of ways. With chronically ill parents or guardians, children may have to forgo education for work or household duties to support themselves and family members.

Economic hardship and reduced parental care and protection mean that orphans and vulnerable children are likely to lose out on education about how to avoid HIV infection and may be more susceptible to abuse and exploitation than others. Education is a basic human right for all children, as recognised in the Convention on the Rights of the Child. Education is critically important to children's social integration and psychosocial well-being. Orphans and vulnerable children stand in particular need of such an education intervention as they are amongst the children most in danger of becoming infected with HIV due to economic hardship, reduced parental care and protection and increased susceptibility to abuse and exploitation. Within the school there is often stigmatisation and discrimination. An especial concern for programmes seeking to enable the access to quality education of orphans and vulnerable children is the needs of girl children. In addition to the more general Millennium Development Goals, global partners have recently signed on to a number of commitments specific to orphans and vulnerable children.[16]

Like adults, children are grieved by the loss of their parents. However, unlike adults children often do not feel the full impact of the loss simply because they may not immediately understand the finality of death. Death of parents introduces a major change in the life of a vulnerable child. This change may involve moving from a middle or upper-class urban home to a poor rural relative's home. Death of parents makes children vulnerable and predisposes them to physical and psychological risks over which they have no control.[17]

Compared to adults, all children are vulnerable by virtue of their younger age, smaller size, and limited life experience, maturity and means, but some children are more vulnerable than others. While the death of a parent places challenges on children, the sickness of a parent also has an impact on health and development. Street children are considered to be among the most vulnerable children "*because they are absolutely desperate and are ready to do anything in order to survive. They are also extremely naive and not equipped to face the realities of street life and without guidance children often make dangerous choices and decisions.*" The actual number of children victims of abuse, including sexual abuse, and exploitation is not known because there is no reliable national system of reporting. Sexual violence and sexual exploitation of children is recognised as a significant issue.[18]

The 1994 Declaration from the Paris Summit on AIDS (1994) calls for increased mobilisation of resources and the development of partnerships to reduce the impact of the HIV/AIDS pandemic on the world's children and youth. The Paris Declaration also calls for greater attention to be paid to the ethical and human rights concerns associated with AIDS. As a result of this summit in January 1995, the United Nations established the joint United Nations Programme on AIDS (UNAIDS) to coordinate the six UN agencies that have been active in responding to the AIDS epidemic. UNICEF is represented at UNAIDS to promote, protect and support the rights of children affected by AIDS. Malawi is currently ranked as one of the poorest sub-Saharan states. Malawi ratified the CRC in 1991.[19]

In all countries, there should be laws that specifically protect the rights of children, such as national constitutions and child-specific laws, as well as laws that focus on specific issues and rights such as education and nutrition. The laws should promote equality and prohibit discrimination in access to rights and services, like education and healthcare; protect children from abuse and exploitation from harmful practices (such as exploitative child labour and some harmful traditional/ cultural practices); protect their rights to inheritance; promote appropriate models of alternative care for children without adequate family care; and define roles and responsibilities of duty bearers.[20]

Conclusion

Today, 153 million children worldwide are orphans. There are serious consequences for the rights and development of such children. An orphan is a child who has one or two deceased parents. One of the major causes of children being orphaned is the HIV/AIDS epidemic. Children can also lose parent due to natural disasters, famine, and war. The latter factor also contributes to the displacement of children across borders. Extreme poverty, illness, abuse and incest can also tear nuclear families apart and, in the end, lead to abandonment. Millions of children around the world have been orphaned by the AIDS crisis. About 20 million children, about four per cent of the total population of India i.e. more than the total population of greater Delhi, are orphans. Government of India policy recognises the central importance of civil society groups, NGOs and the private sector, in coordination with government structures, to serve children affected by AIDS. USAID/India has been a catalyst, advocate, and supporter of the Government of India's vision and policies. They have provided innovative OVC programme funding to strengthen NGOs, work directly with National AIDS Control Organisation (NACO), and forge new public-private partnerships.

References

1. Orphan, Retrieved from http://www.humanium.org/en/orphans/
2. Care for orphans, children affected by HIV/AIDS and other vulnerable children: A Strategic framework, Retrieved from http://www.hivpolicy.org/Library/HPP000531.pdf
3. The Role of the Education Sector in Providing Care and Support for Orphans and Vulnerable Children in Lesotho and Swaziland, Retrieved from http://www.osisa.org/sites/default/files/openlearninglesothoswaziland.pdf
4. Promoting Quality Education for Orphans and Vulnerable Children: A Sourcebook of Programme Experiences in Eastern and Southern Africa, Retrieved from http://www.unicef.org/spanish/education/files/Promoting_Quality_Education_for_Orphans_and_Vulnerable_ Children_Programmes_from_Eastern_and_Southern_Africa.pdf
5. http://www.healthpolicyinitiative.com/Publications/Documents/1346_1_OVC_Global_Fund_Desk_Rev_FINAL_August_2010_acc.pdf
6. Orphan (2015), Retrieved from http://en.wikipedia.org/wiki/Orphan
7. Orphan, Retrieved from http://www.humanium.org/en/orphans/
8. Vinod Mishra (2008), Orphans and Vulnerable Children in High HIV-Prevalence Countries in Sub-Saharan Africa, Retrieved from http://dhsprogram.com/pubs/pdf/as15/as15.pdf
9. Tania Boler and Kate Carroll, and Addressing the educational needs of orphans and vulnerable children Policy and Research: issue 2, Retrieved from http://www.actionaid.org.uk/sites/default/files/doc_lib/129_2_orphans_vulner able_children.pdf
10. Chetan Chauhan, 20 Million Young Orphans: India's Abandoned Children, Retrieved from http://www.sikhchic.net/current_events/20_million_ young_orphans_indias_abandoned_children
11. Orphans and vulnerable children's in India: Understanding the Context and the Response (2003), Retrieved from http://www.saathii.org/ovc/context_and_response/i-01-Synergy_OVCReportFinal.pdf
12. India's HIV Orphans and Vulnerable Children: Generating Evidence for Policy and Practice (2012), Retrieved from http://www.bu.edu/cghd/files/2012/02/IndiaOVCreport-100212-copy1.pdf

13. Kathleen Beegle, Joachim De Weerdt, Stefan Dercon (2007), Orphanhood and the long-run impact on children, Retrieved from http://www.csae.ox.ac.uk/workingpapers/pdfs/2007-08text.pdf
14. Orphans and Other Vulnerable Children Programming Guidance for United States Government In-Country Staff and Implementing Partners (2006), Retrieved from http://www.pepfar.gov/documents/organisation/83298.pdf
15. National policy on Orphans and vulnerable children, Retrieved from http://www.africanchildforum.org/clr/policy%20per%20country/lesotho/lesotho_ovc_en.pdf
16. Education Programming for Orphans and Vulnerable Children Affected by or Vulnerable to HIV, Retrieved from http://pdf.usaid.gov/pdf_docs/PNADP105.pdf
17. James Sengendo and Janet Nambi, Health Transition Review, Supplement to Volume 7, 1997, 105-124, Retrieved from http://ceped.org/cdrom/orphelins_sida_2006/pdf/sengend1.pdf
18. Orphans, Children Affected by HIV and Other Vulnerable Children in Cambodia: A Situation and Response Assessment, 2007, Retrieved from http://www.unicef.org/eapro/OVC_Situation_Assess_June_2008.pdf
19. Starting from strengths community care for orphaned children in Malawi, Retrieved from http://community.eldis.org/.59ee4585/Orphaned%20children.pdf
20. Rose Smart (2003), Policies for Orphans and Vulnerable Children: A Framework for Moving Ahead, Retrieved from http://www.policyproject.com/pubs/generalreport/ovc_policies.pdf
21. Read more at http://www.brainyquote.com/quotes/keywords/human.html#AcLeDlkFalwK9b4S.99

10

Minority Rights

"The moment I have realised God sitting in the temple of every human body, the moment I stand in reverence before every human being and see God in him - that moment I am free from bondage, everything that binds vanishes, and I am free."

- Swami Vivekananda

Introduction

Religion in India is characterised by a diversity of religious beliefs and practices. India is the birthplace of four of the world's major religions; namely Hinduism, Buddhism, Jainism and Sikhism. The Constitution of India declares the nation to be a secular republic that must uphold the right of citizens to freely worship and propagate any or no religion or faith. There are six religions in India which have been awarded "National minority" status: Muslims, Christians, Sikhs, Jains, Buddhists and Zoroastrians. According to the 2011 census, 78.35 per cent of the population of India practice Hinduism. Islam (14.88 per cent), Christianity (2.5 per cent), Sikhism (1.9 per cent), Buddhism (0.8 per cent) and Jainism (0.4 per cent) are the other major religions followed by the people of India. The preamble to the Constitution of India proclaims India a "sovereign socialist secular democratic republic".

Religion plays a major role in the Indian way of life. The vast majority of Indians engage in religious rituals on a daily basis. Communal conflicts have periodically plagued India since it became independent in 1947. The roots of such strife lie largely in the underlying tensions between sections of its majority Hindu and minority Muslim communities, which emerged under the Raj and during the bloody Partition of India. Occasions like birth, marriage, and death involve what are often elaborate sets of religious customs.[1]

Who are Minority?

A minority group is a sociological category within a demographic. The term "minority group" often occurs alongside a discourse of civil rights and collective rights which gained prominence in the 20th century. Feagin (1984) states that a minority group has five characteristics: (1) suffering discrimination and subordination, (2) physical and/or cultural traits that set them apart, and which are disapproved by the dominant group, (3) a shared sense of collective identity and common burdens, (4) socially shared rules about who belongs and who does not determine minority status, and (5) tendency to marry within the group. Sociologist Louis Wirth defined a minority group as "a group of people who, because of their physical or cultural characteristics, are singled out from the others in the society in which they live for differential and unequal treatment and who therefore regard themselves as objects of collective discrimination."[2]

Minority People in India

In Indian Constitution, minority can be classifying as two ways: (a) Religious minority, and (b) Linguistic minority. Muslims, Christians, Sikhs, Buddhists and Zoroastrians (Parsis) have been notified as minority communities by the Union Government. Further vide notification detail 27th Jan 2014; Jains have also been notified as minority community. Linguistic minorities are those who have different first language than the first language of majority of the people in that state. Thus, for example, Gujarati speaking people living in Maharashtra are linguistic minorities in Maharashtra and Marathi speaking people living in Gujarat are linguistic minorities in Gujarat. There are about five million Jains in India, mostly in Maharashtra, Rajasthan, Madhya Pradesh, Gujarat, Karnataka, Uttar Pradesh and Delhi. The literacy rate among Jains is about 90 per cent. The Muslim community has been the major beneficiary of scholarships from the ministry for minority affairs (which account for most of the ministry's annual budget of about Rs 3,000 crore), as their population is the highest among minority communities.[3]

Islam is the second-largest religion in India, making up 14.88 per cent of the country's population with about 180 million adherents

(2011 census). India's Muslim population is the world's third largest and the world's largest Muslim-minority population. Officially, India has the third largest Muslim population next to Indonesia and Pakistan. India is home to 10 per cent of the world's Muslim population. Muslims represent a majority of the local population in Lakshadweep and Jammu and Kashmir. The largest concentration about 47 per cent of all Muslims in India, live in the three states of Uttar Pradesh, West Bengal, and Bihar. High concentrations of Muslims are found in states of Assam, Kerala, Maharashtra, Jharkhand and Karnataka. Muslims in India have a much higher total fertility rate compared to that of other religious communities in the country. There are many denominations amongst Indian Muslims; the majority belongs to the Sunni branch of Islam, while a substantial minority belongs to the Shia branch[4].

Social mobility in the new India has not entirely excluded Muslims. Many Indian Muslims have become sports heroes (the long-serving cricket captain Mohammed Azharuddin, for instance), film stars, politicians (including the recent ex-president A P J Abdul Kalam), academics, professional leaders, business tycoons or journalists. But the great majority languishes.[5] Christianity is India's third-largest religion according to the census of 2001, with approximately 24 million followers, constituting 2.3 per cent of India's population. Christians are found all across India and in all walks of life, with major populations in parts of South India, the Konkan Coast, North-East. Indian Christians have contributed significantly to and are well represented in various spheres of national life.

Minority Rights in Indian Constitution

In Indian constitution various articles are discuss about minority rights. Article 14: The State shall not deny to any person equality before the law or the equal protection of the laws within the territory of India. Article 15: (1) The State shall not discriminate against any citizen on grounds only of religion, race, caste, sex, place of birth or any of them. (2) No citizen shall, on grounds only of religion, race, caste, sex, place of birth or any of them, be subject to any disability, liability, restriction or condition with regard to— (a) access to shops, public restaurants, hotels and places of public entertainment; or (b) the use of wells, tanks, bathing ghats, roads and places of public resort maintained wholly or partly out of State funds or dedicated to the use of the general public. (3) Nothing in this article shall prevent the State from making any special provision for women and children.

Article 21: No person shall be deprived of his life or personal liberty except according to procedure established by law. Article 25: (1) Subject to public order, morality and health and to the other provisions of this Part, all persons are equally entitled to freedom of conscience and the right freely to profess, practise and propagate religion. Article 26: Subject to public order, morality and health, every religious denomination or any section thereof shall have the right. Article 29: (1) Any section of the citizens residing in the territory of India or any part thereof having a distinct language, script or culture of its own shall have the right to conserve the same. (2) No citizen shall be denied admission into any educational institution maintained by the State or receiving aid out of State funds on grounds only of religion, race, caste, language or any of them.[6]

Article 30(1) – the "*minorities only*" clause that is at the centre of all this. *All minorities, whether based on religion or language, shall have the right to establish and administer educational institutions of their choice.* Article 19(1) (g) the ***"secular provision"*** that has gained traction as one that protects All citizens including Hindus and minorities from engaging in any activity including education, *(g) All citizens shall have the right, to practice any profession, or to carry on any occupation, trade or business. Art 29(1) under "Protection of interests of Minorities" says any section of citizens having a distinct culture, language, or script of its own shall have the right to conserve the same.*[7] Article 30 speaks about two categories of minorities — religious and linguistic - while Article 350 relates to linguistic minorities only.

Article 46 of the Constitution states that, "*The State shall promote, with special care, the education and economic interests of the weaker sections of the people, and, in particular of the Scheduled Castes and Scheduled Tribes, and shall protect them from social injustice and all forms of social exploitation.*" Articles 330, 332, 335, 338 to 342 and the entire Fifth and Sixth Schedules of the Constitution deal with special provisions for implementation of the objectives set forth in Article 46. Similarly, Articles 30 (1) provides for the rights of the Minorities to establish and administer educational institutions of their choice. These provisions need to be fully utilised for the benefit of these weaker sections in our society.[8]

The linguistic reorganisation of regional state boundaries has been a major instrument for protecting and nurturing linguistic diversity. The creation of linguistic identity based units, each with political rights to govern itself within the framework of the federal system, meant that a specific linguistic community became a majority within a region. Its language became the official language of that state and the medium of instruction, public examination, communication and media networks. Besides religious and linguistic diversity, India paid some attention to the diversity embodied in tribal ways of life. The constitution identified some areas where tribal communities lived with some form of 'protective segregation' as 'excluded' or 'partially excluded' regions.[9]

The Constitution (103rd Amendment) Bill, 2004 to grant constitutional status to the National Commission for Minorities envisages a change in the way minorities are specified. The Cabinet has reportedly approved a proposal (May 2007) to define minorities State-wise in line with several Supreme Court judgments, most notably that in *T.M.A. Pai*.[10]

Ministry of Minority Affairs

The Ministry of Minority Affairs, a ministry of the Government of India established in 2006. It is the apex body for the central government's regulatory and developmental programmes for the minority communities in India, which include Muslims, Sikhs, Christians, Buddhists, Zoroastrians (Parsis) and Jains notified as minority communities under Section 2 (c) of the National Commission for Minorities Act, 1992. The ministry is also involved with the linguistic minorities and of the Office of the Commissioner for Linguistic Minorities.[11] Besides The Minority Commission of India, there are State Minority Commissions in following states of India: Andhra Pradesh, Assam, Bihar, Chhattisgarh, Delhi, Jharkhand, Karnataka, Maharashtra, Madhya Pradesh, Manipur, Rajasthan, Tamil Nadu, Uttarakhand, Uttar Pradesh and West Bengal.[12]

Violation of Minority Rights

There have been relatively fewer conflicts between Muslims and Christians in India in comparison to those between Muslims and Hindus, or Muslims and Sikh. Historically, Hindus and Christians have lived in relative peace since the arrival of Christianity in India from the early part of the first millennium. There has been an increase in anti-Christian violence in recent years, particularly in the states of Odisha, which is usually perpetrated by opposition to Pentecostalism. In 2007, 19 churches were burned by Hindu right-wingers in Odisha following conflicts between Hindus and Christians regarding Christmas celebrations in the Kandhamal district.[13]

Three ethnic or religious conflicts have stood out of late: two occurred in the states of "Assam and Punjab; another, the more widely known Hindu-Muslim conflict continues to persist. Of the three conflicts mentioned, Assam has attracted the largest attention of late.[14] Not since the 1947 partition of India have so many people been killed and uprooted as a result of ethnic or communal violence. Starting in August 1980, mounting communal tension between Hindus and Sikhs in the state of Punjab led to violent clashes, in the last year in particular. Unlike Assam, Punjab is a state with the highest per capita income.[15]

A 1999 Human Rights Watch report states increasing levels of religious violence on Christians in India, perpetrated by Hindu organisations.[16] Despite widespread poverty and repeated conflicts with its neighbour Pakistan, India under Prime Minister Jawaharlal Nehru and his successors, emerged as a secular democracy in a vibrant political environment, though it has suffered periodic episodes of deadly sectarian violence. In 1984, Prime Minister Indira Gandhi sent the army to remove Sikh militant separatists from Amritsar's Golden Temple, resulting in hundreds of civilian deaths, her assassination by her Sikh bodyguards, and retaliatory anti-Sikh pogroms. The destruction of the Babri Mosque in Ayodhya by Hindu nationalists in 1992 led to riots that killed thousands, as did religious riots in Gujarat in 2002.[17]

Government Efforts

All the people falling under Minority communities in India get benefits in education and employment opportunities. Regional Minorities have set up various education schools and institutions to promote their culture and language. In addition, they are entitled to reserve a specific quota of seats (for students and teachers) for people belonging to their own communities. There are various Government schemes which provide direct aid to educational institutions promoting regional communities in India.[18]

Religious minorities get special benefits, especially in the field of education and educational institutions. Minority communities can establish their own educational institutions, and can reserve 50 per cent seats of the students for own community members. In addition, they can recruit 100 per cent staff from their own community. Beside this, scholarships and other help is offered to minority students by Central and state Governments.

According to 'Sachar Committee Report' *"one-fourth of Muslim children in the age group of 6-14 years has either never attended school or are drop-outs. For children above the age of 17 years, the educational attainment of Muslims at matriculation is 17 per cent, as against national average at 26 per cent. Only 50 per cent of Muslims who complete middle school are likely to complete secondary education, compared to 62 per cent at national level".* The Report has also drawn attention to the low levels of educational attainment among Muslim women, Muslims in rural areas as well as in technical and higher education. Ministry of Human Resource Development has also constituted a National Monitoring Committee on Minorities' Education (NMCME) under the Chairmanship of Hon'ble Minister of Human Resource Development.[19]

Conclusion

Minority group is a sociological category within a demographic. The term "minority group" often occurs alongside a discourse of civil rights and collective rights which gained prominence in the 20th century. In Indian Constitution, minority can be classifying as two ways: (a) Religious minority, and (b) Linguistic minority. Muslims, Christians, Sikhs, Buddhists and Zoroastrians (Parsis) have been notified as minority communities by the Union Government. Further vide notification detail 27th Jan 2014; Jains have also been notified as minority community. Linguistic minorities are those who have different first language than the first language of majority of the people in that state. The linguistic reorganisation of regional state boundaries has been a major instrument for protecting and nurturing linguistic diversity. The creation of linguistic identity based units, each with political rights to govern itself within the framework of the federal system, meant that a specific linguistic community became a majority within a region. The Ministry of Minority Affairs, a ministry of the Government of India established in 2006. Regional Minorities have set up various education schools and institutions to promote their culture and language.

References

1. Religion in India, Retrieved frim http://en.wikipedia.org/wiki/Religion_in_India
2. Minority group, Retrieved from http://en.wikipedia.org/wiki/Minority_group
3. *Business Standard* (Jan 22, 2014), What minority status will mean for Jains, Retrieved from http://www.business-standard.com/article/economy-policy/what-minority-status-will-mean-for-jains-114012100944_1.html

4. Islam in India (2015), Retrieved from http://en.wikipedia.org/wiki/Islam_in_India
5. See http://www.newstatesman.com/politics/2007/08/india-muslims-pakistan-hindu
6. Religious Minorities and the Indian Constitution, Retrieved from https://www.nls.ac.in/csseip/Files/Material%20for%20uploading/Minorities.pdf
7. See https://realitycheck.wordpress.com/2013/01/15/article30-series/
8. See http://mhrd.gov.in/educational-development-minorities
9. Gurpreet Mahajan, Negotiating Cultural Diversity and Minority Rights in India, Retrieved from http://www.idea.int/publications/dchs/upload/dchs_vol2_sec3_4.pdf
10. See http://lawandotherthings.blogspot.in/2007/07/defining-minorities-in-india.html
11. Ministry of Minority Affairs (20150, Retrieved from http://en.wikipedia.org/wiki/Ministry_of_Minority_Affairs
12. Mahaveer Sanglikar, Minorities communities in India, Retrieved from http://jainismus.hubpages.com/hub/Minority-Communities-in-India
13. http://www.pbs.org/wnet/religionandethics/2002/05/24/may-24-2002-hindu-muslim-conflict-in-india/12044/
14. See http://www.culturalsurvival.org/ourpublications/csq/article/ethnic-and-religious-conflicts-india
15. See http://www.culturalsurvival.org/ourpublications/csq/article/ethnic-and-religious-conflicts-india
16. http://study.com/academy/lesson/muslim-and-hindu-conflict-in-india-and-the-partition-of-india-and-pakistan.html
17. http://berkleycenter.georgetown.edu/essays/india-religious-pluralism-and-religious-conflict
18. Minority Communities in India, Retrieved from http://www.indiaonlinepages.com/population/minorities/index.html
19. Official website of Ministry of Human Resource Development, Minority Education, Retrieved from http://mhrd.gov.in/educational-development-minorities

11

Environmental Rights

"My eyes are constantly wide open to the extraordinary fact of existence. Not just human existence, but the existence of life and how this breathtakingly powerful process, which is natural selection, has managed to take the very simple facts of physics and chemistry and build them up to redwood trees and humans."

-Richard Dawkins

Introduction

There is an increasing trend in environmental pollution. Water is polluted by four kinds of substances: traditional organic waste, waste generated from industrial processes, chemical agents for fertilizers and pesticides for crop protection and silt from degraded catchments. Ambient air quality trends in the major cities indicate that levels of suspended particulate matter are higher than the prescribed standards or limits, especially in summer months. It is not enough for the Government to notify laws which are to be complied with. A positive attitude on the part of everyone in society is essential for the prevention of pollution and wide consultation has been held with those who will ultimately implement the policy.[1]

The Ministry of Environment and Forests is primarily concerned with the implementation of policies and programmes relating to conservation of the country's natural resources including lakes and rivers, its biodiversity, forests and wildlife, ensuring the welfare of its animals and prevention and abatement of pollution. While implementing these policies and programmes, the Ministry is guided by the principle of sustainable development and enhancement of human well-being. The main objectives of the Ministry are conservation and survey of flora, fauna, forest and wildlife, prevention and control of pollution, afforestation and regeneration of degraded areas, protection of environment and ensuring the welfare of animals.[2]

The land serves as storage for water and nutrients required for plants and other living micro-macro-organisms. Management of industrial and municipal waste is the major cause of soil pollution and is a serious challenge in terms of magnitude and resources required. India has participated in major international events on the environment since 1972. The country has signed and ratified a number of key multilateral agreements on environment issues in recognition of the trans-boundary nature of several environmental problems, impact on chemical industry and trade and has made efforts to comply with its commitments. The ultimate goal of combating water pollution is to restore the quality of water in all the natural water bodies to a level which can support human use and functions of the ecosystems that depend directly or indirectly on them.[3]

Significance of Environmental Acts

According to Section 2(a) of the Environmental Protection Act, 1986, Environment' includes: (a) Water, air and land; (b) The inter-relationship which exists among and between (i) water, air, land, and (ii) human beings, other living creatures, plants, microorganisms and property.[4] The global atmospheric concentration of CO_2 has increased from a pre-industrial value of about 280 to 379 ppm in 2005. The temperature increases during 2090-99 relative to 1980-99 may range from 1.1 to 6.4 and sea-level rise from 0.18 to 0.59 metres. The need is to identify and prioritize strategies that promote development goals while also serving climate change objectives.[5]

Environmental Policies in India[6]

India is one of the very few countries of the world where forest policy is in operation since 1894. In 1952 and 1988, revisions were made in the forest policy of 1894. The National Forest Policy of 1952 recommended that the country should aim at coverage of one-third of the total land area under forest (60 per cent in hilly and mountainous areas, and 25 per cent in the plains).[7] The National Forest Policy lays emphasis on (1) weaning the tribal people, by persuasion, from the baneful practice of shifting cultivation, (2) increasing the efficiency of forest administration by having adequate forest laws, (3) providing adequate facilities for the management of forest resources, (4) promoting research in forestry, (5) controlling grazing of cattle in the forests, (6) providing fuel wood to the rural areas, (7) improving the availability of commercial wood for industrial uses, and (8) increasing the area under man-made forests.[8]

The National Forest Policy, 1988

The Indian National Forest Policy of 1988 emphasised the protective role of forests in maintaining ecological balance and environmental stability. The basic objectives that should govern the National Forest Policy were enlisted as follows: (i) Maintenance of environmental stability through preservation and, where necessary, restoration of the ecological balance that has been adversely disturbed by serious depletion of the forests of the country. (ii) Conserving the natural heritage of the country by preserving the remaining natural forests with the vast variety of flora and fauna, which represent the remarkable biological diversity and genetic resources of the country; (iii) Checking soil erosion and denudation in the catchment areas of rivers, lakes and reservoirs in the interest of soil and water conservation, for mitigating floods and droughts (iv) Checking the extension of sand dunes in the desert areas of Rajasthan and along the coastal tracts.[9]

National Conservation Strategy and Policy Statement on Environment and Development, 1992

The National Conservation Strategy and the Policy Statement on Environment and Development are in response to the need for laying down the guidelines that will help to weave environmental considerations into the fabric of national life and of development process.[10]

Environmental Acts in India[11]

The present legislative framework is broadly contained in the umbrella Environment (Protection) Act, 1986; the Water (Prevention and Control of Pollution) Act, 1974; the Water Cess Act, 1977; and the Air (Prevention Control of Pollution) Act, 1981. The law in respect of management of forests and bio-diversity is contained in the Indian Forest Act, 1927; the Forest (Conservation) Act, 1980; the Wild Life (Protection) Act, 1972 and the Bio-diversity Act, 2002.[12]

The Water (Prevention and Control of Pollution) Act, 1974

The Water (Prevention and Control of Pollution) Act was enacted in 1974 to provide for the prevention and control of water pollution, and for the maintaining or restoring of wholesomeness of water in the country. The Act was amended in 1988. The Water (Prevention and Control of Pollution) Cess Act was enacted in 1977, to provide for the levy and collection of a cesson water consumed by persons operating and carrying on certain types of industrial activities. This cess is collected with a view to augment the resources of the Central Board and the State Boards for the prevention and control of water pollution constituted under the Water (Prevention and Control of Pollution) Act, 1974.[13]

Pollution means such contamination of water or such alteration of the physical, chemical or biological properties of water or such discharge of any sewage or trade effluent or of any other liquid, gaseous or solid substance into water (whether directly or indirectly) as may or is likely to, create a nuisance or render such water harmful or injurious to public health or safety, or to domestic, commercial, industrial, agricultural or other legitimate uses, or to the life and health of animals or plants or of aquatic organisms.[14] The Central Pollution Control Board, and State Pollution Control Boards composition, terms and conditions of service of members are defined in Sections 3-12 of water (prevention and control of pollution) act, 1974. The Board advises the government on any matter concerning the prevention and control of water pollution. It coordinates the activities and provides technical assistance and guidance. This policy sets the standards and penalties for non-compliance for polluting bodies. The Government has power to restrict any unit, and to take samples of effluents and get them analysed in Central or State laboratories. Whoever fails to comply with any provision of this Act is punishable with imprisonment, fine or with both.[15]

No person shall knowingly cause or permit any poisonous, noxious or polluting matter determined in accordance with such standards as may be laid down by the State Board to enter (whether directly or indirectly) into any stream or well or sewer or on land. No person shall knowingly cause or permit to enter into any stream any other matter which may tend, either directly or in combination with similar matters, to impede the proper flow of the water of the stream in a manner leading or likely to lead to a substantial aggravation of pollution due to other causes or of its consequence.

Any person empowered by a State Board in this behalf shall have a right at any time to enter, with such assistance as he considers necessary, any place: (a) for the purpose of performing any of the functions of the Board entrusted to him; (b) for the purpose of determining whether and if so in what manner, any such functions are to be performed or whether any provisions of this Act or the rules made there under or any notice, order, direction or authorisation served, made, given, or granted under this Act is being or has been complied with; (c) For the purpose of examining any plant, record, register, document or any other material object or for conducting a search of any place in which he has reason to believe that an offence under this Act or the rules made there under has been or is being or is about to be committed and for seizing any such plant, record, register, document or other material object, if he has reason to believe that it may furnish evidence of the commission of an offence punishable under this Act or the rules made there under.[16]

The Air (Prevention and Control of Pollution) Act, 1981

This is an Act to provide for prevention, control and abatement of air pollution in the country so as to preserve the quality of air. Central and State Boards constituted u/s 3 and 4 of Water [Prevention and Control and Pollution] Act, 1974 were deemed also as Central and State Boards for prevention and control of air pollution. An Act to provide for the prevention, control and abatement of air pollution, for the establishment, with a view to carrying out the aforesaid purposes, of Boards, for conferring on and assigning to such Boards powers and functions relating thereto and for matters connected therewith.

Any person empowered by State Board shall have right to enter the industry premises for determining status of pollution control equipment or otherwise compliance of the Act, and the person concerned of the industry shall be bound to render all assistance as deemed necessary for ensuring measures, and carrying out functions laid down in the Act. State Board or any person empowered by it shall have power to samples of air or emissions from any chimney, flue or any duct or any other outlet in such manner as may be prescribed. State Board may direct the industry for its closure, prohibition or regulation can also issue directives for the stoppage or regulation of supply of electricity.[17]

The State Government may, after consultation with the State Board, by notification in the Official Gazette, declare in such manner as may be prescribed, any area or areas within the State as air pollution control area or areas for the purposes of this Act. The State Government may, after consultation with the State Board, by notification in the Official Gazette, - (a) after any air pollution control area whether by way of extension or reduction; (b) declare a new air pollution control area in which may be merged one or more existing air pollution control areas of any part or parts thereof. If the State Government, after consultation with the State Board, is of opinion that the use of any fuel, other than an approved fuel, in any air pollution control area or part thereof, may cause or is likely to cause air pollution, it may, by notification in the Official Gazette, prohibit the use of such fuel in such area or part thereof with effect from such date (being not less months from the date of publication of the notification) as may be specified in the notification.

The State Government may, after consultation with the State Board, by notification in the Official Gazette, direct that with effect from such date as may be specified therein, no appliance, other than an approved appliance, shall be used in the premises situated in an air pollution control area provided that different dates may be specified for different parts of an air pollution control area or for the use of different appliances. If the State Government after consultation with the State Board, is of opinion that the burning of any material (not being fuel) in any air pollution control area or part thereof may cause or is likely to cause air pollution, it may, by notification in the Official Gazette, prohibit the burning of such material in such area or part thereof.[18]

The Environment (Protection) Act, 1986

Environment Protection Act, 1986 is an Act of the Parliament of India. In the wake of the Bhopal Tragedy, the Government of India enacted the Environment Protection Act of 1986 under Article 253 of the Constitution. The purpose of the Act is to implement the decisions of the United Nations Conference on the Human Environments they relate to the protection and improvement of the human environment and the prevention of hazards to human beings, other living creatures, plants and property. The main objectives of this act are: (a) to co-ordinate the activities of the various regulatory agencies already in existence; (b) creation of an authority or authorities with adequate powers for environmental protection; (c) regulation of discharge of environmental pollutants and handling of hazardous substance; (d) speedy response in the event of accidents threatening environmental and deterrents punishment to those who endanger human environment, safety and health.[19]

The Environment (Protection) Rules, 1986

In exercise of powers conferred by Sec. 6 and 25 of the Environment (Protection) Act, 1986 (29 of 1986), the Central Government hereby makes the following rules, namely: It is well settled in law that every subordinate law-making authority has a power to frame subordinate legislation only provided it is reasonable that very subordinate law-making authority has a power to frame subordinate legislation only provided it is reasonable and within the limits of the rule-making power of that body. For the purposes of protecting and improving the quality of the environment and preventing and abating environment pollution, the standards for emission or discharge of environmental pollutants from the industries, operations or processes shall be as specified in [Schs. I to IV].[20]

Notwithstanding any thing contained in any other law but subject to the provisions of this Act, the Central Government may in exercise of its powers and performance of its functions under this Act issue directions in writing to any person officer or any such person, officer or authority shall be bound to comply with such direction. No person carrying on any industry operation or process shall discharge or emit or permit to be discharged or emitted any environmental pollutant in excess of such standards as may be prescribed. No person shall handle or cause to be handled any hazardous substance expert in accordance with such procedure and after complying with such safeguards may be prescribed.

Every person carrying on any industrial operation or process or handling any hazardous substance shall be bound to render all assistance to the person empowered by the Central Government under sub-section to do so without any reasonable cause or excuse, he shall guilty of an offence under this Act. If any person willfully delays or obstructs any person empowered by the Central Government under the sub-section (1) in the performance of this function, he shall be guilty of an offence under this Act. The Central Government or any officer empowered by it in this behalf, shall have power to take, for the purpose of analysis samples of air water, soil or other substance from any factory, premises or other place in such manner as prescribed. Where any offence under this Act has been committed by a company, every person who at the time offence was committed, was directly in charge of and was responsible to the company for the conduct of the business of the company, as well as company shall be deemed to guilty of the offence and shall be liable to be proceeded against and punish accordingly.

No suit prosecution or other legal proceeding shall lie against the Government or any officer or other employee of the Government or any authority constituted under this Act or any member, officer or other employee of such authority in respect of anything which is done or intended to be done in good faith in pursuance of this Act or the rules made or orders or directions issued thereunder. No court shall take cognizance of any offence under this Act except on complaint made by: (a) the Central Government or any authority or officer authorised in this behalf by that Government; or (b) any person who has given the notice of not less than sixty days in the manner prescribed of the alleged offence and of his intention to make a complaint to the Central Government or the authority of the officer authorised as aforesaid.

The Central Government may in relation to its functions under this Act, from the time to time require any person, officer, State Government or authority to furnish to it or any prescribed authority or officer any reports, returns, statistics, accounts and other information and such person, officer, State Government or other authority shall be bound to do so. No civil court shall have jurisdiction enter win any suit or proceeding in respect of any thing done action taken or order or direction issued by the Central Government or any other authority or officer in pursuance of any power conferred by or in relation to its or his functions under this Act. The Central Government may, by notification in the Official Gazette, make rule for carrying out the purposes of this Act.

Every rule made under this Act shall be laid, as soon as may be after it is made, before each House of Parliament, while it is in session, for a total period of thirty days which may be comprised in one session or in two or more successive session or the successive sessions aforesaid, both Houses agree in making any modification in rule or both Houses agree that the rule should not be made, the rule shall thereafter have effect only in such modified from or be no effect as the case may be; so, however, that any such modification or annulment shall be without prejudice to the validity of anything previously done under that rule.[21]

Hazardous Wastes (Management and Handling) Rules, 1989

Hazardous Waste Management Rules are notified to ensure safe handling, generation, processing, treatment, package, storage, transportation, use reprocessing, collection, conversion, and offering for sale, destruction and disposal of Hazardous Waste. These Rules came into effect in the year 1989 and have been amended later in the years 2000, 2003 and with final notification of the Hazardous Waste (Management, Handling and Transboundary Movement) Rules, 2008 in supersession of former notification.[22]

"Hazardous wastes site" means a place for collection, reception, treatment, storage and disposal of hazardous wastes which has been duly approved by the competent authority. "Environmentally sound management of hazardous wastes" means taking all steps to ensure that the hazardous wastes are managed in a manner which will protect human health and the environment against the adverse effects which may result from such wastes. It shall be the duty of the occupier and the operator of a facility to take adequate steps while handling hazardous waste to (i) Contain contaminants and prevent accidents and limit their consequences on human and the environment; and (ii) provide persons working on the site with information, training and equipment necessary to ensure their safety.

The occupier or operator of a facility shall ensure that the hazardous wastes are packaged, based on the composition in a manner suitable for handling, storage and transport and the labeling and packaging shall be easily visible and be able to withstand physical conditions and climatic factors. Packaging, labeling and transport of hazardous wastes shall be in accordance with the provisions of the rules made by Central Government under the Motor Vehicles Act, 1988 and other guidelines issued from time to time. The occupier or any operator of a facility shall be responsible for identifying sites for establishing hazardous wastes disposal facility. The State Government, operator of a facility or any association of occupiers shall identify sites for common hazardous wastes disposal facility in the state. The State Government, occupier or any association shall after preliminary impact assessment studies identify possible sites for disposal facility. They shall then undertake an Environmental Impact Assessment of these sites for selecting an appropriate site for hazardous waste disposal facility.

Import of hazardous wastes from any country to India and export of hazardous wastes from India to any country for dumping or disposal shall not be permitted. The exporting country or the exporter as the case may be, of hazardous wastes shall communicate in Form 6 to the Central Government (the Ministry of Environment and Forests) of the proposed trans-boundary movement of hazardous wastes. Every occupier importing hazardous waste shall apply to the State Pollution Control Board, one hundred twenty days in advance in Form 6 for permission to import along with a minimum fee of rupees thirty thousand payable to Ministry of Environment and Forests, Govt. of India for imports upto five hundred metric tonnes and for every additional five hundred metric tonnes or part thereof of waste imported an additional sum of rupees five thousand will be payable. The State Pollution Control Board shall examine the application received from the occupier within thirty days and forward the application with recommendation and requisite stipulations for safe transport, storage and processing, to the Ministry of Environment and Forests.[23]

The new 2003 Amendment rules excluded the following three categories from the list of hazardous waste:

1. Bio-medical wastes, covered under the Bio-Medical Wastes (Management and Handling) Rules, 1998;
2. Wastes covered under the Municipal Solid Wastes (Management and Handling) Rules, 2000;
3. The lead acid batteries covered under the Batteries (Management and Handling) Rules, 2001.[24]

Manufacture, Storage and Import of Hazardous Chemical Rules, 1989

Govt. of India has promulgated "Manufacture, Storage, and Import of Hazardous Chemicals (MSIHC) Rules, 1989" under the Environment (Protection) Act, 1986. The Central Pollution Control Board (CPCB) or the State Pollution Control Boards / Pollution Control Committees have been identified as the Authority for enforcement of directions and procedures in respect of isolated storage of hazardous chemicals and Import of hazardous Chemicals and enforcement of directions and procedures on import of hazardous chemicals as per Rule 18.[25]

The Forest (Conservation) Act, 1980

The Parliament has enacted the Forest (Conservation) Act, 1980, to check further deforestation and conserve forests and to provide for matters connected therewith or ancillary or incidental thereto. This Act has five Sections which deal with conservation of forests. The Act was enacted with the twin objectives under Section 2 of restricting the use of forest land for non-forest purposes, and preventing the de-reservation of forests that have been reserved under the Indian Forest Act, 1927. However, in 1988 the Act was further amended to include two new provisions under Section 2, where it sought to restrict leasing of forest land to private individuals, authority, corporations not owned by the Government, and to prevent clear felling of naturally grown trees. The Act empowers the Central Government to constitute a committee to advise the Government with a grant of approval under Section 2, as also on any other matter connected with the conservation of forest and referred to it by the Central Government. The Act provides for the punishment of imprisonment, extendable to fifteen days for the contravention of the provisions of the Act.[26]

The Wildlife Protection Act, 1972

The Wildlife Protection Act, 1972 is an Act of the Parliament of India enacted for protection of plants and animal species. Before 1972, India only had five designated national parks. Among other reforms, the Act established schedules of protected plant and animal species; hunting or harvesting these species was largely outlawed. The Act provides for the protection of wild animals, birds and plants; and for matters connected therewith or ancillary or incidental thereto. It extends to the whole of India, except the State of Jammu and Kashmir which has its own wildlife Act. It has six schedules which give varying degrees of protection.[27]

The Wild Life (Protection) Amendment Bill, 2013 was introduced in the Rajya Sabha on August 5, 2013. The Bill has been referred to the Standing Committee on Environment and Forests. The Bill seeks to amend the Wild Life (Protection) Act, 1972. This Act provides for the protection and conservation of wild animals, birds and plants. It also covers the management of their habitats and regulation and control of trade or commerce linked to wild life. Under the Act, destruction, exploitation or removal of any wildlife including forest produce from a sanctuary is not permitted, except with a permit. The amendment allows certain activities such as grazing or movement of livestock, bona fide use of drinking and household water by local communities, and hunting under a permit.[28]

The Public Liability Insurance Act, 1991[29]

Where death or injury to any person (other than a workman) or damage to any property has resulted from an accident, the owner shall be liable to give such relief as is specified in the Schedule for such death, injury or damage. In any claim for relief under sub-section (1) (hereinafter referred to in this Act as claim for relief), the claimant shall not be required to plead and establish that the death, injury or damage in respect of which the claim has been made was due to any wrongful act, neglect or default of any person."

The Central Government may, by notification, establish a fund to be known as the Environmental Relief Fund. The Relief Fund shall be utilised for paying, in accordance with the provisions of this Act. The Central Government may, by notification, make a scheme specifying the authority in which the Relief Fund shall vest, the manner in which the Relief Fund shall be administered, the form and the manner in which money shall be drawn from the Relief Fund and for all other matters connected with or incidental to the administration of the Relief Fund and the payment of relief there from. Any person authorised by the Central Government may, for the purposes of ascertaining whether any requirements of this Act or of any rule or of any direction given under this Act have been complied with, require any owner to submit to that person such information as that person may reasonably think necessary.

Any person, authorised by the Central Government in this behalf, shall have a right to enter, at all reasonable times with such assistance as he considers necessary, any place, premises or vehicle, where hazardous substance is handled for the purpose of determining whether any provisions of this Act or of any rule or of any direction given under this Act is being or has been complied with and such owner is bound to render all assistance to such person. If a person, authorised by the Central Government in this behalf, has reason to believe that handling of any hazardous substance is taking place in any place, premises or vehicle, in contravention of subsection (1) of section 4, he may enter into and search such place, premises or vehicle for such handling of hazardous substance.

Notwithstanding anything contained in any other law but subject to the provisions of this Act, the Central Government may, in exercise of its powers and performance of its functions under this Act, issue such directions in writing as it may deem fit for the purposes of this Act to any owner or any person, officer, authority or agency and such owner, person, officer, authority or agency shall be bound to comply with such directions. If the Central Government or any person authorised by that Government in this behalf has reason to believe that any owner has been handling any hazardous substance in contravention of any of the provisions of this Act, that Government or, as the case may be, that person may make an application to a

Court not inferior to that of a Metropolitan Magistrate or a Judicial Magistrate of first class for restraining such owner from such handling.

The National Environment Tribunal Act, 1995

The National Environmental Tribunal Act has been enacted to provide for strict liability for damages arising out of any accident occurring while handling any hazardous substance and for the establishment of a National Environment Tribunal for effective and expeditious disposal of cases arising from such accidents, with a view to giving relief and compensation for damages to persons, property and the environment and for matters connected therewith or incidental thereto. The Act has not yet been brought into force.[30]

The National Environment Appellate Authority Act, 1997

The National Environmental Appellate Authority Act has been brought with the purpose of providing for the establishment of a National Environmental Appellate Authority to hear appeals with respect to restriction of areas in which any industries, operations or processes or class of industries, operations or processes shall not be carried out or shall be carried out subject to certain safeguards under the Environment (Protection) Act, 1986 and for matters connected therewith or incidental thereto.[31]

National Green Tribunal Act, 2010

National Green Tribunal Act, 2010 is an Act of the Parliament of India which enables creation of a special tribunal to handle the expeditious disposal of the cases pertaining to environmental issues. It was enacted under India's constitutional provision of Article 21, which assures the citizens of India the right to a healthy environment. The Tribunal's dedicated jurisdiction in environmental matters shall provide speedy environmental justice and help reduce the burden of litigation in the higher courts. The Tribunal shall not be bound by the procedure laid down under the Code of Civil Procedure, 1908, but shall be guided by principles of natural justice. The Tribunal has Original Jurisdiction on matters of substantial question relating to environment and damage to environment due to specific activity. Also Tribunal is competent to hear cases for several acts such as Forest (Conservation) Act, Biological Diversity Act, Environment (Protection) Act, Water and Air (Prevention and control of Pollution) Acts etc. and also have appellate jurisdiction related to above acts after establishment of Tribunal within a period of 30 days of award or order received by aggrieved party.[32]

Indian Penal Code for Environmental Protection

The Indian Penal Code has a chapter on offences affecting Public Health, Safety, Convenience (Chapter XIV). Sec. 268 provides that *"a person is guilty of a public nuisance who does any act or is guilty of an illegal omission which causes any common injury, danger or annoyance to the public or to the people in general who dwell or occupy property in the vicinity, or which must necessarily cause injury, obstruction, danger, or annoyance to persons who may have occasion to use any public right."*[33]

Indian Council of Forestry Research and Education

It is an autonomous organisation or governmental agency under the Ministry of Environment and Forests, Government of India. The Council is the apex body in the national research system in the area of forestry. Indian Council of Forestry Research and Education has numerous responsibilities which include the development of holistic forestry research through a well-organised system of coordinated research, education and extension in all areas of forestry.[34] The council has nine research institutes and four advanced centres to cater to the research needs of different bio-geographical regions. These are located at Dehradun, Shimla, Ranchi, Jorhat, Jabalpur, Jodhpur, Bangalore, Coimbatore, Allahabad, Chhindwara, Aizawl, Hyderabad and Agartala.[35]

Existing Schemes and Programmes

There are various centrally sponsored and central sector schemes undertaken for Pollution Abatement. The major activities initiated under the various schemes on pollution abatement are:

1. *Central Pollution Control Board:* The CPCB undertakes the projects and programmes through various institutions, research organisations relating to assessment and monitoring of air and water quality.
2. *Industrial Pollution Abatement through Preventive Strategies:* The scheme consists of three components namely; Environmental Audit, Adoption of Clean Technology in Small Scale Industries and Environmental Statistics.
3. *Establishment of Environment Protection Authorities and Environment Commission and Tribunal:* Under this programme, Authorities have been constituted as per various orders of Hon'ble Supreme Court for environmental compliance and enforcement of various activities.

4. *Assistance for Abatement of Pollution and Environment Policy and Law:* This scheme is to strengthen various State Pollution Control Boards (SPCBs) and the State Environment Departments for enforcing the statutory provisions for initiating pollution abatement measures, upgradation of facilities for analysis, capacity building etc.
5. *Clean Technology:* The objective of the scheme is to provide support to introduction of cleaner production and cleaner technologies through setting up of demonstration projects and initiation of relevant R&D activities.
6. *Creation of Management Structure for Management Substances:* Under the scheme, the activities are carried out under three thrust areas namely; chemical safety, chemical accident prevention and sound management of hazardous waste and municipal solid wastes.[36]

Joint Forest Management

Joint Forest Management often abbreviated as JFM is the official and popular term in India for partnerships in forest management involving both the state forest departments and local communities. Joint Forest Management originated in West Bengal accidentally at the Arabari Forest Range in West Midnapore, near Midnapore town in 1971. The major hardwood of Arabari is sal, a commercially profitable forest crop. After the initial successes in West Bengal and Haryana, the JFM schemes received national importance in the legislation of 1988 and thrust in the Guidelines of 1990. As of 2005, 27 states of the Indian Union had various JFM schemes with over 63,000 FPCs involved in the joint management of over 140,000 km^2 of forested land.[37]

The JFM programme in the country was reviewed by Government of India from time to time in consultation with State Governments, NGO's and other stakeholders in view of several emerging issues. In order to further strengthen the programme, the State Governments may take action on the following suggested lines. Government of India on June 1, 1990 issued guidelines to the state governments for involving local communities in the protection and development of the degraded forests. Based on this, the JFM programme has now been widely adopted in twenty two states of the country. These states are Andhra Pradesh, Arunachal Pradesh, Assam, Bihar, Gujarat, Himachal Pradesh, Haryana, Jammu & Kashmir, Karnataka, Kerala,

Madhya Pradesh, Maharashtra, Mizoram, Nagaland, Orissa, Punjab, Rajasthan, Sikkim, Tamil Nadu, Tripura, Uttar Pradesh and West Bengal.[38]

Under joint forest management (JFM), village communities are entrusted with the protection and management of nearby forests. The areas concerned are usually degraded or even deforested areas. However, in Andhra Pradesh and Madhya Pradesh all village fringe forests can come under JFM. The communities are required to organise forest protection committees, village forest committees, village forest conservation and development societies, etc. Each of these bodies has an executive committee that manages its day-to-day affairs. Non-wood forest products (NWFPs) have a key role in JFM efforts.[39] While the primary objective of the JFM programme continues to be rehabilitation of degraded forestlands with peoples organisations (Village Forest Committees - VFCs), in the course of evolution, approaches like village resource development, micro watershed development have got integrated into JFM as most State governments are attempting to improve the socio-economic status of forest dependant communities in order to reduce pressure on forests.[40]

Conclusion

India is one of the very few countries of the world where forest policy is in operation since 1894. In 1952 and 1988, revisions were made in the forest policy of 1894. The National Forest Policy of 1952 recommended that the country should aim at coverage of one-third of the total land area under forest. The Ministry of Environment and Forests is primarily concerned with the implementation of policies and programmes relating to conservation of the country's natural resources including lakes and rivers, its biodiversity, forests and wildlife, ensuring the welfare of its animals and prevention and abatement of pollution. The National Conservation Strategy and the Policy Statement on Environment and Development are in response to the need for laying down the guidelines that will help to weave environmental considerations into the fabric of national life and of development process.

The present legislative framework is broadly contained in the umbrella Environment (Protection) Act, 1986; the Water (Prevention and Control of Pollution) Act, 1974; the Water Cess Act, 1977; and the Air (Prevention Control of Pollution) Act, 1981. The law in respect of management of forests and bio-diversity is contained in the Indian

Forest Act, 1927; the Forest (Conservation) Act, 1980; the Wild Life (Protection) Act, 1972 and the Bio-diversity Act, 2002.

References

1. Policy Statement for Abatement of Pollution, Retrieved from http://envfor.nic.in/sites/default/files/introduction-psap.pdf
2. Environment and Forests, Retrieved from http://www.archive.india.gov.in/sectors/environment/index.php
3. Report of the Working Group on Environment and Environmental Regulatory mechanisms in Environment and Forests for the Eleventh Five Year Plan (2007-2012), Retrieved from http://planningcommission. nic.in/aboutus/committee/wrkgrp11/wg_envtal.pdf
4. Environmental laws in India, Retrieved from http://www.environmentallawsofindia.com/the-environment-definitions-and-acts.html
5. Ecology and Environment: conservation and protection (2015), Retrieved from http://www.teluguaspirant.com/ecology-and-environment-conservation-and-protection/2284/
6. Environmental laws in India, Retrieved from http://www.environmentallawsofindia.com/the-environment-definitions-and-acts.html
7. The national forest policy of India, Retrieved from http://www.vajiramandravi.in/the-national-forest-policy-of-india.html
8. K.Raja, Short essay on National Forest Policy, Retrieved from http://www.preservearticles.com/2012013021986/short-essay-on-national-forest-policy.html
9. The Indian National Forest Policy of 1988, Retrieved from http://www.conservationindia.org/resources/review-of-national-forest-policy-1998-inviting-comments
10. National Conservation Strategy and Policy Statement on Environment and Development, 1992, See http://iced.cag.gov.in/?page_id=1030
11. Environmental laws in India, Retrieved from http://www.environmentallawsofindia.com/the-environment-definitions-and-acts.html
12. See http://planningcommission.nic.in/aboutus/committee/wrkgrp11/wg_envtal.pdf
13. See http://www.moef.nic.in/division/water-pollution
14. See https://www.elaw.org/node/1917
15. See http://www.indiawaterportal.org/articles/water-prevention-and-control-pollution-act-1974
16. http://www.advocatekhoj.com/library/bareacts/waterprevention/index.php?Title=Water%20%28Prevention%20and%20 Control%20of%20Pollution%29%20Act,%201974

17. See http://hspcb.gov.in/Air_Act.html
18. http://nbaindia.org/uploaded/Biodiversityindia/Legal/23.%20Air%20%28Prevention%20and%20control%20of%20Pollution% 29%20Act%201981.pdf
19. The Environment (Protection) Act, 1986, Retrieved from http://en.wikipedia.org/wiki/Environment_Protection_Act,_1986
20. See http://jkforest.gov.in/act/Environment_Protection_Rules.pdf
21. The Environment (Protection) Rules, 1986, Retrieved from http://icmr.nic.in/ihd/THE%20ENVIRONMENT% 20%28PROTECTION%20ACT%29,1986.pdf
22. See http://www.cpcb.nic.in/Hazardous_waste.php
23. http://www.commoncause.in/EnvironmentProtection/Hazardous%20Waste%20 Managementand%20Handling% 20Rules%201989.pdf
24. See http://www.cseindia.org/dte-supplement/WASTES.PDF
25. See http://cpcb.nic.in/upload/NewItems/NewItem_158_MSIHC-REPORT.pdf
26. See http://www.vanashakti.in/resources_law2.html
27. Wildlife Protection Act, 1972, Retrieved from http://en.wikipedia.org/wiki/Wildlife_Protection_Act,_1972
28. The Wild Life (Protection) Amendment Bill, 2013, Retrieved from http://www.prsindia.org/billtrack/the-wildlife-protection-amendment-bill-2013-2829/
29. The Public Liability Insurance Act, 1991, Retrieved from http://himachal.nic.in/WriteReadData/l892s/3_l892s/The_Public_Liability_Insurance_Act_1991-57952667.pdf
30. Environmental laws in India, National Environmental Appellate Authority, Environmental Tribunal and Green Benches, Retrieved from http://www.environmentallawsofindia.com/national-environmental-appellate-authority.html
31. Environmental laws in India, National Environmental Appellate Authority, Environmental Tribunal and Green Benches, Retrieved from http://www.environmentallawsofindia.com/national-environmental-appellate-authority.html
32. National Green Tribunal Act, 2010, Retrieved from http://en.wikipedia.org/wiki/National_Green_Tribunal_Act
33. Environmental laws in India, Retrieved from http://www.environmentallawsofindia.com/the-environment-definitions-and-acts.html
34. See http://www.mapsofindia.com/dehradun/indian-council-of-forestry-research-and-education.html

35. Indian Council of Forestry Research and Education (2015), Retrieved from http://en.wikipedia.org/wiki/Indian_Council_of_ Forestry_Research_and_Education
36. Report of the Working Group on Environment and Environmental Regulatory Mechanisms in Environment and Forests for the Eleventh Five Year Plan (2007-2012), Retrieved from http://planningcommission.nic.in/aboutus/committee/wrkgrp11/wg_envtal.pdf
37. Joint Forest Management (2015), Retrieved from http://en.wikipedia.org/wiki/Joint_Forest_Management
38. Joint Forest Management Programme, Retrieved from http://agritech.tnau.ac.in/forestry/forest_jfm_index.html
39. R. Prasad, Joint forest management in India and the impact of state control over non-wood forest products, Retrieved from http://www.fao.org/docrep/x2450e/x2450e0c.htm
40. Study on Joint Forest Management conducted by TERI for Ministry of Environment and Forests, Retrieved from http://www.moef.nic.in/sites/default/files/Document1_3.pdf

12

Rights of Consumer

"A consumer is the most important visitor on our premises. He is not dependent on us, we are on him. He is not an interruption to our work; he is the purpose of it. We are not doing a favour to a consumer by giving him an opportunity. He is doing us a favour by giving us opportunity to serve him"

- Mahatma Gandhi

Introduction

Customer purchases goods and consumer uses them. An ultimate customer may be a consumer as well, but just as equally may have purchased items for someone else to consume. An intermediate customer is not a consumer at all. Customer is the recipient of a good, service, product, or idea, obtained from a seller, vendor, or supplier for a monetary or other valuable consideration.[1] Customer satisfaction is a term frequently used in marketing. It is a measure of how products and services supplied by a company meet or surpass customer expectation. It is essential for businesses to effectively manage customer satisfaction. To be able to do this, firms need reliable and representative measures of satisfaction. The importance of customer satisfaction diminishes when a firm has increased bargaining power. Customer satisfaction provides a leading indicator of consumer purchase intentions and loyalty. Organisations need to retain existing customers while targeting non-customers.[2]

Customer service is the provision of service to customers before, during and after a purchase. The importance of customer service may vary by product or service, industry and customer. From the point of view of an overall sales process engineering effort, customer service plays an important role in an organisation's ability to generate income and revenue. Customer support is a range of customer services to assist customers in making cost-effective and correct use of a product.[3] Relationship marketing refers to an arrangement where both the buyer and seller have an interest in providing a more satisfying exchange. This approach tries to disambiguiously transcend the simple post purchase-exchange process with a customer to make more truthful and richer contact by providing a more holistic, personalised purchase, and uses the experience to create stronger ties. Relationship marketing has also been strongly influenced by reengineering[4]. Consumer behaviour is the study of individuals, groups, or organisations and the processes they use to select, secure, use, and dispose of products, services, experiences, or ideas to satisfy needs and the impacts that these processes have on the consumer and society.[5]

Who are Consumer?

Consumer is a person that uses economic services or commodities. The consumer is the one who pays to consume goods and services produced. The law primarily uses the notion of the consumer in relation to consumer protection laws, and the definition of consumer is often restricted to living persons (i.e. not corporations or businesses) and excludes commercial users. In India, the Consumer Protection Act 1986 differentiates the consummation of a commodity or service for personal use or to earn a livelihood.[6] Simply speaking, consumer is a person who consumes or uses various goods and services. Goods may include consumable goods (like wheat flour, salt, sugar, fruits, etc.) or durable consumer goods (like television, refrigerator, toaster, mixer, bicycle, etc.). Services that we buy may include electric power, telephone, transport service, theatre service, etc.[7]

Section 2(*d*) of the Consumer Protection Act says that consumer means any person who: (a) buys any goods for a consideration which has been paid or promised or partly paid and partly promised, or under any system of deferred payment, and includes any user of such goods other than the person who buys such goods for consideration paid or promised or partly paid or partly promised, or under any system of deferred payment when such use is made with the approval of such person, but does not include a person who obtains such goods for resale or for any commercial purpose; or (b) hires or avails of any services for a consideration which has been paid or promised or partly paid and partly promised, or under any system of deferred payment, and includes any beneficiary of such services other than the person who hires or avails of the services for consideration paid or promised, or partly paid and partly promised, or under any system of deferred payment, when such services are availed of with the approval of the first mentioned person.

Consumerism as a social and economic order and ideology encourages the acquisition of goods and services in ever-greater amounts. Consumerism is sometimes used in reference to the anthropological and biological phenomena of people purchasing goods and consuming materials in excess of their basic needs, which would make it recognisable in any society including ancient civilisations. The Industrial Revolution dramatically increased the availability of consumer goods, although it was still primarily focused on the capital goods sector and industrial infrastructure. Consumerism has long had intentional underpinnings, rather than just developing out of capitalism.[8] Specifically, the responsibilities of consumers may include the followings:

1. *Responsibility of self-help:* It is always desirable that a consumer should not depend on the seller for information and choice as far as possible.
2. *Proof of Transactions:* The second responsibility of every consumer is that the proof of purchase and documents relating to purchase of durable goods should be invariable obtained and preserved.
3. *Proper claim:* Another responsibility that consumers are expected to bear in mind is that while making complaints and claiming compensation for loss or injury, they should not make unreasonably large claims.
4. *Proper use of Product/services:* Some consumers, especially during the guarantee period, make rough use of the product, thinking that it will be replaced during the guarantee period.[9]

Consumer Protection

Consumer protection is a group of laws and organisations designed to ensure the rights of consumers as well as fair trade, competition and accurate information in the marketplace. The laws are designed to prevent businesses that engage in fraud or specified unfair practices from gaining an advantage over competitors. In order to safeguard consumer interest, six consumer rights were initially envisioned by consumer rights activists of the West, namely: Right to Safety; Right to Information; Right to Choice; Right to be Heard; Right to Redress; Right to Consumer Education. Consumer protection law or consumer law is considered an area of law that regulates private law relationships between individual consumers and the businesses that sell those goods and services.

In India, The Consumer Protection Act of 1986 is the law governing consumer protection. Under this law, Separate Consumer Dispute Redressal Forums have been set up throughout India in each and every district in which a consumer [complaint can be filed by both the consumer of a goods as well as of the services] can file his complaint on a simple paper with nominal court fees and his complaint will be decided by the Presiding Officer of the District Level.[10]

Consumer Rights in India

Some of the laws which were passed during the British regime concerning consumer interests are: the Indian Contract Act of 1872, the Sale of Goods Act of 1930, the Indian Penal Code of 1860, the Drugs and Cosmetics Act of 1940, the Usurious Loans Act of 1918, and the Agriculture Procedure (Grading and Marketing Act) of 1937. These laws provided specific legal protection for consumers. For fifty-five years, the Sale of Goods Act of 1930 [SGA] was the exclusive source of consumer protection in India. The SGA, drafted with precision, is an admirable piece of legislation. The Indian Penal Code of 1860 has a number of provisions to deal with crimes against consumers. Consumer protection legislation enacted after India's independence from Britain include: the Essential Commodities Act of 1955, the Prevention of Food Adulteration Act of 1954 and the Standard of Weights and Measures Act of 1976. The Indian legal system experienced a revolution with the enactment of the Consumer Protection Act of 1986, which was specifically designed to protect consumer interests. The CPA was passed with avowed objectives.[11]

According to the Consumer Protection Act 1986, the consumer right is referred to as '*right to be protected against marketing of goods and services which are hazardous to life and property*'. It is applicable to specific areas like healthcare, pharmaceuticals. According to this law, everybody, including individuals, a firm, a Hindu undivided family and a company, have the right to exercise their consumer rights for the purchase of goods and services made by them. It is significant that, as consumer, one knows the basic rights as well as about the courts and procedures that follow with the infringement of one's rights.

Consumer rights and consumer protection law provides a way for individuals to fight back against abusive business practices. These laws are designed to hold sellers of goods and services accountable when they seek to profit by taking advantage of a consumer's lack of information or bargaining power. Consumer rights laws also protect the public from false or misleading advertising. For example, automobile dealers have been known to advertise a vehicle at a reduced price in order to draw shoppers to the dealership. Once they arrive, however, that vehicle or sales price is no longer available.[12] Consumer rights awareness is about making the consumer aware of products or services; however, this is largely unknown to many citizens irrespective of whether they are educated or uneducated. With an enormous population along with high levels of poverty, unemployment and poor literacy levels, consumer rights awareness continues to remain low. Education is a lifelong process of constantly acquiring relevant information, knowledge and skills.[13]

An effective, efficient and fair implementation of the Consumer Protection Act is one of the conditions precedents for promoting the culture of good governance and thereby ensuring the better promotion and protection of the rights of the consumers. If the rights of the consumers in relation to the quality of goods and services are assured and taken care of then there will be no cause for complaints.[14] Businessman is aware of his social responsibilities even then we come across many cases of consumer exploitation. The Government of India has included consumer education in the school curriculum and in various university courses. Government is also making use of media to make the consumers aware of their rights and make wise use of their money.[15] In general, the consumer rights in India are listed below:

1. The right to be protected from all kind of hazardous goods and services.
2. The right to be fully informed about the performance and quality of all goods and services.
3. The right to free choice of goods and services.
4. The right to be heard in all decision-making processes related to consumer interests.
5. The right to seek redressal, whenever consumer rights have been infringed.
6. The right to complete consumer education.[16]

The Drugs Control Act, 1950

In 1950, the Drugs (Control) Act was passed which also provides for the control of the sale, supply and distribution of drugs. This Act briefly provides for fixing of maximum prices and maximum quantities which may be held or sold, general limitation on quantity which may be possessed at any one time, duty to declare possession of excess stocks, marking of prices and exhibiting list of prices and stocks.[17]

Industries (Development and Regulation) Act, 1951

Industries (Development and Regulation) Act, 1951 is another example on the part of the union government to make some attempts in implementing the objectives of consumerism. The act provides for the development and regulations of certain industries. The Act specifically deals with the central government's power to control supply, distributing price etc. of certain articles.[18]

The Presentation of Food Adulteration Act, 1954

The Act, keeping in view the menace of adulteration to the society and to make the machinery provided under it more effective to curb the increasing tendencies in adulteration, was amended in 1964. The amendment provides that for the proper enforcement of the provision of the Act that the central government also should have power to appoint food inspectors.[19]

Consumer Protection Act, 1986

Consumer Protection Act, 1986 is an Act of the Parliament of India enacted in 1986 to protect interests of consumers in India. It makes provision for the establishment of consumer councils and other authorities for the settlement of consumers' disputes and for matters connected therewith. Consumer Protection Councils are established at the national, state and district level to increase consumer awareness.[20] When goods are bought for commercial purposes and such purchase satisfy the following criteria: the goods are used by the buyer himself; exclusively for the purpose of earning his livelihood; by means of self-employment, then such use would not be termed as use for commercial purposes under the Act, and the user is recognised as a consumer.

The intention of the legislature is to exclude big business houses carrying on business with profit motive from the purview of the Act. At the same time it is pertinent to save the interests of small consumers who buy goods for self-employment to earn their livelihood, like a rickshaw puller buying rickshaw for self-employment, or a farmer purchasing fertiliser for his crops, or a taxi driver buying a car to run it as a taxi, etc. When a person hires services, he may hire it for himself or for any other person. In such cases the beneficiary (or user) of these services is also a consumer.

An aggrieved consumer seeks redressal under the Act through the instrumentality of complaint. It does not mean that the consumer can complain against his each and every problem. The Act has provided certain grounds on which complaint can be made. Similarly, relief against these complaints can be granted within the set pattern. Complaint is a statement made in writing to the National Commission, the State Commission or the District Forum by a person competent to file it, containing the allegations in detail, and with a view to obtain relief provided under the Act. At the outset it is clear that a person who can be termed as a consumer under the Act can make a complaint. To be specific on this account, following are the persons who can file a complaint under the Act: (a) a consumer; or (b) any voluntary consumer association registered under the Companies Act, 1956 or under any other law for the time being in force, or (c) the Central Government or any State Government, (d) one or more consumers, where there are numerous consumers having the same interest.

A complaint must contain any of the following allegations: (a) An unfair trade practice or a restrictive trade practice has been adopted by any trader; (b) The goods bought by him or agreed to be bought by him suffer from one or more defects; (c) The services hired or availed of or agreed to be hired or availed of by him suffer from deficiency in any respect. Section 24A of the Act provides that a consumer dispute can be filed within two years from the date on which the cause of action arises. The point of time when cause of action arises is an important factor in determining the time period available to file a complaint. There are no set rules to decide such time. It depends on the facts and circumstances of each case. The Act says that, "unfair trade practice" means a trade practice which, for the purpose of promoting the sale, use or supply of any goods or for the provision of any service, adopts any unfair method or unfair or deceptive practice including any of the following practice. Section 2(1)(*nn*) of the Act provides that, "restrictive trade practice" means "any trade practice which requires a consumer to buy, hire or avail of any goods or, as the case may be, services as a condition precedent for buying, hiring or availing of other goods or services".

A consumer can make complaint when he comes across defective goods. Here it is required to understand that are the items which can be considered as 'goods' and what constitutes 'defect' under the Act. Section 2(1) (*f*) of the Act provides that, "defect" means any fault, imperfection or shortcoming in the quality, quantity, potency, purity or standard *which is required to be maintained* by or under any law of the time being in force under any contract, express or implied or as is claimed by the trader in any manner whatsoever *in relation to any goods*. When a service is found deficient by a consumer, he can make a complaint under the Act. Thus, the prime requirement is that the matter must fall within the definition of service, and it must entail a deficiency as per the norms given by the Act. Section 2(1)(*o*) of the Act provides that "service" means service of any description which is made available to potential users and includes the provision of facilities in connection with *banking, financing, insurance, transport, processing, supply of electrical or other energy, board or loading or both, housing construction, entertainment, amusement or the purveying of news or other information,* but does not include the rendering of any service free of charge or under a contract of personal service.

Section 2(1) (*g*) of the Act provides that, "deficiency" means any fault, imperfection, shortcoming or inadequacy in the quality, nature and manner of performance which is required to be maintained by or under any law for the time being in force or has been undertaken to be performed by a person in pursuance of a contract or otherwise in relation to any service. One interesting aspect is that deficiency in service should occur during the happening of performance. Thus it is crucial to determine when the performance of a service commenced. When a person finds any defect in the goods, be it manufacturing defect, or excessive price, or lack of information about hazardous nature, or restrictive or unfair trade practice, he can make a complaint against the trader. Thus it is very important to know who can be termed as a trader under the Act. Generally when a consumer finds defect in the goods, he sues the person from whom he bought the goods. If the defect is a manufacturing defect, the consumer may sue the manufacturer also along with the seller. This is an option with the consumer. Thus, the manufacturer is a possible party, and not a necessary party.

It may be noted that when price of an article is not fixed by law, or when the same is not displayed on goods or on the package containing goods, no complaint can be made under the Act for excess pricing. The term hazardous goods have not been defined in the Act. The dictionary meaning of the term is - dangerous or risky. However, the term is used in context of 'goods' only, *i.e.*, a person can make a complaint if he is not informed about the hazardous nature of the goods but the same is not true in case of hazardous services. The rationale behind this provision is to ensure physical safety of the consumers. The law seeks to ensure that those responsible for bringing goods to the market, in particular, suppliers, exporters, importers, retailers and the like should ensure that while in their care these goods are not rendered unsafe through improper handling or storage.

Consumers should be instructed in the proper use of goods and should be informed of the risks involved in intended or normally foreseeable use. Vital safety information should be conveyed to consumers. Adequate information is very important in order to make a right choice. In our country, however, consumers do not get adequate comparative information about the quality, quantity, potency, purity, standard and price of different kinds of goods or services which are available. As a result buying decisions become difficult. Therefore, consumers need to be given maximum information about the wide variety of competing goods available in the market.

1. ***Right to choose*** - The right to choose can be made meaningful by ensuring access to a variety of goods and services at competitive prices. Fair and effective competition must be encouraged so as to provide consumers with the widest range of products and services at the lowest cost.
2. ***Right to represent*** - It is right to be heard and to be assured that consumer's interests will receive due consideration at appropriate forums. The Consumer Protection Act, 1986 has well taken care of this right by making available the instrumentality of Redressal Forums. Every consumer has a right to file complaint and be heard in that context.
3. ***Right to redressal*** - It is a right to seek redressal against unfair trade practices or restrictive trade practices or unserpulous exploitation of consumers. When consumers are wronged in a market place transaction, appropriate and adequate redress must be available. The Act has ensured this right by establishing Consumer Forums and recognising restrictive and unfair trade practices as a ground to make a complaint.
4. ***Right to education*** - The right to consumer education is a right which ensures that consumers are informed about the practices

prevalent in the market and the remedies available to them. For spreading this education, media, or school curriculum, or cultural activities, etc. may be used as a medium.[21]

Standards of Weights and Measures Act, 1976

This Act was enacted to establish standards of weights and measures, to regulate inter-State trade or commerce in weights, measures and other goods which are sold or distributed by weight, measure or number, to provide for matters connected therewith or incidental thereto. Under the Act, weight and measures also include 'weighing or measuring instrument' which means "any object, instrument, apparatus or device, or any combination thereof, which is, or is intended to be, used, exclusively or additionally, for the purpose of making any weighment or measurement, and includes any appliance, accessory or part associated with any such object, instrument, apparatus or device.[22]

Standards of Weights and Measures (Enforcement) Act 1985

This Act was enacted to provide for the enforcement of the standards of weights and measures established by or under the Standards of Weights and Measures Act, 1976, and for matters connected therewith or incidental thereto. As per the Act, in relation to any goods or things which are sold, transferred, distributed or delivered, or any service rendered (except those permitted under the Standards Act), no person is allowed to- (i) quote, or make announcement of, whether by word of mouth or otherwise, any price or charge; or (ii) issue or exhibit any price list, invoice, cash memo or other document; or (iii) mention any weight or measure in any advertisement, poster or other document; or (iv) indicate the weight or measure or number of the net contents of any package; or (v) express any quantity or dimension, in relation to any transaction, industrial production or protection. The Act further states that no person shall make, manufacture, repair or sell, or offer, expose or possess for repair or sale, any weight or measure unless he holds a valid license issued in this behalf by the Controller authorising such person to do so.[23]

Standards of Weights and Measures (Packaged Commodities) Rules, 1977

Provisions of the Act relating to packaged commodities and the relevant rules, namely, the Standards of Weights and Measures

(Packaged Commodities) Rules, 1977 were brought into force, since September 1977. According to these provisions every package intended for retail sale is required to carry information as regards the name of the commodity, name and address of manufacturer or packer, net quantity, month and year of manufacture/packing and retail price.[24]

Ministry of Consumer Affairs

The Ministry of Consumer Affairs is a government ministry of India. The Ministry is headed by a minister of Cabinet rank. The current Minister of State with Independent Charge is Ram Vilas Paswan. The objectives of the Department are to ensure: (a) The remunerative rates for the farmers; and (b) Supply of food grains at reasonable prices to the consumers through the public distribution system. The Department of Consumer affairs administers the policies for Consumer Cooperatives, Monitoring Prices, availability of essential commodities, Consumer Movement in the country and Controlling of statutory bodies like Bureau of Indian Standards (BIS) and Weights and Measures.[25]

Consumer Court

Consumer Court is the special purpose court, mainly in India, that deals with cases regarding consumer disputes and grievances. These are judiciary set ups by the government to protect the consumer rights. Its main function is to maintain the fair practices by the sellers towards consumers. Consumers can file a case against a seller if they are harassed or exploited by sellers. The main function of consumer court is to provide some extra privilege to the consumers and to maintain fair practice by the seller or the service provider towards the consumer.[26]

National Consumer Disputes Redressal Commission

It is a quasi-judicial commission in India which was set up in 1988 under the Consumer Protection Act, 1986. Its head office is in New Delhi. The commission is headed by a sitting or retired judge of the Supreme Court of India. Section 21 of Consumer Protection Act, 1986 describes, the National Consumer shall have jurisdiction: to enter a complaint valued more than one crore and also have Appellate and Revisional jurisdiction from the orders of State Commissions. Section 23 of Consumer Protection Act, 1986, provides that any person aggrieved by an order of NCDRC, may prefer an Appeal against such order to Supreme Court of India within a period of 30 days.[27]

Consumer Redressal Forum

To provide cheap, speedy and simple redressal to consumer disputes, quasi-judicial machinery is set up at each District, State and National levels called District Forums, State Consumer Disputes Redressal Commission and National Consumer Disputes Redressal Commission respectively. There are 604 District Forums, 35 State Commission and States and Union Territories and a apex body of National Consumer Disputes Redressal Commission (NCDRC) having its office at Janpath Bhawan, A Wing, 5th Floor, Janpath, New Delhi. The National Commission was constituted in 1988. It is headed by Sitting Retired Judge of Supreme Court and other members chosen by Government in consultation with Chairperson. At least one member should be a Woman. Similarly, while State Commission is headed by a sitting retired High Court Judge and at least three members, one woman.[28]

Bureau of Indian Standards

The Bureau of Indian Standards (BIS) may be made the national standards body and repository of all voluntary national standards. Wherever voluntary standards are being formulated by other standards development organisations which are recognised as national (like Indian Roads Congress or Agmark), these may be published as national standards by BIS while these bodies continue to make these standards.[29]

Constitutional Perspectives

The Constitution of India in Articles 38, 39, 42, 43, 46 and 47 provides that the state shall strive to secure a social order for the promotion of welfare of the people; it shall direct its policies in such a way that operation of economic system does not result in the concentration of wealth and means of production to the common detriment, it shall make provision for securing just and humane conditions of work and for maternity relief. Article 46 of the Indian constitution provides that state shall endeavour to protect the economic interest of the weaker section of its population and also protect them from social injustice and all forms of exploitation which means all kinds of harassments and frauds in the market place.[30]

The Indian Penal Code

Sections 264 to 267 of the Indian penal code relate to fraudulent use of false instrument for weighing, fraudulent use of false weight and measures, anyone in possession of false weight or measure respectively. The penal code further provides sections 269 to 271 on spreading of infections and in sections 272 to 276 on adulteration of food or drink, adulteration of drugs, sale of adulterated drugs and sale of drugs as a different drug or preparation are punishable with imprisonment or with both.[31]

Conclusion

Consumer is a person that uses economic services or commodities. Customer service is the provision of service to customers before, during and after a purchase. The importance of customer service may vary by product or service, industry and customer. From the point of view of an overall sales process engineering effort, customer service plays an important role in an organisation's ability to generate income and revenue. Consumerism as a social and economic order and ideology encourages the acquisition of goods and services in ever-greater amounts. In India, The Consumer Protection Act of 1986 is the law governing consumer protection. Under this law, Separate Consumer Dispute Redressal Forums have been set up throughout India in each and every district in which a consumer [complaint can be filed by both the consumer of a goods as well as of the services] can file his complaint on a simple paper with nominal court fees and his complaint will be decided by the Presiding Officer of the District Level.

References

1. Customer (2015), Retrieved from http://en.wikipedia.org/wiki/Customer
2. Customer satisfaction (2015), Retrieved from http://en.wikipedia.org/wiki/Customer_satisfaction
3. Customer service (2015), Retrieved from http://en.wikipedia.org/wiki/Customer_service
4. Relationship marketing (2015), Retrieved from http://en.wikipedia.org/wiki/Relationship_marketing
5. Consumer behavior (2015), Retrieved from http://en.wikipedia.org/wiki/Consumer_behaviour
6. Consumer (2015), Retrieved from http://en.wikipedia.org/wiki/Consumer
7. Lesson 25 Rights and Responsibilities of Consumers, Retrieved from http://old.nios.ac.in/Secbuscour/25.pdf
8. Consumerism (2015), Retrieved from http://en.wikipedia.org/wiki/Consumerism
9. Lesson 25 Rights and Responsibilities of Consumers, Retrieved from http://old.nios.ac.in/Secbuscour/25.pdf

10. Consumer protection (2015), Retrieved from http://en.wikipedia.org/wiki/Consumer_protection
11. Historical Evolution of Consumer Protection and Law in India, Retrieved from http://www.jtexconsumerlaw.com/v11n3/jccl_india.pdf
12. Consumer Rights - Consumer Protection Law, See http://www.hg.org/consume.html
13. Consumer rights awareness: Problems and prospects, Retrieved from http://shodhganga.inflibnet.ac.in/bitstream/10603/13130/10/10_chapter%201.pdf
14. Consumer Protection in India: Some Reflections, Retrieved from http://www.consumereducation.in/monograms/1_consumer_orotection_%20in_India.pdf
15. Utkarsh Daya, Consumer Rights under the Consumer Protection Act, India, Retrieved from http://www.yourarticlelibrary.com/consumers/consumer-rights-under-the-consumer-protection-act-india/8786/
16. Consumer Rights (2015), Retrieved from http://www.consumerrights.org.in/rights.htm
17. Aman Chatterjee and Sheetal Sahoo, Consumer Protection: Problems and Prospects, Postmodern Openings, 2011, Year 2, Vol. 7, September, pp. 157-182, Retrieved from http://postmodernopenings.com/wp-content/uploads/2011/10/PO-7-112.pdf
18. *Ibid.*
19. *Ibid.*
20. Consumer Protection Act, 1986, Retrieved from http://en.wikipedia.org/wiki/Consumer_Protection_Act,_1986
21. Consumer Protection Act, see http://ncdrc.nic.in/1_1_2.html
22. 'Weights and Measures, Retrieved from http://business.gov.in/consumer_rights/measures_act.php
23. *Ibid.*
24. See http://www.archive.india.gov.in/sectors/consumer_affairs/index.php?id=7
25. Ministry of consumer affairs (2015), Retrieved from http://en.wikipedia.org/wiki/Ministry_of_Consumer_Affairs,_Food_and_Public_Distribution
26. Consumer court (2015), Retrieved from http://en.wikipedia.org/wiki/Consumer_Court
27. National Consumer Disputes Redressal Commission (2015), Retrieved from http://en.wikipedia.org/wiki/National_Consumer_Disputes_Redressal_Commission
28. Dr. Partap Singh and Joginder Grewal, Consumer Protection in India: Some Issues and Trends, International Journal of Latest Trends in Engineering and Technology (IJLTET), Retrieved from http://ijltet.org/wp-content/uploads/2013/02/42.pdf

29. Consumer Protection and Competition Policy, Retrieved from http://planningcommission.nic.in/plans/planrel/fiveyr/11th/11_v1/11v1_ch11.pdf
30. Aman Chatterjee and Sheetal Sahoo, Consumer Protection: Problems and Prospects, Postmodern Openings, 2011, Year 2, Vol. 7, September, pp. 157-182, Retrieved from http://postmodernopenings.com/wp-content/uploads/2011/10/PO-7-112.pdf
31. *Ibid.*

13

Rights of Prisoner

"We must become bigger than we have been: more courageous, greater in spirit, larger in outlook. We must become members of a new race, overcoming petty prejudice, owing our ultimate allegiance not to nations but to our fellow men within the human community."

- Haile Selassie

Introduction

Prison is a facility in which inmates are forcibly confined and denied a variety of freedoms under the authority of the state as a form of punishment. The beginning of prisons can be traced back to the rise of the state as a form of social organisation. Some Ancient Greek philosophers, such as Plato, began to develop ideas of using punishment to reform offenders instead of simply using it as retribution. The Romans were among the first to use prisons as a form of punishment, rather than simply for detention. During the middle Ages in Europe, castles, fortresses, and the basements of public buildings were often used as makeshift prisons. The theory of the modern prison system was born in London, influenced by the utilitarianism of Jeremy Bentham. The first state prison in England was the Millbank Prison, established in 1816 with a capacity for just fewer than 1000 inmates.

Prisons are normally surrounded by fencing, walls, earthworks, geographical features, or other barriers to prevent escape. Remotely controlled doors, CCTV monitoring, alarms, cages, restraints, nonlethal and lethal weapons, riot-control gear and physical segregation of units and prisoners may all also be present within a prison to monitor and control the movement and activity of prisoners within the facility. Generally, when an inmate arrives at a prison, they go through a security classification screening and risk assessment that determines where they will be placed within the prison system. Female inmates experience high rates of rape and sexual violence while incarcerated. As of 2010, it is estimated that at least 10.1 million people are currently imprisoned worldwide. In the United States alone, more than $760 billion per year is spent on prisons, with over 800,000 people employed in the prison industry (Wikipedia).[1]

Prison in India

As of 31 December 2011, there are 1382 functioning jails in India having a total capacity to house 332,782 prisoners. As of the same date, there were 372,926 inmates in jails across in India. Males at 356,902 make up 95.7 per cent of prisoners while females at 16,024 represent 4.3 per cent. Prison establishments in India comprise eight categories of jails. The most common and standard jail institutions are Central Jails, District Jails and Sub Jails. The other types of jail establishments are Women Jails, Borstal Schools, Open Jails and Special Jails. The Supreme Court of India, in its judgments on various aspects of prison administration, has laid down three broad principles regarding imprisonment and custody. Firstly, a person in prison does not become a non-person. Secondly, a person in prison is entitled to all human rights within the limitations of imprisonment. Lastly, there is no justification for aggravating the suffering already inherent in the process of incarceration.[2]

Tihar Prisons is a prison complex in India and the largest complex of prisons in South Asia. Originally, Tihar was a maximum security prison run by the State of Punjab. It is located in Tihar village, approximately seven kms from Chanakya Puri, to the west of New Delhi, India. The surrounding area is called Hari Nagar. As of December 2012, Tihar jail has 10,533 inmates against the sanctioned capacity of 5,200.[3]

Two of every three persons incarcerated in India have not yet been convicted of any crime, and Muslims are over-represented among such under trials, new official data show. Despite repeated Supreme Court orders on the rights of under trials, the jails are filling ever faster with them, shows Prisons Statistics for 2013 released by the National Crime Records Bureau. The number of convicts grew by

1.4 per cent from 2012 to 2013, but the number of under trials shot up by 9.3 per cent during the period. Men make up 96 per cent of all prison inmates. Nearly 2,000 children of women inmates live behind bars, 80 per cent of those women being under trials. A sharp increase in the number of under trials charged with crimes against women contributes to the rise in the number of all under trials. The number of those incarcerated on charges of rape rose by over 30 per cent from 2012 to 2013, and the number facing charges of molestation grew by over 50 per cent. The number of men convicted of rape raised dramatically too, by 16 per cent — the biggest increase among major sections of the Indian Penal Code.[4]

Muslims, dalits and adivasis, three of the most vulnerable sections of Indian society make up more than half of India's prison population. Former chief justice of Delhi High Court Rajinder Sachar, who headed the committee that brought out a report on the condition of Muslim community in India in 2006, pointed out that there had been several cases of Muslim youths being acquitted after years in prison. Ramesh Nathan of the National Dalit Movement for Justice alleged that false cases are filed against dalits in order to intimidate them, causing this disturbingly high number of prisoners among vulnerable sections. Prison statistics are published annually by the National Crime Records Bureau since 1995, although caste breakup is available since 1999. The proportions of Muslims, dalits and adivasis have remained virtually unchanged over the past 15 years indicating that this is a systemic problem.[5]

Prison Institutions are one of the three main constituents of the criminal justice system. In recent times there has been considerable change in social perception towards the prisoners.[6] Uttar Pradesh accounted for the highest number of convicted prisoners (25,310) at the end of 2013 among the States and UTs. Other States which have reported considerably large number of convicts were Madhya Pradesh (16,869), Punjab (8,936), Maharashtra (8,041), Haryana (7,020), Chhattisgarh (6,586), Rajasthan (6,044), West Bengal (5,590), Tamil Nadu (4,648), Andhra Pradesh (4,598), Jharkhand (4,162) and Gujarat (3,808). The proportion of under trial male inmates to total inmates was observed as 95.4 per cent while that of female inmates was 4.6 per cent during 2013. A total of 4,820 inmates were reported as mentally ill out of total 4,11,992 inmates lodged in various jails in the country.[7]

A total of 15,822 convicts were lodged in various jails of the country for committing offences under Special and Local Laws.[8] Death of a prisoner is always a matter of serious concern for prison administration. A total of 1,597 prisoners were reported dead in jails due to natural and unnatural causes during 2013 in the country out of which 1,482 were natural deaths and 115 were due to unnatural causes. Among the unnatural deaths, Uttar Pradesh has reported the highest number (18) of deaths followed by Rajasthan (11), Tamil Nadu (10), Haryana, Madhya Pradesh and Punjab (nine each), Delhi (eight), Assam, Gujarat and West Bengal (five each).[9]

Prisoner Rights in India

In India, the idea of rights of prisoners was long suppressed under the colonial rule and has only recently emerged in public discourse. The Constitution of India confers a number of fundamental rights upon citizens. There are many United Nations codified standards of treatment for prisoners across different economic, social and cultural contexts in a number of documents. Article 21 of the Constitution of India guarantees the right of personal liberty and thereby prohibits any inhuman, cruel or degrading treatment to any person whether he/she is a national or foreigner. Article 21, Protection of Life and Personal Liberty; *"No person shall be deprived of his life or personal liberty except according to procedure established by law"*. Any violation of this right attracts the provisions of Article 14 of the Constitution, which enshrines right to equality and equal protection of law. In addition to this, the question of cruelty to prisoners is also dealt with, specifically by the Prison Act, 1894 and the Criminal Procedure Code. The Indian Supreme Court has been active in responding to human right violations in Indian jails and has, in the process, recognised a number of rights of prisoners by interpreting Articles 21, 19, 22, 32, 37 and 39A of the Constitution in a positive and humane way.[10] Rights of Prisoner are: [11]

1. Right to be lodged appropriately based on Proper Classification.
2. Special Right of young prisoners to be segregated from adult prisoners.
3. Rights of women prisoners.
4. Right to healthy environment.
5. Right to bail.
6. Right to speedy trial.
7. Right to free legal services.
8. Right to basic needs such as food, water and shelter.
9. Right to have interviews with one's Lawyer.

10. Right against being detained for more than the period of sentence imposed by the court.
11. Right to protection against being forced into sexual activities.
12. Right against arbitrary use of handcuffs and fetters.
13. Right against torture, cruel and degrading punishment.
14. Right not to be punished with solitary confinement for a prison offence.
15. Right against arbitrary prison punishment.
16. Right to air grievances and to effective remedy.
17. Right to evoke the writ of habeas corpus against prison authorities for excesses.
18. Right to be compensated for violation of human rights.
19. Right to visits and access by family members of prisoners.
20. Right to write letters to family and friends and to receive letters, magazines, etc.
21. Right to rehabilitation and reformative programmes.
22. Right in the context of employment of prisoners and to prison wages.
23. Right to information about prison rules.
24. Right to emergency and reasonable healthcare.

The Code of Criminal Procedure

It is the main legislation on procedure for administration of substantive criminal law in India. It was enacted in 1973 and came into force on 1 April 1974. It provides the machinery for the investigation of crime, apprehension of suspected criminals, collection of evidence, determination of guilt or innocence of the accused person and the determination of punishment of the guilty. The Criminal Procedure Code is applicable in the whole of India except in the State of Jammu and Kashmir. The Parliament's power to legislate in respect of Jammu and Kashmir is curtailed by Article 370 of the Constitution of India. There is no definition of the term "bail" under the code though the terms "bailable" and "non-bailable" have been defined. Section 260, Clause 2 of the Code lists certain offences which may be summarily tried by any Chief Judicial Magistrate, any Metropolitan Magistrate or any Judicial Magistrate First Class. A First Class Magistrate must first be authorised by the respective High Court to that effect before he may try cases summarily under this Section.[12]

Prison Act, 1894

"Prison" means any jail or place used permanently or temporarily under the general or special orders of a State Government for the detention of prisoners, and includes all lands and buildings appurtenant thereto, but does not include— (a) any place for the confinement of prisoners who are exclusively in the custody of the police; (b) any place specially appointed by the State Government under section 541 of the Code of Criminal Procedure, 1882; or (c) any place which has been declared by the State Government, by general or special order, to be a subsidiary jail. "Criminal prisoner" means any prisoner duly committed to custody under the writ, warrant or order of any Court or authority exercising criminal jurisdiction, or by order of a Court-martial.

Prison Act, 1894

Section	*Explanation*
	Chapter I [Preliminary]
1	This Act may be called the Prisons Act, 1894. [(2) It extends to the whole of India except [the territories which, immediately before the 1st November, 1956, were comprised in Part B States]; and. (3) It shall come into force on the first day of July, 1894. (4) Nothing in this Act shall apply to civil jails in the State of Bombay [as it existed immediately before the 1st November, 1956] outside the city of Bombay, and those jails shall continue to be administered under the provisions of section 9 to 16 (both inclusive) of Bombay Act 2 of 1874, as amended by subsequent enactments.
2	Repealed by the Repealing Act, 1938 (1 of 1938), section 2 and Schedule.
3	"Convicted criminal prisoner" means any criminal prisoner under sentence of a Court or Court-martial, and includes a person detained in prison under the provisions of Chapter VIII of the Code of Criminal Procedure, 1882, (10 of 1882) or under the Prisoners Act, 1871 (5 of 1871). "Civil prisoner" means any prisoner who is not a criminal prisoner. "Remission system" means the rules for the time being in force regulating the award of Marks to, and the consequent shortening of

(Contd.)

(Contd. Table)

Section	*Explanation*
	sentences of, prisoners in jails. "History-ticket" means the ticket exhibiting such information as is required in respect of each prisoner by this Act or the rules thereunder. "Inspector General" means the Inspector General of Prisons. "Medical subordinate" means an Assistant Surgeon, Apothecary or qualified hospital Assistant: and "prohibited article" means an article the introduction or removal of which into or out of a prison is prohibited by any rule under this Act.
	Chapter II [Maintenance and Officers of Prisons]
4	The State Government shall provide, for the prisoners in the territories under such Government, accommodation in prisons constructed and regulated in such manner as to comply with the requisitions of this Act in respect of the separation of prisoners.
5	An Inspector General shall be appointed for the territories subject to each State Government and shall exercise, subject to the orders of the State Government the general control and superintendence of all prisons situated in the territories under such Government.
6	For every prison there shall be a superintendent, a Medical Officer (who may also be the Superintendent), a Medical Subordinate, a Jailer and such other officers as the State Government thinks necessary: Provided that [the State Government of Bombay] may ***** declare by order in writing that in any prison specified in the order the office of Jailer shall be held by the person appointed to be Superintendent.
7	Whenever it appears to the Inspector General that the number of prisoners in any prison is greater than can conveniently or safely be kept therein, and it is not convenient to transfer the excess number to some other prison, or whenever from the outbreak of epidemic disease within any prison, or for any other reason, it is desirable to provide for the temporary shelter and safe custody of any prisoners, provision shall be made, by such officer and in such manner as the State Government may direct, for the shelter and safe custody in

(Contd.)

(Contd. Table)

Section	*Explanation*
	temporary prisons of so many of the prisoners as cannot be conveniently or safely kept in the prison.
	Chapter III [Duties of Officers]
8	All officers of a prison shall obey the directions of the Superintendent; all officers subordinate to the Jailer shall perform such duties as may be imposed on them by the Jailer with the sanction of the Superintendent or be prescribed by rules under Section 59.
9	No officer of a prison shall sell or let, nor shall any person in trust for or employed by him, sell or let or derive any benefit from selling or letting, any article to any prisoner or have any money or other business dealings directly or indirectly with any prisoner.
10	No officer of a prison shall, nor shall any person in trust for or employed by him, have any interest, direct or indirect, in any contract for the supply of the prison; nor shall he derive any benefit, directly or indirectly, from the sale or purchase of any article on behalf of the prison or belonging to a prisoner.
11	Subject to the orders of the Inspector General the Superintendent shall manage the prison in all matters relating to discipline, labour, expenditure, punishment and control. Subject to such general or special directions as may be given by the State Government, the Superintendent of a prison other than a central prison or a prison situated in a presidency-town shall obey all orders not inconsistent with this Act or any rule thereunder which may be given respecting the prison by the District Magistrate, and shall report to the Inspector General all such orders and the action taken thereon.
12	The Superintendent shall keep, or cause to be kept, the following records:- (1) a register of prisoners admitted; (2) a book showing when each prisoner is to be released; (3) a punishment-book for the entry of the punishments inflicted on prisoners for prison offences; (4) a visitors' book for the entry of any observations made by the visitors touching any matters connected with the administration of the prison; (5) a

(Contd.)

(Contd. Table)

Section	*Explanation*
	record of the money and other articles taken from prisoners; and all such other records as may be prescribed by rules under Section 59.
13	Subject to the control of the Superintendent, the Medical Officer shall have charge of the sanitary administration of the prison, and shall perform such duties as may be prescribed by rules made by the State Government under Section 59.
14	Whenever the Medical Officer has reason to believe that the mind of a prisoner is, or is likely to be, injuriously affected by the discipline or treatment to which he is subjected, the Medical Officer shall report the case in writing to the Superintendent, together with such observations as he may think proper. This report, with the orders of the Superintendent thereon, shall forthwith be sent to the Inspector General for information.
15	On the death of any prisoner, the Medical Officer shall forthwith record in a register the following particulars, so far as they can be ascertained, namely: (1) the day on which the deceased first complained of illness or was observed to be ill, (2) the labour, if any, on which he was engaged on that day, (3) the scale of his diet on that day, (4) the day on which he was admitted to hospital, (5) the day on which the Medical Officer was first informed of the illness, (6) the nature of the disease, (7) when the deceased was last seen before his death by the Medical Officer or Medical Subordinate, (8) when the prisoner died, and (9) (in cases where a post-mortem examination is made) an account of the appearances after death, together with any special remarks that appear to the Medical Officer to be required.
16	The Jailer shall reside in the prison, unless the Superintendent permits him in writing to reside elsewhere. The Jailer shall not, without the Inspector General's sanction in writing, be concerned in any other employment.
17	Upon the death of a prisoner, the Jailer shall give immediate notice thereof to the Superintendent and the Medical Subordinate.

(Contd.)

(Contd. Table)

Section	*Explanation*
18	The Jailer shall be responsible for the safe custody of the records to be kept under Section 12, for the commitment warrants and all other documents confined to his care, and for the money and other articles taken from prisoners.
19	The Jailer shall not be absent from the prison for a night without permission in writing from the Superintendent; but, if absent without leave for a night from unavoidable necessity, he shall immediately report the fact and the cause of it to the Superintendent.
20	Where a Deputy Jailer or Assistant Jailer is appointed to a prison, he shall, subject to the orders of the Superintendent, be competent to perform any of the duties, and be subject to all the responsibilities, of a Jailer under this Act or any rule thereunder.
21	The officer acting as gate-keeper, or any other officer of the prison, may examine anything carried in or out of the prison, and may stop and search or cause to be searched any person suspected of bringing any prohibited article into or out of the prison, or of carrying out any property belonging to the prison, and if any such article or property be found, shall give immediate notice thereof to the Jailer.
22	Officers subordinate to the Jailer shall not be absent from the prison without leave from the Superintendent or from the Jailer.
23	Prisoners who have been appointed as officers of prisons shall be deemed to be public servants within the meaning of the Indian Penal Code (45 of 1860).
	Chapter IV: Admission, Removal and Discharge of Prisoners
24	Whenever a prisoner is admitted into prison, he shall be searched, and all weapons and prohibited articles shall be taken from him. Every criminal prisoner shall also, as soon as possible after admission, be examined under the general or special orders of the Medical Officer, who shall enter or cause to be entered in a book, to be kept by the Jailer, a record of the state of the prisoner's health, and of any wounds or marks on his person, the class of labour he is fit for if

(Contd.)

(Contd. Table)

Section	*Explanation*
	sentenced to rigorous imprisonment, and any observations which the Medical Officer thinks fit to add. In the case of female prisoners the search and examination shall be carried out by the matron under the general or special orders of the Medical Officer.
25	All money or other articles in respect whereof no order of a competent Court has been made, and which may with proper authority be brought into the prison by any criminal prisoner or sent to the prison for his use, shall be placed in the custody of the Jailer.
26	All prisoners, previously to being removed to any other prison, shall be examined by the Medical Officer. No prisoner shall be removed from one prison to another unless the Medical Officer certifies that the prisoner is free from any illness rendering him unfit for removal. No prisoner shall be discharged against his will from prison, if labouring under any acute or dangerous distemper, nor until, in the opinion of the Medical Officer, such discharge is safe.
	Chapter V [Discipline of Prisoners]
27	The requisitions of this Act with respect to the separation of prisoners are as follows:- (1) in a prison containing female as well as male prisoners, the females shall be imprisoned in separate buildings, or separate parts of the same building, in such manner as to prevent their seeing, or conversing or holding any intercourse with, the male prisoners; (2) in a prison where male prisoners under the age of [twenty-one] are confined, means shall be provided for separating them altogether from the other prisoners and for separating those of them who have arrived at the age of puberty from those who have not; (3) unconvicted criminal prisoners shall be kept apart from convicted criminal prisoners; and (4) civil prisoners shall be kept apart from criminal prisoners.
28	Subject to the requirements of the last foregoing section, convicted criminal prisoners may be confined either in association or individually in cells or partly in one way and partly in the other.

(Contd.)

(Contd. Table)

Section	*Explanation*
29	No cell shall be used for solitary confinement unless it is furnished with the means of enabling the prisoner to communicate at any time with an officer of the prison, and every prisoner so confined in a cell for more than twenty-four hours, whether as a punishment or otherwise, shall be visited at least once a day by the Medical Officer or Medical Subordinate.
30	Every prisoner under sentence of death shall, immediately on his arrival in the prison after sentence, be searched by, or by order of, the Jailer and all articles shall be taken from him which the Jailer deems it dangerous or inexpedient to leave in his possession. Every such prisoner shall be confined in a cell apart from all other prisoners, and shall be placed by day and by night under the charge of a guard.
31	A civil prisoner or an unconvicted criminal prisoner shall be permitted to maintain himself, and to purchase, or receive from private sources at proper hours, food, clothing, bedding or other necessaries, but subject to examination and to such rules as may be approved by the Inspector General.
32	No part of any food, clothing, bedding or other necessaries belonging to any civil or unconvicted criminal prisoner shall be given, hired or sold to any other prisoner; and any prisoner transgressing the provisions of this section shall lose the privilege of purchasing food or receiving it from private sources, for such time as the Superintendent thinks proper.
33	Every civil prisoner and unconvicted criminal prisoner unable to provide himself with sufficient clothing and bedding shall be supplied by the Superintendent with such clothing and bedding as may be necessary. When any civil prisoner has been committed to prison in execution of a decree in favour of a private person, such person, or his representative, shall, within forty-eight hours after the receipt by him of a demand in writing, pay to the Superintendent the cost of the clothing and bedding so supplied to the prisoner; and in default of such payment the prisoner may be released.

(Contd.)

(Contd. Table)

Section	*Explanation*
	Chapter VII [Employment of Prisoners]
34	Civil prisoners may, with the Superintendent's permission, work and follow any trade or profession. Civil prisoners finding their own implements, and not maintained at the expense of the prison, shall be allowed to receive the whole of their earnings; but the earnings of such as are furnished with implements or are maintained at the expense of the prison shall be subject to a deduction, to be determined by the Superintendent, for the use of implements and the cost of maintenance.
35	No criminal prisoner sentenced to labour or employed on labour at his own desire shall, except on an emergency with the sanction in writing of the Superintendent, be kept to labour for more than nine hours in any one day. The Medical Officer shall from time to time examine the labouring prisoners while they are employed, and shall at least once in every fortnight cause to be recorded upon the history-ticket of each prisoner employed on labour the weight of such prisoner at the time. When the Medical Officer is of opinion that the health of any prisoner suffers from employment on any kind or class of labour, such prisoner shall not be employed on that labour but shall be placed on such other kind or class of labour as the Medical Officer may consider suited for him.
36	Provision shall be made by the Superintendent for the employment (as long as they so desire) of all criminal prisoners sentenced to simple imprisonment; but no prisoner not sentenced to rigorous imprisonment shall be punished for neglect of work excepting by such alteration in the scale of diet as may be established by the rules of the prison in the case of neglect of work by such a prisoner.
	Chapter VIII [Health of Prisoners]
37	The names of prisoners desiring to see the Medical Subordinate or appearing out of health in mind or body shall, without delay, be reported by the officer in immediate charge of such prisoners to the Jailer. The Jailer shall, without delay, call the attention of the Medical Subordinate to any prisoners

(Contd.)

(Contd. Table)

Section	*Explanation*
	desiring to see him, or who is ill, or whose state of mind or body appears to require attention, and shall carry into effect all written directions given by the Medical Officer or Medical Subordinate respecting alterations of the discipline or treatment of any such prisoner.
38	All directions given by the Medical Officer or Medical Subordinate in relation to any prisoner, with the exception of orders for the supply of medicines or directions relating to such matters as are carried into effect by the Medical Officer himself or under his superintendence, shall be entered day by day in the prisoner's history-ticket or in such other record as the State Government may by rule direct, and the Jailer shall make an entry in its proper place stating in respect of each direction the fact of its having been or not having been complied with, accompanied by such observations, if any, as the Jailer thinks fit to make, and the date of the entry.
39	In every prison an hospital or proper place for the reception of sick prisoners shall be provided.
	Chapter IX [Visits of Prisoners]
40	Due provision shall be made for the admission, at proper times and under proper restrictions, into every prison of persons with whom civil or unconvicted criminal prisoners may desire to communicate, care being taken that, so far as may be consistent with the interests of justice, prisoners under trial may see their duly qualified legal advisers without the presence of any other person.
41	The Jailer may demand the name and address of any visitor to a prisoner, and, when the Jailer has any ground for suspicion, may search any visitor, or cause him to be searched but the search shall not be made in the presence of any prisoner or of another visitor. In case of any such visitor refusing to permit himself to be searched, the Jailer may deny him admission; and the grounds of such proceeding, with the particulars thereof, shall be entered in such record as the State Government may direct.

(Contd.)

(Contd. Table)

Section	*Explanation*
	Chapter X [Offences in Relation to Prisons]
42	Whoever, contrary to any rule under section [59] introduces or removes, or attempts by any means whatever to introduce or remove, into or from any prison, or supplies or attempts to supply to any prisoner outside the limits of a prison, any prohibited article, and every officer of a prison who, contrary to any such rule, knowingly suffers any such article to be introduced into or removed from any prison, to be possessed by any prisoner, or to be supplied to any prisoner outside the limits of a prison, and whoever, contrary to any such rules, communicates or attempts to communicate with any prisoner, and whoever abets any offence made punishable by this section, shall, on conviction before a Magistrate, be liable to imprisonment for a term not exceeding six months, or to fine not exceeding two hundred rupees, or to both.
43	When any person, in the presence of any officer of a prison, commits any offence specified in the last foregoing section, and refuses on demand of such officer to state his name and residence, or gives a name or residence which such officer knows, or has reason to believe, to be false, such officer may arrest him, and shall without unnecessary delay make him over to a Police-officer, and thereupon such Police-officer shall proceed as if the offence had been committed in his presence.
44	The Superintendent shall cause to be affixed, in a conspicuous place outside the prison, a notice in English and the Vernacular setting forth the acts prohibited under section 42 and the penalties incurred by their commission.
	Chapter XI [Prisons Offences]
45	The following acts are declared to be prison-offences when committed by a prisoner:- (1) such wilful disobedience to any regulation of the prison as shall have been declared by rules made under Section 59 to be a prison-offence; (2) any assault or use of criminal force; (3) the use of insulting or threatening language; (4) immoral or indecent or disorderly

(Contd.)

(Contd. Table)

Section	Explanation
	behaviour; (5) wilfully disabling himself from labour; (6) Contumaciously refusing to work; (7) filing, cutting, altering or removing handcuffs, fetters or bars without due authority; (8) wilful idleness or negligence at work by any prisoner sentenced to rigorous imprisonment. (9) wilful mismanagement of work by any prisoner sentenced to rigorous imprisonment; (10) wilful damage to prison property; (11) tampering with or defacing history-tickets, records or documents; (12) receiving, possessing or transferring any prohibited article; (13) feigning illness; (14) wilfully bringing a false accusation against any officer or prisoner; (15) omitting or refusing to report, as soon as it comes to his knowledge, the occurrence of any fire, any plot or conspiracy, any escape, attempt or preparation to escape, and any attack or preparation for attack upon any prisoner or prison-official; and (16) conspiring to escape, or to assist in escaping, or to commit any other of the offences aforesaid.
46	The Superintendent may examine any person touching any such offence, and determine thereupon, and punish such offence by- (1) a formal warning: (2) change of labour to some more irksome or severe form [for such period as may be prescribed by rules made by the State Government; (3) hard labour for a period not exceeding seven days in the case of convicted criminal prisoners not sentenced to rigorous imprisonment; (4) such loss of privileges admissible under the remission system for the time being in force as may be prescribed by rules made by the State Government; (5) the substitution of gunny or other coarse fabric for clothing of other material, not being woollen, for a period which shall not exceed three months; (6) imposition of handcuffs of such pattern and weight, in such manner and for such period, as may be prescribed by rules made by the State Government; (7) imposition of fetters of such pattern and weight, in such manner and for such period, as may be prescribed by rules made by the State Government; (8) separate confinement for

(Contd.)

(Contd. Table)

Section	*Explanation*
	any period not exceeding [three] months; (9) penal diet, that is, restriction of diet in such manner and subject to such conditions regarding labour as may be prescribed by the State Government: Provided that such restriction of diet shall in no case be applied to a prisoner for more than ninety-six consecutive hours, and shall not be repeated except for a fresh offence nor until after an interval of one week; (10) cellular confinement for any period not exceeding fourteen days.
47	Any two of the punishments enumerated in the last foregoing section may be awarded for any such offence in combination, subject to the following exceptions, namely:- (1) formal warning shall not be combined with any other punishment except loss of privileges under clause (4) of that section; (2) penal diet shall not be combined with change of labour under clause (2) of that section, nor shall any additional period of penal diet awarded singly be combined with any period of penal diet awarded in combination with [cellular] confinement; [(3) cellular confinement shall not be combined with separate confinement, so as to prolong the total period of seclusion to which the prisoner shall be liable]; (4) whipping shall not be combined with any other form of punishment except cellular or separate confinement [or] loss of privilege admissible under the remission system; [(5) no punishment shall be combined with any other punishment in contravention of rules made by the State Government.
48	The Superintendent shall have power to award any of the punishments enumerated in the two last foregoing sections, subject, in the case of separate confinement for a period exceeding one month, to the previous confirmation of the Inspector General. No officer subordinate to the Superintendent shall have power to award any punishment whatever.
49	Except by order of a Court of Justice, no punishment other than the punishments specified in the foregoing sections shall

(Contd.)

(Contd. Table)

Section	Explanation
	be inflicted on any prisoner, and no punishment shall be inflicted on any prisoner otherwise than in accordance with the provisions of those sections.
50	No punishment of penal diet, either singly or in combination, or of whipping, or of change of labour under Section 46, clause (2), shall be executed until the prisoner to whom such punishment has been awarded has been examined by the Medical Officer, who, if he considers the prisoner fit to undergo the punishment, shall certify accordingly in the appropriate column of the punishment-book prescribed in Section 12. If he considers the prisoner unfit to undergo the punishment, he shall in like manner record his opinion in writing and shall state whether the prisoner is absolutely unfit for punishment of the kind awarded, or whether he considers any modification necessary.
51	In the punishment-book prescribed in Section 12 there shall be recorded, in respect of every punishment inflicted, the prisoner's name, register number and the class (whether habitual or not) to which he belongs, the prison-offence of which he was guilty, the date on which such prison-offence was committed, the number of previous prison-offences recorded against the prisoner, and the date of his last prison-offence, the punishment awarded, and the date of infliction. In the case of every serious prison-offence, the names of the witnesses proving the offence shall be recorded, and, in the case of offences for which whipping is awarded, the Superintendent shall record the substance of the evidence of the witnesses, the defence of the prisoner, and the finding with the reasons therefor. Against the entries relating to each punishment the Jailer and Superintendent shall affix their initials as evidence of the correctness of the entries.
52	If any prisoner is guilty of any offence against prison-discipline which, by reason of his having frequently committed such offences or otherwise, in the opinion of the Superintendent, is not adequately punishable by the infliction of any punishment which he has power under this Act to award, the

(Contd.)

(Contd. Table)

Section	*Explanation*
	Superintendent may forward such prisoner to the Court of the District Magistrate or of any Magistrate of the first class [or Presidency Magistrate] having jurisdiction, together with a statement of the circumstances, and such Magistrate shall thereupon inquire into and try the charge so brought against the prisoner, and, upon conviction may sentence him to imprisonment which may extend to one year, such term to be in addition to any term for which such prisoner was undergoing imprisonment when he committed such offence, or may sentence him to any of the punishments enumerated in Section 46.
53	No punishment of whipping shall be inflicted in installments, or except in the presence of the Superintendent and Medical Officer or Medical Subordinate. Whipping shall be inflicted with a light ratan not less than half an inch in diameter on the buttocks, and in case of prisoners under the age of sixteen it shall be inflicted, in the way of school discipline, with a lighter ratan.
54	Every Jailer or officer of a prison subordinate to him who shall be guilty of any violation of duty or wilful breach or neglect of any rule or regulation or lawful order made by competent authority or who shall withdraw from the duties of his office without permission, or without having given previous notice in writing of his intention for the period of two months, or who shall wilfully overstay any leave granted to him, or who shall engage without authority in any employment other than his prison-duty, or who shall be guilty of cowardice, shall be liable, on conviction before a Magistrate, to fine not exceeding two hundred rupees, or to imprisonment for a period not exceeding three months, or to both. No person shall under this section be punished twice for the same offence.
	Chapter 12 [Miscellaneous]
55	A prisoner, when being taken to or from any prison in which he may be lawfully confined, or whenever he is working

(Contd.)

(Contd. Table)

Section	*Explanation*
	outside or is otherwise beyond the limits of any such prison in or under the lawful custody or control of a prison-officer belonging to such prison, shall be deemed to be in prison shall be subject to all the same incidents as if he were actually in prison.
56	Whenever the Superintendent considers it necessary (with reference either to the state of the prison or the character of the prisoners) for the safe custody of any prisoners that they should be confined in irons, he may, subject to such rules and instructions as may be laid down by the Inspector General with the sanction of the State Government, so confine them.
57	Prisoners under sentence of transportation may, subject to any rules made under Section [59], be confined in fetters for the first three months after admission to prison. Should the Superintendent consider it necessary, either for the safe custody of the prisoner himself or for any other reason, that fetters should be retained on any such prisoner for more than three months, he shall apply to the Inspector General for sanction to their retention for the period for which he considers their retention necessary, and the Inspector General may sanction such retention accordingly.
58	No prisoner shall be put in irons or under mechanical restraint by the Jailer of his own authority, except in case of urgent necessity, in which case notice thereof shall be forthwith given to the superintendent.
59	[The State Government may] make rules consistent with this Act— (1) defining the act which shall constitute prison-offences; (2) determining the classification of prison-offences into serious and minor offences; (3) fixing the punishments admissible under this Act which shall be awardable for commission of prison-offences or classes thereof; (4) declaring the circumstances in which acts constituting both a prison-offence and an offence under the Indian Penal Code (Act 45 of 1860) may or may not be dealt with as a prison-offence; (5) for the award of marks and the shortening of sentences; (6) regulating the use of arms against any prisoner or body

(Contd.)

(Contd. Table)

Section	*Explanation*
	of prisoners in the case of an outbreak or attempt to escape; (7) defining the circumstances and regulating the conditions under which prisoners in danger of death may be released; [(8) for the classification of prisons, and description and construction of wards, cells and other places of detention; (9) for the regulation by numbers, length or character of sentences, or otherwise, of the prisoners to be confined in each class of prisons]; (10) for the government of prisons and for the appointment of all officers appointed under this Act; (11) as to the food, bedding and clothing of criminal prisoners and of civil prisoners maintained otherwise than at their own cost; (12) for the employment, instruction and control of convicts within or without prisons; (13) for defining articles the introduction or removal of which into or out of prisons without due authority is prohibited; (14) for classifying and prescribing the forms of labour and regulating the periods of rest from labour; (15) for regulating the disposal of the proceeds of the employment of prisoners; (16) for regulating the confinement in fetters of prisoners sentenced to transportation; (17) for the classification and the separation of prisoners; (18) for regulating the confinement of convicted criminal prisoners under Section 28; (19) for the preparation and maintenance of history-tickets; (20) for the selection and appointment of prisoners as officers of prisons; (21) for rewards for good conduct; (22) for regulating the transfer of prisoners whose term of transportation or imprisonment is about to expire; subject, however, to the consent of the State Government of any other State to which a prisoner is to be transferred; (23) for the treatment, transfer and disposal of criminal lunatics or recovered criminal lunatics confined in prisons; (24) for regulating the transmission of appeals and petitions from prisoners and their communications with their friends; (25) for the appointment and guidance of visitors of prisons; (26) for extending any or all of the provisions of this Act and of the rules thereunder to subsidiary jails or special places of confinement appointed under Section 541

(Contd.)

(Contd. Table)

Section	*Explanation*
	of the Code of Criminal Procedure, 1882 (10 of 1882), and to the officers employed, and the prisoners confined, therein; (27) in regard to the admission, custody, employment, dieting, treatment and release of prisoners; and (28) generally for carrying into effect the purposes of this Act.
60	[*Power of Local Government to make rules*] Omitted by the Government of India (Adaptation of Indian Laws) Order, 1937.
61	Copies of rules, under [Section 59] so far as they affect the government of prisons, shall be exhibited, both in English and in the Vernacular, in some place to which all persons employed within a prison have access.

The Identification of Prisoners Act, 1920

Section	*Explanation*
1	This Act may be called the Identification of Prisoners Act, 1920
2	In this Act, unless there is anything repugnant in the subject or context, (a) "measurements" include finger-impressions and foot-point impressions; (b) "Police Officer" means an officer in charge of a police station, a police officer making an investigation under Chapter XIV of the Code of Criminal Procedure, 1898, or any other police officer not below the rank of Sub-Inspector; and (c) "prescribed" means prescribed by rules made under this Act.
3	Every person who has been, (a) convicted of any offence punishable with rigorous imprisonment for a term of one year or upwards, or of any offence which would render him liable to enhanced punishment on a subsequent conviction, or (b) ordered to give security for his good behaviour under Section 118 of the Code of Criminal Procedure, 1898, shall, if so required, allow his measurements and photograph to be taken by a Police Officer in the prescribed manner.
4	Any person who has been arrested in connection with an offence punishable with rigorous imprisonment for a term of

(Contd.)

(Contd. Table)

Section	*Explanation*
	one year or upwards shall, if so required by a police officer, allow his measurements to be taken in the prescribed manner.
5	If a Magistrate is satisfied that, for the purposes of any investigation or proceeding under the Code of Criminal Procedure, 1898, it is expedient to direct any person to allow his measurements or photograph to be taken, he may make an order to the effect, and in that case the person to whom the order relates shall be produced or shall attend at the time and place specified in the order and shall allow his measurements or photograph to be taken, as the case may be, by a police officer:
6	If any person who under this Act is required to allow his measurements or photograph to be taken resists or refuses to allow the taking of the same, it shall be lawful to use all means necessary to secure the taking thereof. Resistance to or refusal to allow taking of measurements or photograph under this Act shall be deemed to be an offence under Section 186 of the Indian Penal Code.
7	Where any person who, not having been previously convicted of an offence punishable with rigorous imprisonment for a term of one year or upwards, has had his measurements taken or has been photographed in accordance with the provisions of this Act is released without trial or discharged or acquitted by any court, all measurements and all photographs (both negatives and copies) so taken shall, unless the court or (in a case where such person is released without trial) the District Magistrate or Sub-divisional Officer for reasons to be recorded in writing otherwise directs, be destroyed or made over to him
8	The State Government may make rules for the purpose of carrying into effect the provisions of this Act. In particular and without prejudice to the generality of the foregoing provision, such rules may provide for, —(a) restriction on the taking of photographs of persons under Section 5; (b) the places at which measurements and photographs may be taken; (c) The nature of the measurements that may be taken; (d) the

(Contd.)

(Contd. Table)

Section	*Explanation*
	method in which any class or classes or measurements shall be taken; (e) the dress to be worn by a person when being photographed under Section 3; and (f) the preservation, safe custody, destruction and disposal of records of measurements and photographs.
9	No suit or other proceedings shall lie against any person for anything done, or intended to be done in good faith under this Act or under any rule made thereunder.

Vocational Training in Prisons

Training of prisoners in various vocational skills in the Prison Institution has received a lot of importance in almost all the States/UTs. These training programmes provide opportunities for the prison inmates to engage themselves in fruitful pursuits during the term of their sentence in jails. The training facilities available in the jails depend on the local conditions. The training of jail inmates in the vocational trades resulted in production of articles which have the market value. The number of jail inmates involved in various training programmes in the States/UTs of Punjab, Madhya Pradesh, Rajasthan, Delhi, Gujarat, Maharashtra, Uttar Pradesh, Jharkhand, Tamil Nadu and Bihar were 10,352, 9,944, 6,475, 5,666 4,714, 3,458, 3,346, 3,325, 3,010 and 2,678 respectively during the year 2013.[13]

Prison Litigation Reform Act

The Prison Litigation Reform Act (PLRA) is a USA federal law that was enacted in 1996. Congress enacted PLRA in response to a significant increase in prisoner litigation in the federal courts; the PLRA was designed to decrease the incidence of litigation within the court system. The most pointed provision of the PLRA in this context is the so-called "automatic stay" section, which states that a motion to terminate prospective relief "shall operate as a stay" of that relief during the period beginning 30 days after the filing of the motion (extendable to up to 90 days for "good cause") and ending when the court rules on the motion. Another way Congress tried to curb prison litigation was by setting up an "exhaustion" requirement.[14]

Prisoners' Rights in International Law

Prisoners' rights in international law are found in a number of international treaties. The Third Geneva Convention defines humanitarian protections for prisoners of war. The Third Geneva Convention, relative to the treatment of prisoners of war, is one of the four treaties of the Geneva Conventions. The Geneva Convention relative to the Treatment of Prisoners of War was first adopted in 1929, but significantly revised and replaced by the Third Geneva Convention of 1949. A prisoner of war is a person, whether combatant or non-combatant, who is held in custody by a belligerent power during or immediately after an armed conflict. The United States Military Code of Conduct was promulgated in 1955 via Executive Order 10631 under President Dwight D. Eisenhower to serve as a moral code for United States service members who have been taken prisoner. During World War I, about eight million men surrendered and were held in POW camps until the war ended. The Geneva Convention (1929) was signed at Geneva, July 27, 1929. Its official name is the Convention relative to the Treatment of Prisoners of War, Geneva July 27, 1929. It entered into force 19 June 1931.

Provisions concerning the treatment of prisoners of war are contained in the Hague Regulations of 1899 and 1907. In the course of World War I they revealed several deficiencies as well as a lack of precision. Such defects were partly overcome by special agreements made between belligerents in Berne in 1917 and 1918. In 1921, the International Red Cross Conference held at Geneva expressed the wish that a special convention on the treatment of prisoners of war be adopted.[15]

The International Covenant on Civil and Political Rights (ICCPR) remains the core international treaty on the protection of the rights of prisoners. India ratified the Covenant in 1979 and is bound to incorporate its provisions into domestic law and state practice. The International Covenant on Economic, Social and Cultural Rights (ICESR) states that prisoners have a right to the highest attainable standard of physical and mental health. The UN standard Minimum Rule also made it mandatory to provide separate residence for young and child prisoners from the adult prisoners. The modern prison in India originated with the Minute by TB Macaulay in 1835. A committee namely, Prison Discipline Committee, was appointed, which submitted its report on 1838. The committee recommended increased rigorousness of treatment while rejecting all humanitarian needs and reforms for the prisoners.[16]

Human Rights and Prisoner

International human rights law is binding on all States and their agents, including prison officials. All human beings are born free and equal in dignity and rights. The main aim of the prison authorities in their treatment of prisoners should be to encourage personal reformation and social rehabilitation. Vocational training shall be provided, especially for young prisoners. Education in prisons should be aimed at developing the whole person, taking account of prisoners' social, economic and cultural background. No one shall be subjected to arbitrary interference with his or her privacy, family, home or correspondence. All persons are equal before the law and are entitled, without discrimination, to equal protection of the law. Prisoners who are foreign nationals shall be allowed reasonable facilities to communicate with diplomatic representatives of their State. Women prisoners shall not suffer discrimination and shall be protected from all forms of violence or exploitation.

Women prisoners shall be supervised and searched only by female officers and staff. The death penalty shall not be imposed for crimes committed by persons below the age of eighteen and shall not be carried out on pregnant women, new mothers or persons who have become insane. All arrested or detained persons shall have access to a lawyer or other legal representative and adequate opportunity to communicate with that representative.[17] Prisoners and detainees in many local, state and federal facilities, including those run by private contractors, confront conditions that are abusive, degrading and dangerous. Soaring prison populations due to harsh sentencing laws which legislators have been reluctant to change and immigrant detention policies coupled with tight budgets have left governments unwilling to make the investments in staff and resources necessary to ensure safe and humane conditions of confinement.[18] Prisoners, just like all other people, are entitled to enjoy their human rights. Prisoners can make complaints to the Commission about human rights breaches and discrimination that occurs in prison.[19]

Conclusion

As of 31 December 2011, there are 1382 functioning jails in India having a total capacity to house 332,782 prisoners. As of the same date, there were 372,926 inmates in jails across in India. Males at 356,902 make up 95.7 per cent of prisoners while females at 16,024 represent 4.3 per cent. Two of every three persons incarcerated in

India have not yet been convicted of any crime, and Muslims are over-represented among such under trials, new official data show. Muslims, dalits and adivasis, three of the most vulnerable sections of Indian society make up more than half of India's prison population. There are many United Nations codified standards of treatment for prisoners across different economic, social and cultural contexts in a number of documents. Any violation of this right attracts the provisions of Article 14 of the Constitution, which enshrines right to equality and equal protection of law. In addition to this, the question of cruelty to prisoners is also dealt with, specifically by the Prison Act, 1894 and the Criminal Procedure Code.

References

1. Prison (2015), Retrieved from wikipedia.org/wiki/Prison
2. Prisons in India (2015), Retrieved from http://en.wikipedia.org/wiki/Prisons_in_India
3. Tihar jail, Retrieved from http://en.wikipedia.org/wiki/Tihar_Jail
4. *The Hindu* (Oct 30, 2014), Two-thirds of prison inmates in India are undertrials, Retrieved from http://www.thehindu.com/news/national/twothirds-of-prison-inmates-in-india-are-undertrials/article6545617.ece
5. *The Times of India* (Nov, 24, 2014), Muslims, dalits and tribals make up 53% of all prisoners in India, Retrieved from http://timesofindia.indiatimes.com/india/Muslims-dalits-and-tribals-make-up-53-of-all-prisoners-in-India/articleshow/45253329.cms
6. Prison Institutions, chapter 1, Retrieved from http://ncrb.gov.in/PSI-2013/CHAPTER-1.pdf
7. Types of prison inmates, chapter 3, Retrieved from http://ncrb.gov.in/PSI-2013/CHAPTER-3.pdf
8. Distribution of Convicted and Undertrials prisoners under IPC and SLL (Special and Local laws), chapter 4, Retrieved from http://ncrb.gov.in/PSI-2013/CHAPTER-4.pdf
9. Deaths in jails, chapter 9, Retrieved from http://ncrb.gov.in/PSI-2013/CHAPTER-9.pdf
10. Rights of prisoners, Retrieved from http://www.nimhans.kar.nic.in/prison/chapter_10-r_he_prisoners.pdf
11. Rights of prisoners, Retrieved from http://www.nimhans.kar.nic.in/prison/chapter_10-r_he_prisoners.pdf
12. The Code of Criminal Procedure (2015), Retrieved from http://en.wikipedia.org/wiki/Code_of_Criminal_Procedure,_1973
13. Vocational training in prisons, chapter 8, Retrieved from http://ncrb.gov.in/PSI-2013/CHAPTER-8.pdf

14. Prison Litigation Reform Act (2015), Retrieved from http://en.wikipedia.org/wiki/Prison_Litigation_Reform_Act
15. See https://www.icrc.org/ihl/INTRO/305?OpenDocument
16. Prisons in India: An overview of reforms and current situation, Retrieved from http://www.nimhans.kar.nic.in/prison/chapter_2.pdf
17. Human rights and prisons: A Pocketbook of International Human Rights Standards for Prison Officials (2005), Retrieved from http://www.ohchr.org/Documents/Publications/training11Add3en.pdf
18. See http://www.hrw.org/united-states/us-program/prison-and-detention-conditions
19. See https://www.humanrights.gov.au/our-work/rights-and-freedoms/projects/prisoners-rights

14

Reproductive Rights

"Social media are a catalyst for the advancement of everyone's rights. It's where we're reminded that we're all human and all equal. It's where people can find and fight for a cause, global or local, popular or specialised, even when there are hundreds of miles between them."

- Queen Rania of Jordan

Introduction

Rights function to protect the vulnerable from the powerful. The twentieth century has seen an expansion in the social acceptance of women as legitimate bearers of human rights in many countries in the world.[1] In the human reproductive process, two kinds of sex cells, or gametes, are involved. The male gamete, or sperm, and the female gamete, the egg or ovum, meet in the female's reproductive system to create a new individual.[2] Humans are sexual, meaning a male and a female are needed to reproduce. Each is equipped with specific organs capable of producing specific cells to procreate. Together with a woman's reproductive organs, sexual intercourse can lead to the reproduction of human life. As a man ages, sexual function typically diminishes.[3]

Human rights violations are common in both natural and man-made crisis situations. States are responsible for protecting the human rights of their citizens, but during crises, states may be temporarily incapable of providing protection (in the case of a natural disaster, for example), or may be failed (in the case of an armed conflict). The human rights of adolescents, including vulnerable sub-groups, are protected under several declarations and conventions in international law. Adolescents are entitled to rights under the Convention on the Rights of the Child until age 18.[4]

What are Reproductive Rights?

Reproductive rights are legal rights and freedoms relating to reproduction and reproductive health. Reproductive rights may include some or all of the following: the right to legal and safe abortion; the right to birth control; freedom from sterilisation and contraception; the right to access good-quality reproductive healthcare; and the right to education and access in order to make free and informed reproductive choices.[5] It usually include the right to control one's reproductive functions, the right to access quality reproductive healthcare, and the right to education and access in order to make reproductive choices free from coercion, discrimination, and violence.[6]

Reproductive rights were clarified and endorsed internationally in the Cairo Consensus that emerged from the 1994 International Conference on Population and Development. This constellation of rights, embracing fundamental human rights established by earlier treaties, was reaffirmed at the Beijing Conference and various international and regional agreements since, as well as in many national laws.[7] The World Health Organisation defines reproductive rights as *"resting on the recognition of the basic right of all couples and individuals to decide freely and responsibly the number, spacing, and timing of their children and to have the information and means to do so, and the right to attain the highest standard of sexual and reproductive health."*[8]

Importance of Reproductive Rights

Good health is essential to leading a productive and fulfilling life, and the right of all women to control all aspects of their health, in particular their own fertility, is basic to empowerment. Neglect of women's reproductive rights severely limits their opportunities in public and private life, including opportunities for education, economic and political empowerment. The ability of women to control their own fertility forms an important basis for the enjoyment of other rights.[9]

Reproductive rights are a subset of sexual and reproductive health and rights. In the September 2005 World Summit, the goal of universal access to reproductive health was endorsed at the highest level. Reproductive rights are recognised as valuable ends in themselves, and essential to the enjoyment of other fundamental rights. Special emphasis has been given to the reproductive rights of women and adolescent girls, and to the importance of sex education and reproductive health programmes.[10]

Reproductive Rights in India

India began grappling with the magnitude of its population even before it became independent in 1947; it was labelled a crisis in the 1970s when the government of Indira Gandhi carried out mandatory sterilisations. But since those dark days, the country has emerged as a leader in the field, adopting the language of "reproductive health and rights. In the words of the World Health Organisation, that India is committed to ensuring its people have "the capability to reproduce and the freedom to decide if, when and how often to do so" – and that their decision be "free of discrimination, coercion and violence."

China's one-child campaign, adopted in 1979, forced women to have abortions if they conceived again without state approval, or fined couples heavily, especially in urban areas. India's policy involves no such direct punishments, but its impact can be harsh in a place such as Kamrora. Parents with more than two children are denied access to everything from a subsidy for babies delivered in hospital and school nursaries to the right to run for political office. Many of the more punitive policies in place today have been set by state governments, but the two-child norm also applies to a number of benefits, such as nutritional support for pregnant women, that come from the national government.[11]

In India, the Medical Termination of Pregnancy (MTP) Act made abortion legal in 1972, and the legality of abortion has not been in contention. The stated policy and actual implementation of the government family planning programme present a set of contradictions with regard to women's rights and choice in India. Since ICPD 1994, the Indian government has attempted to move from a longstanding policy of achieving specified targets on contraceptive use to greater emphasis on individual need and quality of care, but with uneven and limited success.[12] The Indian perspective on reproductive rights has had to additionally take account of several other inequalities and contradictions in society. On one hand, traditional feudal society has sought to regulate every aspect of women's lives. Religion, caste and cultural values have played important roles in defining and controlling women's fertility.[13]

Maternal and Child Health Policy (MCH), Reproductive and Child Health Policy (RCH), the National Rural Health Mission (NRHM) and the Janani Suraksha Yojana (JSY) have all fallen short in targeting basic gender prejudice and addressing gender-specific needs in health service provision. The RCH policy was launched in 1997 (Ninth Five Year Plan) to incorporate the recommendations of the ICPD. The focus of RCH policy was on participative and community needs-based assessments and its remit included a wide range of services. For the first time, men were also involved as equal partners in taking responsible decisions in regard to family size and the health of the mother and child.[14]

Early pregnancy in India, almost all of which takes place within marriage, is the major cause of poor reproductive health among female adolescents. Girls under 18 are two-five times more likely to die during pregnancy or childbirth. Adolescent pregnant mothers, who are often already poorly nourished before becoming pregnant, run a high obstetric risk for premature delivery, giving birth to a low birth weight baby, prolonged and obstructed labour, and severe intrapartum and postpartum haemorrhage.[15] India's response to the ICPD PoA and MDGs and the progress in the direction of meeting targets set by the MDGs needs to be analysed in the context of the history of Indian population and family welfare programmes. India was the first country to have a national government supported family planning/ welfare programme beginning from 1952 and till the late 1990s, i.e. post-ICPD; the Indian government has focused on sexual and reproductive health mainly through the population control policies.[16]

Reproductive Rights of Women

The United Nations Population Fund and the World Health Organisation advocate for reproductive rights with a primary emphasis on women's rights. The reproductive rights of women are advanced in the context of the right to freedom from discrimination and the social and economic status of women.[17] The mainstream reproductive rights movement has roots in a broader women's rights movement that advocated for women's equality, articulating reproductive and sexual freedom as the means to self-determination, full participation in society, and emancipation from patriarchal control.[18] One of the most challenging goals of the feminist movement has been protecting the rights of women over their own bodies. Reproductive rights, which run the gamut from the right to abstinence, birth control, abortion, and the right to carry a pregnancy to term, must still be protected in the courts.[19]

Gender-based violence violates human rights and affects sexual and reproductive health (SRH). Widely prevalent and socially silenced in most Asian-Pacific countries, GBV is increasingly recognised as a major public health concern in the region. All human rights, which are universal, indivisible and interdependent, make the State responsible for guaranteeing SRH and individual choices regarding reproduction and sexuality.[20] Feminist analysis of patriarchal control over reproduction by the women's movement all over the world has spearheaded individual and collective attempts to fight against it at all levels. At the same time, women's groups in Third World nations have asserted that the debate on women's reproductive rights must account for the fact that reproduction is only one aspect of women's physiology and lives, and cannot be viewed in isolation.[21]

Men's Reproductive Rights

Men's reproductive rights have been claimed by various organisations; both for issues of reproductive health, and other rights related to sexual reproduction.[22] Men should be able to choose whether to have a woman receive an abortion, because that embryo/fetus there is just as much his as it is hers. Reproductive rights are two-fold: women and men. It is essentially unamerican and sexist to offer repro rights to women and not to men.[23]

Adolescents' Reproductive Rights

While adolescents have the same reproductive rights as adults, they face more obstacles to enjoying those rights. Adolescents' age-related low social status and lack of autonomy can make them vulnerable to a host of rights violations. The rights to information and education also provide direct support for adolescents' access to sexual and reproductive health information. Access to reproductive healthcare is crucial for the health and safety of adolescents. Adolescents are increasingly at risk of contracting HIV/AIDS, as well as other STIs. They also face a heightened risk of maternal mortality. To prevent unwanted pregnancy and exposure to STIs, adolescents should have access to reproductive healthcare, including family planning services. Adolescents are particularly vulnerable to violations of their physical integrity through sexual violence and abuse within families, schools, or other institutions.[24]

In order to ensure that adolescents develop into adults whose lives reflect their full potential, governmental and non-governmental organisations must support adolescents' healthy sexual and reproductive development.[25] Despite young people's disproportionate burden of poor sexual and reproductive health outcomes and the powerful economic and development rationales for investing in adolescents and youth, there are currently limited programmatic efforts intended for young people. Today's approximately three billion young people represent three billion assets for sustained economic growth and development. Kenya and Bangladesh provide potential models for how a youth focus can be successfully incorporated into country strategies. Mali, Malawi, and Ethiopia's strategies include explicit mention of young people. Promote multisectoral linkages to comprehensively address the needs of young people, particularly young girls.[26]

There is growing recognition of the importance of addressing the sexual and reproductive health and rights of adolescents and young people.[27] The Millennium Development Goals report published by United Nations in 2011 reiterated the point that: Reaching adolescents is critical to improving maternal health and achieving other Millennium Development Goals. In April 2012, the 45th session of the Commission on Population and Development, on the theme Adolescents and Youth, adopted a landmark resolution urging government and development partners to strengthen health systems and ensure that they prioritise universal access to sexual and reproductive information and health-care services.[28]

Birth Control Movement

Birth control is the practice of taking steps to prevent pregnancy or childbirth as a result of sexual activity. Birth control is often used synonymously with contraception. Easy access to birth control, including its legalisation has led to women being able to more directly and consistently participate in society, both intellectually and economically, and remains a critical aspect of women's overall equality and individual independence.[29]

The birth control movement in the United States was a social reform campaign from 1914 to around 1945 that aimed to increase the availability of contraception in the U.S. through education and legalisation. The movement began in 1914 when a group of political radicals in New York City. Legal victories in the 1930s continued to weaken anti-contraception laws. The practice of birth control was common throughout the US prior to 1914, when the movement to legalise contraception began. Contraception was legal in the United States throughout most of the 19th century, but in the 1870s a social purity movement grew in strength, aimed at outlawing vice in general, and prostitution and obscenity in particular.[30]

Abortion was legal in America until the Second half of the 19th century. The first statutory abortion regulation, passed in Connecticut in 1821, was a poison control measure designed to protect women – not to criminalise abortion or to restrict abortion access. A campaign to outlaw abortion, led by the leader of the newly formed American Medical Association (AMA), began in the 1850s. The Comstock Act, passed in 1873, made it illegal to send anything related to birth control or abortion through the mail. Public outrage at abortion laws began to grow in the 1960s and the movement to decriminalise abortion became one of the fastest growing movements in American history. Since 1973, hundreds of state laws have been passed restricting access to abortion services.[31]

Sexual and Reproductive Rights

Sex refers to the biological characteristics that define humans as female or male. Sexuality is a central aspect of being human throughout life and encompasses sex, gender identities and roles, sexual orientation, eroticism, pleasure, intimacy and reproduction. Sexual health is a state of physical, emotional, mental and social well-being in relation to sexuality; it is not merely the absence of disease, dysfunction or infirmity. Sexual health is a state of physical, emotional, mental and social well-being in relation to sexuality; it is not merely the absence of disease, dysfunction or infirmity.[32] Sexual and reproductive health and rights is the concept of human rights applied to sexuality and reproduction. It is a combination of four fields that in some contexts are more or less distinct from each other, but less so or not at all in other contexts.

The World Health Organisation defines sexual health as: *"Sexual health is a state of physical, mental and social well-being in relation to sexuality. It requires a positive and respectful approach to sexuality and sexual relationships, as well as the possibility of having pleasurable and safe sexual experiences, free of coercion, discrimination and violence."* The Platform for Action from the 1995 Beijing Conference on Women established that human rights include the right of women freely and without coercion, violence or discrimination, to have control over and make decisions concerning their own sexuality, including their own sexual and reproductive health.[33]

Sexual and reproductive health rights including access to sexual and reproductive healthcare and information, as well as autonomy in sexual and reproductive decision-making are human rights; they are universal, indivisible, and undeniable.[34] Reproductive health is a state of complete physical, mental and social well-being and not merely the absence of disease or infirmity, in all matters relating to the reproductive system and to its functions and processes. Reproductive health, therefore, implies that people are able to have a satisfying and safe sex life and that they have the capability to reproduce and the freedom to decide if, when and how often to do so.[35] Sexual and reproductive health and rights can be understood (in theory) as the right for all, whether young or old, women, men or transgender, heterosexual, gay, lesbian or bisexual, HIV positive or negative, to make choices regarding their own sexuality and reproduction, providing these respect the rights of others to bodily integrity.[36] Men's reproductive rights include issues such as false paternity claims or paternity fraud, adoption rights, abortion, rights over frozen embryos, choice for men, etc.[37]

Reproductive Rights are Human Rights

Reproductive rights are very much a part of human rights and are the legal rights and freedoms relating to reproduction and reproductive health. The World Health Organisation (WHO) defines reproductive rights as follows: *"Reproductive rights rest on the recognition of the basic right of all couples and individuals to decide freely and responsibly the number, spacing and timing of their children and to have the information and means to do so, and the right to attain the highest standard of sexual and reproductive health. They also include the right of all to make decisions concerning reproduction free of discrimination, coercion and violence."*[38] Reproductive rights began to develop as a subset of human rights at the United Nation's 1968 International Conference on Human Rights.

The International Conference on Population and Development (ICPD) held in Cairo in 1994 marked the acceptance of a new paradigm in addressing human reproduction and health. For the first time, there was a clear focus on the needs of individuals and on the empowerment of women, and the emergence of an evolving discourse about the connection between human rights and health, linking new conceptions of health to the struggle for social justice and respect for human dignity.[39] The Universal Declaration of Human Rights describes the family as the natural and fundamental unit of society. It follows that any choice and decision with regard to the size of the family must inevitably rest with the family itself, and cannot be made by anyone else. But this right of parents to free choice will remain illusory unless they are aware of the alternatives open to them.[40]

According to the 1994 Cairo Programme of Action "*Reproductive rights embrace certain human rights that are already recognised in national laws, international human rights documents and other relevant United Nations consensus documents. These rights rest on the recognition of the basic right of all couples and individuals to decide freely and responsibly the number, spacing and timing of their children and to have the information and means to do so, and the right to attain the highest standard of sexual and reproductive health. It also includes the right of all to make decisions concerning reproduction free of discrimination, coercion and violence as expressed in human rights documents. In the exercise of this right, they should take into account the needs of their living and future children and their responsibilities towards the community.*"[41]

The interconnection of human rights is reflected in every element of SRH and the rights, policies and funding required for ensuring universal access to SRH. Individuals may be unable to access comprehensive SRH services as a result of poverty, insufficient healthcare or transportation infrastructure, poor governance, inadequate training of healthcare workers or access to reliable supplies and supply chains, and a range of other barriers.[42] Embrace certain human rights that are already recognised in national laws, international humans rights documents and other consensus documents. These rights rest on the recognition of the basic rights for all couples and individuals to decide freely and responsibly the number, spacing and timing of their children and to have the information and means to do so, and the right to the highest attainable standard of sexual and reproductive health.[43] The concept of reproductive rights began to develop as a part of human rights at the United Nation's International Conference on Human Rights in 1968. This resulted in the 'Proclamation of Teheran' which was the first international document to recognise one of these rights. In 1975, the UN International Women's Year Conference also echoed the Proclamation of Teheran.[44]

Conclusion

Reproductive rights are legal rights and freedoms relating to reproduction and reproductive health. Reproductive rights may include some or all of the following: the right to legal and safe abortion; the right to birth control; freedom from sterilisation and contraception; the right to access good-quality reproductive healthcare; and the right to education and access in order to make free and informed reproductive choices. In India, the Medical Termination of Pregnancy (MTP) Act made abortion legal in 1972, and the legality of abortion has not been in contention. The stated policy and actual implementation of the government family planning programme present a set of contradictions with regard to women's rights and choice in India. Maternal and Child Health Policy (MCH), Reproductive and Child Health Policy (RCH), the National Rural Health Mission (NRHM) and the Janani Suraksha Yojana (JSY) have all fallen short in targeting basic gender prejudice and addressing gender-specific needs in health service provision. The reproductive rights of women are advanced in the context of the right to freedom from discrimination and the social and economic status of women.

While adolescents have the same reproductive rights as adults, they face more obstacles to enjoying those rights. In order to ensure that adolescents develop into adults whose lives reflect their full potential, governmental and non-governmental organisations must support adolescents' healthy sexual and reproductive development. Sexual and reproductive health rights including access to sexual and reproductive healthcare and information, as well as autonomy in sexual and reproductive decision-making are human rights; they are universal, indivisible, and undeniable.

References

1. Politics and Fertility: The Evolution of Sexual and Reproductive Rights.
2. See http://www.healthline.com/human-body-maps/male-reproductive-organs
3. See http://www.healthline.com/human-body-maps/male-reproductive-organs
4. Adolescent Sexual and Reproductive Health Toolkit for Humanitarian Settings, Retrieved from http://www.unfpa.org/sites/default/files/pub-pdf/UNFPA_ASRHtoolkit_english.pdf
5. Reproductive rights (2015), Retrieved from http://en.wikipedia.org/wiki/Reproductive_rights
6. Reproductive rights (2015), Retrieved from http://rationalwiki.org/wiki/Reproductive_rights

7. Supporting the Constellation of Reproductive Rights - See more at: http://www.unfpa.org/resources/supporting-constellation-reproductive-rights#sthash.Qs4qndB4.dpuf
8. See https://athefist.wordpress.com/2014/01/17/aethics-male-reproductive-rights/
9. See http://countryoffice.unfpa.org/india/drive/Upholdmyreproductiverights.pdf
10. Supporting the Constellation of Reproductive Rights - See more at: http://www.unfpa.org/resources/supporting-constellation-reproductive-rights#sthash.Qs4qndB4.dpuf
11. Stephanie Nolen, Why India's acclaim for protecting reproductive rights rings hollow, Retrieved from http://www.theglobeandmail.com/news/world/why-indias-acclaim-for-protecting-reproductive-rights-rings-hollow/article12429763/?page=all
12. Anju Malhotra et al. Realising Reproductive Choice and Rights Abortion and Contraception in India, Retrieved from http://www.icrw.org/sites/default/files/publications/Realising-Reproductive-Rights-and-Choice-Abortion-and-Contraception-India.pdf
13. Reproductive rights in the Indian Context: An Introduction, Retrieved from https://sites.google.com/site/saheliorgsite/health/reproductive-rights-in-the-indian-context
14. Sexual and Reproductive Health Rights under the Reproductive and Child Health Policy: Compromising Women's Dignity, Retrieved from http://www.clraindia.org/include/CLRA%20RCH%20Booklet-1.pdf
15. Adolescent Sexual and Reproductive Health and Rights in India, Retrieved from http://files.creaworld.org/files/adolescent_working_paper.pdf
16. Expert Group Meeting Structural and policy constraints in achieving the MDGs for women and girls.
17. Reproductive rights (2015), Retrieved from http://en.wikipedia.org/wiki/Reproductive_rights
18. Hooton: Symposium: A Broader Vision of the Reproductive Rights Movement, Retrieved from http://digitalcommons.wcl.american.edu/cgi/viewcontent.cgi?article=1284&context=jgspl
19. See http://civilliberty.about.com/od/gendersexuality/tp/Reproductive-Rights-History-United-States-Timeline.htm
20. Gender-based Violence and Sexual and Reproductive Health and Rights: Looking at the Health Sector Response in the Asia-Pacific Region, Retrieved from http://arrow.org.my/publications/AFC/v17n2.pdf
21. See http://www.sacw.net/Wmov/saheli_reproductivehealth.pdf
22. Reproductive rights (2015), Retrieved from http://en.wikipedia.org/wiki/Reproductive_rights

23. See http://www.debate.org/opinions/male-reproductive-rights-should-men-have-some-reproductive-rights-with-their-unborn-children
24. Adolescents' Reproductive Rights, Retrieved from https://www.k4health.org/sites/default/files/pub_bo_GG_adolescents.pdf
25. Adolescent Sexual and Reproductive Health and Rights (2002), Retrieved from http://www.ipas.org/~/media/Files/Ipas%20Publications/AdolSexRepoRights.ashx
26. Promoting the Sexual and Reproductive Rights and Health of Adolescents and Youth, Retrieved from http://www.pathfinder.org/publications-tools/pdfs/Promoting-the-sexual-and-reproductive-rights-and-health-of-Adolescents-and-Youth.pdf
27. See http://www.who.int/reproductivehealth/topics/adolescence/en/
28. See http://www.who.int/reproductivehealth/topics/adolescence/background/en/
29. Birth control (2015), Retrieved from http://rationalwiki.org/wiki/Contraception
30. Birth control movement in the United States (2015), Retrieved from http://en.wikipedia.org/wiki/Birth_control_movement_in_the_United_States
31. A Brief History of Reproductive Rights, Retrieved from http://www.fwhc.org/herstory-repro-rights.htm
32. Gender and human rights, Retrieved from http://www.who.int/reproductivehealth/topics/gender_rights/sexual_health/en/
33. Sexual and reproductive health and rights (2015), Retrieved from http://en.wikipedia.org/wiki/Sexual_and_reproductive_health_and_rights
34. Sexual and Reproductive Health Rights, Retrieved from http://www.amnestyusa.org/pdfs/SexualReproductiveRightsFactSheet.pdf
35. Reproductive rights and reproductive health, Retrieved from http://www.iisd.ca/cairo/program/p07002.html
36. Vicci Tallis (2012), Sexual and reproductive health and rights: a useful discourse for feminist analysis and activism? See http://www.osisa.org/buwa/regional/sexual-and-reproductive-health-and-rights-useful-discourse-feminist-analysis-and-activ
37. Reproductive right, Retrieved from http://ncfm.org/2009/01/issues/mens-reproductive-rights/
38. Sayeda Urooj, Reproductive Rights of Women: Issues and Concerns, Retrieved from http://www.isidelhi.org.in/wl/article/sayeda1804.pdf
39. See http://www.un.org/womenwatch/daw/csw/shalev.htm
40. See http://www.un.org/en/development/desa/population/theme/rights/
41. Reproductive rights in India, Retrieved from http://www.hrln.org/hrln/reproductive-rights/433-reproductive-rights-in-india.html

42. Sexual and Reproductive Health Rights, Retrieved from http://www.amnestyusa.org/pdfs/SexualReproductiveRightsFactSheet.pdf
43. http://www.choiceforyouth.org/information/sexual-and-reproductive-health-and-rights/official-definitions-of-sexual-and-reproductiv
44. Sayeda Urooj, Reproductive Rights of Women: Issues and Concerns, Retrieved from http://www.isidelhi.org.in/wl/article/sayeda1804.pdf

15

Digital Rights

"The human brain works as a binary computer and can only analyse the exact information-based zeros and ones (or black and white). Our heart is more like a chemical computer that uses fuzzy logic to analyse information that can't be easily defined in zeros and ones."

- Naveen Jain

Introduction

Digital data is using discrete values. Digital data, in information theory and information systems, are discrete, discontinuous representations of information or works, as contrasted with continuous or analog signals which behave in a continuous manner, or represent information using a continuous function. A symbol input device usually consists of a group of switches that are polled at regular intervals to see which switches are switched.[1] Digital media are any media that are encoded in a machine-readable format. Combined with the Internet and personal computing, digital media has caused disruption in publishing, journalism, entertainment, education, commerce and politics.[2] Digital electronics are electronics that represent signals by discrete bands of analog levels, rather than by continuous ranges.[3] Some information is intrinsically digital, so it is natural to process and manipulate it using purely digital techniques. Examples are numbers and words.[4]

Digital rights are rights given to each individual that is surfing the web. In addition to that the rights are always broken by hackers and other people that break the law. These hackers take advantage of technology and use it to hack into e-mails, credit card numbers, and get free subscriptions.[5] The order of the labs follows most electronic textbooks. The first six labs cover the fundamental circuits of gates, encoders, binary addition, D-latches, ring counters, and JK flip-flops. Many of the VIs are suitable for both classroom demonstration and laboratory exploration. The order of the labs follows most electronic textbooks. The first six labs cover the fundamental circuits of gates, encoders, binary addition, D-latches, ring counters, and JK flip-flops. Many of the VIs are suitable for both classroom demonstration and laboratory exploration.[6]

What are Digital Rights?

The term digital rights describe the human rights that allow individuals to access, use, create, and publish digital media or to access and use computers, other electronic devices, or communications networks. A number of human rights have been identified as relevant with regard to the Internet. These include: freedom of expression, data protection and privacy and freedom of association. Digital rights refer to the relationship between copyrighted digital works (such as film, music and art) and user permissions and rights related to computers, networks and electronic devices. Digital rights also refer to the access and control of digital information.[7]

Importance of Digital Rights

The purpose of DRM is to prevent unauthorised redistribution of digital media and restrict the ways consumers can copy content they've purchased. DRM products were developed in response to the rapid increase in online piracy of commercially marketed material, which proliferated through the widespread use of peer-to-peer file exchange programmes.[8] Essential to organisations, DRM provides intellectual property (IP) protection and is primarily applied by entertainment industries and enterprises. DRM's access control halts copyright violations of music, films, TV shows, PC games and similar Internet entertainment.[9]

Typically, a DRM system protects intellectual property by either encrypting the data so that it can only be accessed by authorised users or marking the content with a digital watermark or similar method so that the content cannot be freely distributed.[10] DRM system manages the appropriate use of content. The major functionalities of this system are numerous. They include facilitating the packaging of raw content into an appropriate form for easy distribution and tracking, protecting the content for tamper-proof transmission, protecting content from unauthorised use, and enabling specifications of suitable rights, which define the modes of content consumption.[11]

DRM ensures that their digital content is only used by those who have paid for it and have thus gained the right a DRM system protects intellectual property by either encrypting the data so that it can only be accessed by authorised users or marking the content with a digital watermark, so that the content can not be freely distributed.[12]

Digital Rights and Responsibilities

The definition of digital rights and responsibilities is having the right and freedom to use all types of digital technology while using the technology in an acceptable and appropriate manner. As a user of digital technology, you also have the right to privacy and the freedom of personal expression. The illegally downloading of music and videos has also been an ongoing problem in our society. Students need to understand that this is not only disrespectful to the artists and producing companies, but it is against the law. As teachers, we too should respect the works of others, such a using YouTube or teacher tube videos within our webpage's; they need to be cited properly on our webpage's so credit given.[13]

Digital Rights and Responsibilities are the *"privileges and freedom extended to all digital technology users, and the behavioural expectations that come with them"*. Using technology responsibly involves an understanding of many issues. Most importantly, parents and educators want students to be safe when using technology. Students must understand the rules for technology use within the school and at home so that they can have safe experiences online. Additionally, students must learn how to act ethically and legally. Students should be taught how to use material they find online appropriately. Cyber bullying and threatening behaviours are two other major issues related to this topic of digital rights and responsibilities.[14]

The Acceptable Use Policy is a set of rules that are applied by networks and website owners that put limitations on ways in which the website or network is used. AUP's at schools describe what students are allowed to do while working on the computers that the school provides.[15] America started a new campaign against cyber bullying. Most of the teenagers spend a lot of time on a cell phone or instant messenger chatting with friends and uploading photos, videos, and music to websites. Cyber bullying is online bullying, and happens when teens use the Internet, cell phones, or other devices to send or post-text or images intended to hurt or embarrass another person. It is a problem that affects almost half of all American teens.[16]

The term "digital citizenship" has become the new catch phrase for identifying digital rights and responsibilities. The focus of digital citizenship is how Internet users should manage online relationships, provide personal protection from online attacks and show accountability for posted online viewpoints and opinions. The following are five of the personal responsibilities that is associated with becoming a productive digital citizen: Cyber bullying, Internet safety, Netiquette, Reporting Offenders, and Digital Law.[17]

Digital Rights: Global Perspectives

Over 500 leading authors across the world, including five Nobel laureates, signed an open letter challenging the global mass surveillance of Internet and telephone communications by the US National Security Agency, describing the Agency's snooping as a "theft" of data and a force undermining democratic principles. Hailing from 81 different nations the authors, including Margaret Atwood, J.M. Coetzee, Orhan Pamuk, and Günter Grass called on the UN to create an international bill of digital rights that would enshrine the protection of civil rights in the Internet age. They argued that the capacity of intelligence agencies to spy on millions of people's digital communications is turning everyone into potential suspects, with worrying implications for the way societies work. The debate also comes as privacy advocates within the US have pressed for surveillance reform and the US Congress has grilled intelligence community bosses over whether any violations of laws occurred.[18]

Back in 1995, Bill Clinton's copyright tsar Bruce Lehman - a copyright lawyer, late of Microsoft - wrote a white paper proposing a new regulatory framework for the internet. It was bonkers. Under Lehman's plan, every copy of every work would have to be explicitly permitted and a license fee collected. Lehman submitted his paper to then-Vice President Al Gore, who was holding hearings on the demilitarisation of the internet - the National Information Infrastructure (NII) or "information superhighway" hearings. In the USA, the First Amendment of the Constitution gives broad protection to free expression, and prohibits government from making laws that abridge Americans' free speech rights. In 1997's Bernstein vs. United States, another US appeals court found that code was protected expression.[19]

Digital Rights in India

The Copyright (Amendment) Act 2012 has introduced some digital rights management (DRM) provisions in the Indian Copyright law. While a comparative analysis of the new DRM provisions with similar legislation in the US and the EU shows a relatively better approach that reduces the detrimental effects posed by DRM provisions.[20] The rapid advances in digital technology have meant that digitised content is now readily available to most people. However, content owners and commercial stakeholders face a constant battle to protect their intellectual property and commercial rights.[21] At present, India is not a signatory to the WIPO Internet Treaties, but the government has proposed amendments to the extant legislation to incorporate Digital Rights Management (DRM) as enshrined in them. Conventionally the western entertainment industry has viewed DRM as an important tool to combat piracy pervasive on the internet.[22]

There have been no provisions in the Indian Copyright Act, 1957 which deal with Digital Rights Management (DRM). The Copyright (Amendment) Bill, 2010 is, however, poised to change this: it includes three sections [viz. Sections 2(xa), 65A and 65B] which deal with DRM. The provisions in the Copyright (Amendment) Bill which deal with DRM are soporific. And to the average person, they seem to mean nothing. They are, nonetheless, provisions which are industry-oriented. They could control the locations (i.e. countries) in which a copyrighted work is enjoyed consider a DVD of a film which is playable in just one continent.[23]

In the Indian context, the decision to introduce DRM-protection measures has been justified by the government which reasons that DRM-protection was necessary to bring India's copyright law in line with WIPO's Copyright (WCT) and Performances and Phonograms (WPPT) treaties.[24] The digital rights for the Indian Premier League (IPL), the T20 tournament organised by the Board for Control of Cricket in India (BCCI), for the years 2015, 2016 and 2017, have gone to Novi Digital Entertainment Pvt. Ltd, a subsidiary of Star India Pvt Ltd. The BCCI had set a cumulative reserve price of Rs 120 crores for this time period, and says that they received bids from Times Internet Ltd*, which owns Cricbuzz and video service Box TV (we checked, and it's still around), Multi Screen Media (which owns video service Sony Liv) and Novi Digital. Star India streams sports on StarSports.com, and other content on HotStar.com.[25]

At present India is one of the fastest growing economies in the world especially in ICTE area. As India is enriched with a rich cultural heritage, a huge potential is foreseen as far as copyright is concerned. A main benefit of DRM conferred by the law is that it can be enforced by the copyright holders of digital media or software themselves through technological means for preventing access and infringement of copyright.[26] Digital rights management protected content comes with an associated license that defines your rights to use the content.[27]

Digital Right Management includes techniques which have been developed to control duplication, modification and distribution of original works. The authors or the creators of the original works contend that DRM techniques are necessary in order to protect their interest by preventing free and unauthorised copying and distribution of their work.[28] Encryption Schemes allow creators to prevent any unauthorised access to their original work. Digital Watermarks are the best techniques that help authors to trace the source of a work and any unauthorised duplication or distribution of their original work. There are other various technological protection measures by way of which the infringement of copyright work can be prevented and the interest of the authors can be secured.[29]

Rights to Internet Access

National constitutions are supposed to enshrine fundamental rights for everyone and for generations. Such documents are also products of moments in time and reflect perceptions of life in those moments.[30] The right to Internet access is the view that all people must be able to access the Internet in order to exercise and enjoy their rights to Freedom of expression and opinion and other fundamental human rights. The right to Internet access is closely linked to the right of freedom of speech which can be seen to encompass freedom of expression too. Implementing the right to Internet access can be accomplished by requiring that universal service providers provide a mandatory minimum connection capability to all desiring home users in the regions of a country they serve. The Internet as a whole is seen as a medium which is outside of any one State's jurisdiction, while portions of the Internet are subject to laws and regulations of the countries in which they operate.[31]

A United Nations report said that disconnecting people from the internet is a human rights violation and against international law. The report, by the United Nations Special Rapporteur on the Promotion and Protection of the Right to Freedom of Opinion and Expression, comes the same day an internet-monitoring firm detected that two thirds of Syria's internet access has abruptly gone dark, in what is likely a government response to unrest in that country.[32] The UN report overwhelmingly supports the internet as a communication platform, a boon to all democratic societies, but it also warns how the internet's unique architecture threatens power brokers in those societies: *"The vast potential and benefits of the Internet are rooted in its unique characteristics, such as its speed, worldwide reach and relative anonymity. At the same time, these distinctive features of the Internet that enable individuals to disseminate information in "real time" and to mobilise people has also created fear amongst Governments and the powerful. This has led to increased restrictions on the Internet through the use of increasingly sophisticated technologies to block content, monitor and identify activists and critics, criminalisation of legitimate expression, and adoption of restrictive legislation to justify such measures."*[33]

Human rights come from the need to protect individuals from the arbitrary power of the state. Human rights are "international norms that help to protect all people everywhere from severe political, legal, and social abuses."[34] A survey of 26 countries conducted by the BBC in March 2010 found that nearly four out of five people (79 per cent, to be exact) believe that access to the Internet is a "fundamental human right." Some countries have taken things one step further. Estonia passed a law in 2000, for example, that declared access to the Internet a basic human right. In 2009, France followed. Legislators in Costa Rica, in 2010, reached a similar decision. In 2009, Finland, the report notes, *"passed a decree ... stating that every Internet connection needs to have a speed of at least one Megabit per second."*[35]

Digital Rights Management

From Wikipedia we say that, Digital rights management is a class of technologies that are used by hardware and software manufacturers, publishers, copyright holders, and individuals with the intent to control the use of digital content and devices after sale. In 1998, the Digital Millennium Copyright Act (DMCA) was passed in the United States to impose criminal penalties on those who make available technologies whose primary purpose and functions are to circumvent content protection technologies. The use of digital rights management is not universally accepted. Computer games sometimes use DRM technologies to limit the number of systems the game can be installed on by requiring authentication with an online server. It is any system used by producers, publishers, and vendors to embed technological controls on what users can do with electronic files – e-books, movies on DVDs, and other media.[36] DRM is not a single technology and it is not even a single philosophy. It refers to a broad range of technologies and standards, many of which are still in the planning and development stage. DRM is not thin copyright, and it isn't even thick copyright; DRM is potentially a nearly absolute protection of works.[37]

Enterprise digital rights management is the application of DRM technology to the control of access to corporate documents such as Microsoft Word, PDF, and AutoCAD files, e-mails, and intranet web pages rather than to the control of consumer media. Electronic books read on a personal computer or an e-book reader typically uses DRM technology to limit copying, printing, and sharing of e-books. The Open Mobile Alliance created a standard for interoperable DRM on mobile devices. Article 11 of the 1996 WIPO Copyright Treaty (WCT) requires nation's party to the treaties to enact laws against DRM circumvention, and has been implemented in most member states of the World Intellectual Property Organisation.[38]

Digital Restrictions Management is the practice of imposing technological restrictions that control what users can do with digital media.[39] It is a general term used to describe any type of technology that aims to stop, or at least ease, the practice of piracy.[40] Corporations claim that DRM is necessary to fight copyright infringement online and keep consumers safe from viruses. But there's no evidence that DRM helps fight either of those. Instead DRM helps big business stifle innovation and competition by making it easy to quash "unauthorised" uses of media and technology.[41]

European *Digital Rights*

European Digital Rights (EDRi) is an international not-for-profit association of 33 digital civil rights organisations from 19 European countries. We defend and promote rights and freedoms in the digital environment, such as the right to privacy, freedom of expression, communication and access to information.[42] EDRi was founded in June 2002 in Berlinby ten NGOs from seven countries. EDRi's objective is to promote, protect and uphold civil rights in the field of information and communication technology. EDRi provides a strong civil society voice and platform to ensure that European policy, which has an impact on the digital environment, is in line with fundamental rights. EDRi launches campaigns to increase public awareness on issues related to information and communication technologies discussed both in the European institutions and on a global level. EDRi is financed by membership fees and donations from the general public.[43]

Digital Millennium Copyright Act

From Wikipedia, we say the Digital Millennium Copyright Act (DMCA) is a United States copyright law that implements two 1996 treaties of the World Intellectual Property Organisation. Passed on October 12, 1998, by a unanimous vote in the United States Senate and signed into law by President Bill Clinton on October 28, 1998, the DMCA amended Title 17 of the United States Code to extend the reach of copyright, while limiting the liability of the providers of online services for copyright infringement by their users. The DMCA's principal innovation in the field of copyright is the exemption from direct and indirect liability of Internet service providers and other intermediaries. The law is currently unsettled with regard to websites that contain links to infringing material; however, there have been a few lower-court decisions which have ruled against linking in some narrowly prescribed circumstances.[44]

Conclusion

Digital rights are rights given to each individual that is surfing the web. In addition to that the rights are always broken by hackers and other people that break the law. These hackers take advantage of technology and use it to hack into e-mails, credit card numbers, and get free subscriptions. The purpose of DRM is to prevent unauthorised redistribution of digital media and restrict the ways consumers can copy content they've purchased. DRM products were developed in response to the rapid increase in online piracy of commercially marketed material, which proliferated through the widespread use of peer-to-peer file exchange programmes. The Copyright (Amendment) Act 2012 has introduced some digital rights management (DRM) provisions in the Indian Copyright law. While a comparative analysis of the new DRM provisions with similar legislation in the US and the EU shows a relatively better approach that reduces the detrimental effects posed by DRM provisions. There have been no provisions in the Indian Copyright Act, 1957 which deal with Digital Rights Management (DRM). The Copyright (Amendment) Bill, 2010 is, however, poised to change this: it includes three sections [viz. Sections 2(xa), 65A and 65B] which deal with DRM.

References

1. Digital data (2015), Retrieved from http://en.wikipedia.org/wiki/Digital_data
2. Digital media (2015), Retrieved from http://en.wikipedia.org/wiki/Digital_media
3. Digital electronics (2015), Retrieved from http://en.wikipedia.org/wiki/Digital_electronics
4. Lecture Notes for Digital Electronics, Retrieved from http://zebu.uoregon.edu/~rayfrey/432/DigitalNotes.pdf
5. Digital Rights and Responsibilities, Retrieved from http://digiteen09-.flatclassroomproject.org/Digital+Rights+and+Responsibilities
6. Professor Barry Paton (1998), Retrieved as http://people.clarkson.edu/~tortmeye/ee211/sequential%20logic/Fundamentals% 20of%20 Digital%20Electronics.pdf
7. See http://www.techopedia.com/definition/24928/digital-rights
8. Margaret Rouse (2009), Digital rights management, Retrieved from http://searchcio.techtarget.com/definition/digital-rights-management
9. Digital rights, Retrieved from http://www.techopedia.com/definition/24928/digital-rights
10. See http://www.webopedia.com/TERM/D/DRM.html
11. Digital rights management, Retrieved from http://mslab.kaist.ac.kr/twiki/pub/ContentNetworking/WebHome/DRM_overview.pdf
12. Emilija Arsenova and MI, RWTH-Aachen, Technical aspects of Digital Rights Management, Retrieved from http://wob.iai.uni-bonn.de/Wob/images/01212504.pdf
13. Digital Rights and Responsibilities, Retrieved from https://sites.google.com/site/digitalcitizenshipdferris/digital-rights-and-responsibilities
14. Digital Rights and Responsibilities, Retrieved from http://areyouadigitalcitizen.weebly.com/digital-rights-and-responsibilities.html
15. Digital Rights and Responsibilities, Retrieved from https://cunedigitalcitizenship.wikispaces.com/Digital+Rights+ %26+Responsibilities
16. Digital Rights and Responsibilities, Retrieved from http://digiteen09-1.flatclassroomproject.org/Digital+Rights+and+Responsibilities
17. 5 Responsibilities that come from digital citizenship (2012), Retrieved from http://education.cu-portland.edu/blog/tech-ed/responsibilities-that-come-with-digital-citizenship/
18. *The Hindu* (December 11, 2013), Leading authors call for bill of digital rights, Retrieved from http://www.thehindu.com/news/international/leading-authors-call-for-bill-of-digital-rights/article5444935.ece

19. *The Guardian* (Feb 4, 2014), What happens with digital rights management in the real world? Retrieved from http://www.theguardian.com/technology/blog/2014/feb/05/digital-rights-management
20. Scaria, Arul George (2012), Does India Need Digital Rights Management Provisions or Better Digital Business Management Strategies? Retrieved from http://nopr.niscair.res.in/handle/123456789/14771
21. See https://www.in.capgemini.com/the-world-beyond-digital-rights-management
22. Browse Journals and Books, Journal of International Trade Law and Policy, Volume 6, Issue 1, The potential impact of digital rights management on the Indian entertainment industry, See http://www.emeraldinsight.com/doi/abs/10.1108/14770020780000549
23. See http://copyright.lawmatters.in/2010/06/drm-and-other-implications-of-copyright.html
24. Tarun Krishnakumar and Kaustav Saha, India's new copyright law: the good, the bad and the DRM, Retrieved from http://jiplp.blogspot.in/2012/12/indias-new-copyright-law-good-bad-and.html
25. See http://www.medianama.com/2015/02/223-ipl-cricket-2015-starsports/
26. See http://ict-ipr.in/index.php/blogs/item/44-digital-rights-management-drm-need-of-time-in-indian-scenario
27. About digital rights management, Retrieved from http://www.microsoft.com/en-in/mobile/support/product/lumia625/userguidance/?action=singleTopic&topic=S-DRM
28. Zoya Nafis (2015), India: Protecting Copyright in the Digital Environment, Retrieved from http://www.mondaq.com/india/x/370058/Copyright/Protecting+Copyright+In+The+Digital+Environment
29. Zoya Nafis (2015), India: Protecting Copyright in the Digital Environment, Retrieved from http://www.mondaq.com/india/x/370058/Copyright/Protecting+Copyright+In+The+Digital+Environment
30. David Rothkopf (2015), Is unrestricted internet access a modern human rights? See http://foreignpolicy.com/2015/02/02/unrestricted-internet-access-human-rights-technology-constitution/
31. Right to Internet access (2015), Retrieved from http://en.wikipedia.org/wiki/Right_to_Internet_access
32. UN Report declares internet access as human rights, Retrieved from http://www.wired.com/category/design
33. Adam clark Esters, The UN. Declares internet access as human rights, Retrieved from http://www.thewire.com/technology/2011/06/united-nations-wikileaks-internet-human-rights/38526/

34. See http://www.ru.idebate.org/debatabase/debates/freespeechdebate/house-believes-internet-access-human-right
35. UN declares internet access as a basic human rights, Retrieved from http://www.theatlantic.com/technology/archive/2011/06/united-nations-declares-internet-access-a-basic-human-right/239911/
36. Digital Rights Management (2012), Retrieved from http://connect.ala.org/files/94226/DRM%20Library%20Education% 20Tip%20Sheet_DEFINITIVE_ 7_11_12.pdf
37. Karen Coyle (2003), The Technology of Rights: Digital Rights Management, Retrieved from http://www.kcoyle.net/drm_basics.pdf
38. Digital rights management (2015), Retrieved from http://en.wikipedia.org/wiki/Digital_rights_management
39. See https://www.defectivebydesign.org/what_is_drm_ digital_restrictions_management
40. See http://computer.howstuffworks.com/drm.htm
41. See https://www.eff.org/issues/drm
42. Diego Naranjo, "We still need to watch you, really": PNR back in the Parliament, Retrieved from https://edri.org/
43. European Digital Rights (2015), Retrieved from http://en.wikipedia.org/wiki/European_Digital_Rights
44. Digital Millennium Copyright Act (2015), Retrieved from http://en.wikipedia.org/wiki/Digital_Millennium_Copyright_Act

16

Rights in Indian Constitution

"If civilisation is to survive, we must cultivate the science of human relationships - the ability of all peoples, of all kinds, to live together, in the same world at peace."

-Franklin D. Roosevelt

Introduction

Constitution is a set of fundamental principles or established precedents according to which a state or other organisation is governed. Constitutions concern different levels of organisations, from sovereign states to companies and unincorporated associations. Generally, every modern written constitution confers specific powers to an organisation or institutional entity, established upon the primary condition that it abides by the said constitution's limitations.[1] The first written constitutions were English colonies constitutions in the North America after its freedom in 1776, USA Constitution in 1787 that still remains. Since written constitutions appeared, the idea of constitution liberty prevailed to be a tool for freedom whereas it remains with specific right for the citizen. The constitutional convention emerges along with written constitution and it consists with physical and spiritual article, i.e. with following up definite custom then is followed till to be binding matter.[2]

There are different types of Constitution; these are the Written Constitution, the Unwritten Constitution, the Conventional or Enacted Constitution, the Cumulative or Evolve Constitution, the Rigid or Inelastic Constitution and the Flexible or Elastic Constitution. All of the above-mentioned constitutions have their different features and characteristics. The Written Constitution is the constitution where the provisions are all contained in a single document. The Unwritten Constitution is the constitution where the provisions are not contained in a single document. The Conventional of Enacted Constitution is the constitution that was created through a constitutional convention; this convention is called to be able to draft the constitution. The Cumulative or Evolve Constitution is the constitution that is developed as a part of the history of a particular nation; it was not created through a national convention. The Rigid or Inelastic Constitution is the kind of constitution that cannot be easily amended. However, if the constitution itself provides that particular amendment, then it could be possible to amend the constitution. The Flexible or Elastic Constitution is the kind of constitution that can be easily be changed.[3]

The Constitution of India offers all citizens, some basic rights. These rights are known as Fundamental Rights. These rights are justifiable which means that if someone is denied these rights he can go to the Supreme Court the following fundamental rights have been guaranteed under the Constitution: The right to equality; the right to freedom; the right to property; the right against exploitation; the right to freedom of religion; Cultural and educational rights.[4]

Importance of Constitution

Today, mostly every democratic country has a constitution which is a vital document, according to which the country carries out its operations. Constitution protects the rights of the citizens of a concerned nation, irrespective of their religion, caste, creed, sex or physical appearance.[5] In the constitution, the people give instructions to their servant, the government. A constitution must therefore be as clear and specific as possible, or else the instructions will be vague. For that reason, the constitution is typically a written document. Once the people have chosen their form of government, then the rulers may not thereafter change it. By choosing the form of government, the people have the right to limit the government officials, who may not depart from the rules laid down by the people.

The constitution contains provisions relating to the powers and duties of government, the relations between government and people and the rights and duties of people. This helps in maintaining discipline in the society, makes government responsible and makes people aware that the government belongs to them. The constitution is the most important legal document of the country. It helps maintain law and order in the country.[6] The purpose of the constitution is to create and outline the powers of its various organs and prescribe the general manner in which these powers are to be exercised. In some constitutions these provisions are fragmentary and very general in character.[7]

The doctrine of the separation of powers, involving a system of checks and balances, is basic to liberal constitutionalism. The system of checks and balances begins with the separation through a constitution of judicial, executive and legislative powers. However, it goes much further. It operates also within each branch of the state, in the division of powers between state and federal governments and the distribution of powers between the state, other institutions and individuals in the community.[8]

Fundamental Rights in India

Fundamental Rights is a charter of rights contained in the Constitution of India. It guarantees civil liberties such that all Indians can lead their lives in peace and harmony as citizens of India. These include individual rights common to most liberal democracies, such as equality before law, freedom of speech and expression, and peaceful assembly, freedom to practice religion, and the right to constitutional remedies for the protection of civil rights by means of writs such as habeas corpus. Fundamental rights for Indians have also been aimed at overturning the inequalities of pre-independence social practices. Specifically, they have also been used to abolish untouchability and thus prohibit discrimination on the grounds of religion, race, caste, sex, or place of birth. They also forbid trafficking of human beings and forced labour.[9]

Fundamental rights guaranteed by the Constitution are, in the absence of specific constitutional provisions, mainly enforceable against 'the State'. The definition of 'the State' in Article 12 being an 'inclusive' one, courts have ruled that where there is pervasive or predominant governmental control or significant involvement in its activity, such bodies, entities and organisations fall within the definition of 'the State'. In Articles 15 and 16, prohibition against discrimination should be extended to "ethnic or social origin; political or other opinion; property or birth". There was a plea on behalf of some minority communities for an express provision for reservation in favour of minorities both in Articles 15 (4) and 16 (4). Article 19(1)(a) refers to 'freedom of speech and expression'. There was a plea on behalf of some minority communities for an express provision for reservation in favour of minorities both in Articles 15 (4) and 16 (4). The Commission, upon due consideration of the representations, felt that no special provision was necessary inasmuch as, under the existing provision of Articles 14, 15 and 16, it is open to the State to make reservation if it is of the opinion that such reservation is necessary and justified.[10]

The Fundamental Rights in Indian Constitution acts as a guarantee that all Indian citizens can and will live their life's in peace as long as they live in Indian democracy. They include individual rights common to most liberal democracies, such as equality before the law, freedom of speech and expression, freedom of association and peaceful assembly, freedom of religion, and the right to constitutional remedies for the protection of civil right.[11] The Constitution guarantees six fundamental rights to Indian citizens as follows: (i) right to equality, (ii) right to freedom, (iii) right against exploitation, (iv) right to freedom of religion, (v) cultural and educational rights, and (vi) right to constitutional remedies.

1. Right to equality is very important in a society like ours. The purpose of this right is to establish the rule of law where all the citizens should be treated equal before the law.
2. The Constitution of India provides Right to Freedom to all its citizens. This Right is stipulated under Articles 19-22.
3. Traditionally, the Indian society has been hierarchical that has encouraged exploitation in many forms. Which is why, the Constitution makes provisions against exploitation. The citizens have been guaranteed the right against exploitation through Articles 23 and 24 of the Constitution.
4. One of the objectives declared in the Preamble is "to secure to all its citizens liberty of belief, faith and worship". Since India is a multi-religion country, where Hindus, Muslims, Sikhs, Christians and many other communities live together, the Constitution declares India as a 'secular state'. It means that Indian State has no religion of its own.
5. India is the largest democracy in the world having diversity of culture, scripts, languages and religions. As we know the democracy is a rule of the majority. But the minorities are also equally important for its successful working.[12]

The Supreme Court has broadened the ambit of right of life to bring in a citizen's right to sleep peacefully under it. A citizen has a right to sound sleep because it is fundamental to life, the Supreme

Court said while ruling that the police action on a sleeping crowd at Baba Ramdev's rally at Ramlila Maidan amounted to violation of their crucial right. "Sleep is essential for a human being to maintain the delicate balance of health necessary for its very existence and survival. Sleep is, therefore, a fundamental and basic requirement without which the existence of life itself would be in peril," the Court said, terming it as a basic human right. Authorities have taken steps to protect citizens from being disturbed while they are asleep, like placing curbs on the playing of music late at night. But order elevates right to sleep in the hierarchy of rights and may goad the authorities to protect it. A bench of Justices B S Chauhan and Swatanter Kumar was unanimous that the police erred gravely by clamping prohibitory orders under Section 144 of Criminal Procedure Code on the night of June 4 when the gathering at Ramdev's yoga camp was sleeping peacefully. Though Justice Kumar wrote the lead judgment, Justice Chauhan elaborated on sleep as a fundamental right crucial to life and put it on the same plane as right to privacy and right to food, consistently held by the Supreme Court as an inviolable right which was part of right to life under Article 21 of the Constitution.[13]

Directive Principle of State Policy

The Directive Principles of State Policy are guidelines/principles given to the central and state governments of India, to be kept in mind while framing laws and policies. Directive Principles are classified under the following categories: Gandhian, economic and socialistic, political and administrative, justice and legal, environmental, protection of monuments and peace and security. The concept of Directive Principles of State Policy was borrowed from the Irish Constitution. The makers of the Constitution of India were influenced by the Irish nationalist movement. The State has made and is making many efforts to implement the Directive Principles. Changes in Directive Principles require a Constitutional amendment which has to be passed by a special majority of both houses of the Parliament. This means that an amendment requires the approval of two-thirds of the members present and voting.[14]

The Directive Principles are indeed the precursor to the Economic, Social and Cultural Rights specified in the International Covenant on Economic, Social and Cultural Rights, 1966 (ICESCR). Article 41 directs the State to make effective provision for securing the right to work, to education and to public assistance in cases of unemployment, old age, sickness and disablement, and in other cases of undeserved want. This is social security in its widest sense. It is a measure of the distance the country still has to travel to build a good society. The present situation, as revealed by successive UNDP reports, is one of hardship and deprivation for very large sections of our people. Poverty eradication continues to be a major challenge for social and economic policy. The 'trickle-down' theory did not work but neither did the direct anti-poverty programmes.[15]

The Constitution lays down certain Directive Principles of State Policy, which though not justiciable, are 'fundamental in governance of the country', and it is the duty of the State to apply these principles in making laws. These lay down that the State shall strive to promote the welfare of people by securing and protecting as effectively as it may, a social order, in which justice-social, economic and political-shall form in all institutions of national life.[16]

The Forty-second Amendment, which came into force in January 1977, attempted to raise the status of the Directive Principles by stating that no law implementing any of the Directive Principles could be declared unconstitutional on the grounds that it violated any of the Fundamental Rights. After the March 1977 general election ended the control of the Congress (Congress (R) from 1969) over the executive and legislature for the first time since independence in 1947, the new Janata-dominated Parliament passed the Forty-third Amendment (1977) and Forty-fourth Amendment (1978). These amendments revoked the Forty-second Amendment's provision that Directive Principles take precedence over Fundamental Rights and also curbed Parliament's power to legislate against "anti-national activities."[17]

The Directive Principles of State Policy contained in Part IV; Articles 36-51 of the Indian constitution constitute the most interesting and enchanting part of the constitution. The Directive Principles may be classified into three broad categories:

1. Socialistic: Principal among this category of directives are (a) securing welfare of the people (Art. 38), (b) securing proper distribution of material resources of the community as to best sub-serve the common-good, equal pay for equal work, protection of childhood and youth against exploitation. etc. (Art.39), (c) curing right to work, education etc. Art. (41), (d) securing just and humane conditions of work and maternity relief (Art. 42) etc.

2. *Gandhian:* Such directives are spread over several Arts. Principal among such directives are (a) to organise village panchayats (Art. 40), (b) to secure living wage, decent standard of life, and to promote cottage industries (Art. 43), (c) to provide free and compulsory education to all children up to 14 years of age (Art. 45), (d) to promote economic and educational interests of the weaker sections of the people, particularly, the scheduled castes and scheduled tribes, (e) to enforce prohibition of intoxicating drinks and cow-slaughter and to organise agriculture and animal husbandry on scientific lines (Arts. 46-48).

3. *Liberal-intellectual:* Principal among such directives are (a) to secure uniform civil code throughout the country (Art. 44), (b) to separate the judiciary from the executive (Art. 50), (c) to protect monuments of historic and national importance and (d) to promote international peace and security.[18]

Rights of Women

The Constitution of India not only grants equality to women but also empowers the State to adopt measures of positive discrimination in favour of women for neutralising the cumulative socio-economic, education and political disadvantages faced by them. Fundamental Rights, among others, ensure equality before the law, equal protection of law, prohibits discrimination against any citizen on grounds of religion, race, caste, sex or place of birth, and guarantee equality of opportunity to all citizens in matters relating to employment Articles 14, 15, 15(3), 16, 39(a), 39(b), 39(c) and 42 of the constitution are of specific importance in this regard.[19] Clause (3) of the Art. 15 of Constitution of India says that the State may make special provisions for women; this is a protectionist strategy and not an equation measure.[20]

To uphold the Constitutional mandate, the State has enacted various legislative measures intended to ensure equal rights, to counter social discrimination and various forms of violence and atrocities and to provide support services especially to working women.[21] Article 14 in the Indian Constitution ensures equality in political, economic and social spheres. Article 16 provides for equality of opportunities in matters of public appointment for all citizens. Article 15 prohibits discrimination against any citizen on the grounds of religion, race, caste, sex etc. Article 15 (3) of the Indian Constitution allows the State to make any special provision for women and children. Article 39(a) mentions that the State will direct its policies towards securing all citizens, men and women, the right to means of livelihood while Article 39 (c) ensures equal pay for equal work. Article 42 directs the State to ensure just and humane working conditions. More often than not, women are exploited by their bosses. The constitution imposes a fundamental duty on every citizen through Article 15 (A) (e) to renounce practices derogatory to the dignity of women.[22]

Rights of Children

The Indian constitution accords rights to children as citizens of the country, and in keeping with their special status the State has even enacted special laws. The Constitution, promulgated in 1950, encompasses most rights included in the UN Convention on the Rights of the Child as Fundamental Rights and Directive Principles of State Policy[23]. Article 39(e) in the Directive Principles in Part IV refers to the duty of the State to direct its policy to see that children of tender age are not abused. Article 39 (f) refers to a similar duty on the State to give opportunities and facilities to children to develop in a healthy manner and with dignity and in conditions which are free and where childhood and youth are protected against exploitation and moral and material abandonment. Art. 24A: Every child shall have the right to care and assistance in basic needs and protection from all forms of neglect, harm and exploitation.

Article 15(3) empowers the state to make special provision for children. Under Part III Fundamentals Rights the following provisions. Article 15(3) empowers the state to make special provisions for children under this clause and it is an exception for children under this clause and it is an exception to the rule against discrimination provided by clauses (1) and (2) of Article 15. Special provisions may be made either by legislation or by executive order. The Constitution (86th amendment) Act, 2002 added this Article 21-A has made education for all children of the age of 6 to 14 years a fundamental right. Article 24: No Child below the age of 14 years shall be employed to work in any factory or mine or engaged in any other hazardous employment. Article 39(f): The Children are given opportunities and facilities to develop in a healthy manner and in conditions of freedom and dignity and that childhood and youth are protected against exploitation and against moral and material abandonment.[24]

The Directive Principles of State Policy laid down in Part-IV of the Constitution also provide some human rights to women. Article 39 provides three specific rights to women. Clause (a) says that the citizen, men and women equally, have the right to an adequate means of livelihood. Clause (d) mandates that there is equal pay for equal work for, both men and women. Clause (e) states that the health and strength of workers, men and women and the tender age of children are not abused and that citizens are not forced by economic necessity to enter avocation unsuited to their age or strength.[25]

In M.C. Mehta Vs State of Tamil Nadu, the Supreme Court noted that menace of child labour was wide spread. Therefore, it issued wide ranging directions in the context of employment and exploitation of children in Sivakasi prohibiting children below the age of 14 and making arrangement for their education by creating a fund and providing employment of the parents of able bodied adults in the family. Article 39 therefore, specifically requires the state to ensure for the people adequate means of livelihood, fair distribution of wealth, equal pay for the equal work and protection of children and labour. Article 45 stated that the state shall endeavour to provide early childhood care and education for all children until they complete the age of six years. Article 47 requires the state to raise the level of nutrition and the standard of living of the people including children. Spelling out the fundamental duties of every citizen in Article 51-A, it is stated that a parent or guardian should provide opportunities for education to his child, or as the case may be, between the age of six and fourteen years.[26]

In India, the law considers anyone less than 18 years to be a child/minor, not competent to take major decisions affecting herself or others for the purposes of the Indian Majority Act, Contract Act, Juvenile Justice Act, Child Marriage Restraint Act, or Representation of Peoples Act. However, under Section 375 of the Indian Penal Code, the girl (aged 16-18) is given the right of consent to sexual intercourse. The courts have held that evidence from a child witness, if found competent to depose facts, could be the basis for a conviction. Under the Child Labour Prohibition and Regulation Act, 1986, a child is a person who has not completed 14 years of age. The Constitution of India protects children below the age of 14 from working in factories and hazardous jobs. But below 14, they can work in non-hazardous industries. An area of concern is that no minimum age for child labour has been specified. But for the purposes of criminal responsibility, the age limit is seven and twelve under the Indian Penal Code, 1860.[27]

Rights of Dalits

Dalits are discriminated against, denied access to land and basic resources, forced to work in degrading conditions, and routinely abused at the hands of police and dominant-caste groups that enjoy the state's protection. Dalit women face the triple burden of caste, class, and gender. Dalit girls have been forced to become prostitutes for dominant-caste patrons and village priests. Sexual abuse and other forms of violence against women are used by landlords and the police to inflict political lessons and crush dissent within the community. Dalits who dare to challenge the social order have often been subject to abuses by their dominant-caste neighbours.[28]

India has systematically failed to uphold its international legal obligations to ensure the fundamental human rights of Dalits, or so-called untouchables, despite laws and policies against caste discrimination, the Center for Human Rights and Global Justice and Human Rights Watch said in a new report released today. A resolution passed by the European Parliament on February 1, 2007 found India's efforts to enforce laws protecting Dalits to be grossly inadequate, adding that atrocities, untouchability, illiteracy, inequality of opportunity, continue to blight the lives of India's Dalits.[29] The fundamental rights were included in the constitution because they were considered essential for the development of the personality of every individual and to preserve human dignity. All people, irrespective of race, religion, caste or sex, have been given the right to move the Supreme Court and the High Courts for the enforcement of their fundamental rights.[30]

Rights of Minorities

Though the Constitution of India does not define the word 'Minority' and only refers to 'Minorities' and speaks of those 'based on religion or language', the rights of the minorities have been spelt out in the Constitution in detail. The Constitution provides two sets of rights of minorities which can be placed in 'common domain' and 'separate domain'. The rights which fall in the 'common domain' are those which are applicable to all the citizens of our country. The rights which fall in the 'separate domain' are those which are applicable to the minorities only and these are reserved to protect their identity. Part IVA of the Constitution, relating to Fundamental Duties as provided in Article 51 A applies in full to all citizens, including those belonging to Minorities.

The Minority Rights provided in the Constitution which fall in the category of 'Separate Domain' are as under: (a) right of 'any section of the citizens' to 'conserve' its 'distinct language, script or culture'; [Article 29(1)]; (b) restriction on denial of admission to any citizen, to any educational institution maintained or aided by the State, 'on grounds only of religion, race, caste, language or any of them'; [Article 29(2)]; (c) right of all Religious and Linguistic Minorities to establish and administer educational institutions of their choice; [Article 30(1)]; (d) freedom of Minority-managed educational institutions from discrimination in the matter of receiving aid from the State; [Article30(2)]; (e) special provision relating to the language spoken by a section of the population of any State; [Article 347]; (f) provision for facilities for instruction in mother-tongue at primary stage; [Article 350 A]; (g) provision for a Special Officer for Linguistic Minorities and his duties; and [Article 350 B]; (h) Sikh community's right of 'wearing and carrying of kirpans'; [Explanation 1 below Article 25].[31]

Conclusion

The constitution contains provisions relating to the powers and duties of government, the relations between government and people and the rights and duties of people. Fundamental Rights is a charter of rights contained in the Constitution of India. It guarantees civil liberties such that all Indians can lead their lives in peace and harmony as citizens of India. The Fundamental Rights in Indian constitution acts as a guarantee that all Indian citizens can and will live their life's in peace as long as they live in Indian democracy. They include individual rights common to most liberal democracies, such as equality before the law, freedom of speech and expression, freedom of association and peaceful assembly, freedom of religion, and the right to constitutional remedies for the protection of civil right. The Directive Principles of State Policy are guidelines/principles given to the central and state governments of India, to be kept in mind while framing laws and policies. Directive Principles are classified under the following categories: Gandhian, economic and socialistic, political and administrative, justice and legal, environmental, protection of monuments and peace and security. The concept of Directive Principles of State Policy was borrowed from the Irish Constitution.

References

1. Constitution (2015), Retrieved from http://en.wikipedia.org/wiki/Constitution

2. Different types of constitution (2015), Retrieved from http://www.lawteacher.net/free-law-essays/constitutional-law/different-types-of-constitutions.php
3. The different types of constitution, Retrieved from https://politics.knoji.com/the-different-types-of-constitution/
4. Mayank Pal, Seven Important fundamental rights that has been guaranteed under Indian constitution to every citizen, Retrieved from http://www.shareyouressays.com/91783/seven-important-fundamental-rights-that-has-been-guaranteed-under-indian-constitution-to-every-citizen
5. Importance of constitution, Retrieved from http://lifestyle.iloveindia.com/lounge/importance-of-constitution-10803.html
6. Arvind Kumar, Short essay on the meaning and importance of constitution, Retrieved from http://www.preservearticles.com/2011100314523/short-essay-on-the-meaning-and-importance-of-constitution.html
7. Suhana Dhawan, Short essay on the importance of Constitution, Retrieved from http://www.shareyouressays.com/88367/short-essay-on-the-importance-of-constitution
8. See http://www.ourcivilisation.com/cooray/constit/
9. Fundamental Rights in India (2015), Retrieved from http://en.wikipedia.org/wiki/Fundamental_rights_in_India
10. See http://lawmin.nic.in/ncrwc/finalreport/v1ch3.htm
11. Fundamental Rights in India, Retrieved from http://www.facts-about-india.com/fundamental-rights-in-India.php
12. Fundamental rights and fundamental duties, Retrieved from http://www.nios.ac.in/media/documents/secsocscicour/english/lesson-16.pdf
13. *The Times of India* (Feb 25, 2012), Right to sleep a fundamental right, says Supreme Court, Retrieved from http://timesofindia.indiatimes.com/india/Right-to-sleep-a-fundamental-right-says-Supreme-Court/articleshow/12025358.cms
14. Directive Principles of State Policy, Retrieved from http://en.wikipedia.org/wiki/Directive_Principles_in_India
15. See http://lawmin.nic.in/ncrwc/finalreport/v1ch3.htm
16. Directive Principle of State Policy, Retrieved from http://www.archive.india.gov.in/knowindia/profile.php?id=18
17. Directive Principles of State Policy, Retrieved from http://www civilserviceindia.com/subject/Law/notes/fundamental-right-principles.html
18. The Directive Principles of State Policy, Retrieved from http://www.importantindia.com/2032/directive-principles-of-state-policy-in-the-indian-constitution/
19. See http://statistics.puducherry.gov.in/new%20update/women%20 and%20 men%202010-11/II-1.pdf

20. See http://wscpedia.org/index.php?option=com_content&view= article&id=161:rights-of-women-under-indian-constitution-for-alleviating-poverty
21. See http://nlrd.org/womens-rights-initiative/legislations-laws-related-to-women/constitutional-and-legal-provisions-for-women-in-india
22. Supriya Prathapan, Constitutional rights of women in India, Retrieved from http://goarticles.com/article/CONSTITUTIONAL-RIGHTS-OF-WOMEN-IN-INDIA/1577722/
23. Constitution of India, Retrieved from http://www.haqcrc.org/constitution-india
24. Prof. B.S. Reddy, Constitution of India, Retrieved from http://elearning.vtu.ac.in/P3/CIP71/1.pdf
25. Patil Jaiprakash Reddy (2013), Women and human rights, Retrieved from http://www.lawyersclubindia.com/articles/Women-and-Human-Rights-5303.asp#.VSXSY9zF8qM
26. Rights of child under Indian Constitution, Retrieved from http://www.easternmirrornagaland.com/2013/09/rights-of-the-child-under-indian-constitution/
27. Asha Bajpai, who is a child? Retrieved from http://infochangeindia.org/agenda/child-rights-in-india/who-is-a-child.html
28. Overview of dalit Human rights solution, Retrieved from http://www.ncdhr.org.in/dalit-rights-situation
29. India: 'Hidden Apartheid' of Discrimination Against Dalits (2007), Retrieved from http://www.hrw.org/news/2007/02/12/india-hidden-apartheid-discrimination-against-dalits
30. *Ibid.*
31. Official website of National commission of minorities, Constitutional rights and safeguards provided to the minorities in India, Retrieved from http://ncm.nic.in/constitutional_provisions.html

Bibliography

- A.B.M. Mafizul Islam Patwari (1995). *Human rights in contemporary international law,* Humanist and Ethical Association of Bangladesh.
- A. Kumar (2006). *Women and Crime: Dimensions and Remedial Measures,* Anmol Publications Pvt. Limited.
- A. S. Garg (1990). *Bride burning: crime against women,* Sandeep Publication.
- A. S. Srinivasar Aiyar (1930). *The Child Marriage Restraint Act, 1929*, Universal Law Publishing.
- Abdon Rwegasira (2012). *Land as a Human Right: A History of Land Law and Practice in Tanzania,* African Books Collective.
- Abdul Matin (1992). *The Law on Dowry Prohibition and Child Marriage Restraint*, Palak Publishers.
- Adam Hibbert (2004). *Children's Rights*, Sea-To-Sea Publisher.
- Aftab Alam (2000), *Human Rights in India: Issues and Challenges,* Raj Publications.
- Ahmed, S.M. (2009). Capability Development among the Ultra Poor in Bangladesh: A Case Study. *Journal of Health, Population, and Nutrition*, 4, 528-535.
- Ajit Gopal Roy (1960). *Commentary on Hindu law, past and present*, Pahuja Bros.
- Alessandro Cigno and Furio Camillo Rosati (2005). *The Economics of Child Labour*, Oxford University Press.
- Alexandra Stiglmayer (1994). *Mass Rape: The War Against Women in Bosnia-Herzegovina,* U of Nebraska Press.
- Al-Mamun, A. Malarvizhi, C.A. Wahab, S.A, and Mazumder, M.N.H. (2011). Investigating The Effect of Microcredit on Microenterprise Income in Peninsular Malaysia. *European Journal of Economic, Finance and Administrative Sciences*, 29, 122-133.

- Amarnath Amarasingam (2010). *Religion and the New Atheism: A Critical Appraisal*, BRILL.
- Amartya Sen (2007). *Identity and Violence: The Illusion of Destiny*, Penguin Books India.
- Anaclaudia Gastal Fassa, David L. Parker, and Thomas J. Scanlon (2010). *Child Labour: A Public Health Perspective*, Oxford University Press.
- Andrea Dworkin (1981). *Pornography: Men Possessing Women,* Women's Press.
- Andrea Warren (1998). *Orphan Train Rider: One Boy's True Story,* Houghton Mifflin Harcourt.
- Andrea Warren (2004). *We Rode the Orphan Trains*, Houghton Mifflin Harcourt.
- Andrea Warren (2011). *Charles Dickens and the Street Children of London*, Houghton Mifflin Harcourt.
- Annaim, Abdullahi, and Francis M. Deng (2000). Human Rights in Africa: Cross-Cultural Perspectives, Brookings Institution Press.
- Anne Digby, and David Wright (2002). *From Idiocy to Mental Deficiency: Historical Perspectives on People with Learning Disabilities,* Taylor and Francis.
- Anne Norton (2013). *On the Muslim Question,* Princeton University Press.
- Anne-Marie Hilsdon (2000). *Human Rights and Gender Politics: Asia-Pacific Perspectives*, Routledge.
- Annemarie Schimmel (1982). *Islam in India and Pakistan*, BRILL.
- Annemarie Schimmel (2000). *Islam in the Indian Subcontinent,* BRILL.
- Arjun Prakash Aggarwal (1992). *Sexual Harassment in the Workplace*, Edition 2, Butterworth Pub Limited.
- Arun Ray (2003). *National Human Rights Commission of India: Formation, Functioning, and Future Prospects,* Atlantic Publishers and Dist.
- Aruna Goel (2009). *Women Empowerment: Myth or Reality*, New Delhi: Deep and Deep Publications.
- Arvind Ganesan, and Patricia Gossman (1996). *Police Abuse and Killings of Street Children in India*, Human Rights Watch Children's Rights Project.
- Arvind Sharma (2010). *Hindu Narratives on Human Rights,* ABC-CLIO.
- Aryeh Neier (2012). *The International Human Rights Movement: A History*, Princeton University Press.

- Asgharali Engineer (1989). *Communalism and Communal Violence in India: An Analytical Approach to Hindu-Muslim Conflict,* Ajanta Publications (India).
- Asha Bajpai (2003). *Child Rights in India: Law, Policy, and Practice,* Oxford University Press.
- Assefa Bekele and Jo Boyden (1988). *Combating Child Labour.* International Labour Organization.
- Assefa Bekele and William E. Myers (1995). *First Things First in Child Labour: Eliminating Work Detrimental to Children*, International Labour Organization.
- B. R. Rodil (1993). *The Lumad and Moro of Mindanao*, Minority Rights Group.
- B. S. Nagi (1993). *Child Marriage in India: A Study of Its Differential Patterns in Rajasthan*, Mittal Publications.
- Bahaudin Ghulam Mujtaba (2006). *Afghanistan: Realities of War and Rebuilding*, Ilead Academy.
- Bella Chagall (1988). *Burning Lights: A Unique Double Portrait of Russia*, Knopf Doubleday Publishing Group.
- Benedicte Ingstad and Susan Reynolds Whyte (1995). *Disability and Culture*, University of California Press.
- Bernard Grofman, Chandler Davidson (2009). *Controversies in Minority Voting: The Voting Rights Act in Perspective*, Brookings Institution Press.
- Bernard Grofman, Chandler Davidson (2009). *Controversies in Minority Voting: The Voting Rights Act in Perspective*, Brookings Institution Press.
- Bernard Lewis (1993). *Islam and the West,* Oxford University Press.
- Bernd Rechel (2010). *Minority Rights in Central and Eastern Europe,* Taylor and Francis.
- Bernie Anderson (2007). *Breaking the Silence: A Pastor Goes Public about His Battle with Pornography,* Autumn House Publishing.
- Bertrand G. Ramcharan (1979). *Human Rights: Thirty Years After the Universal Declaration: Commemorative Volume on the Occasion of the Thirtieth Anniversary of the Universal Declaration of Human Rights*, International Forum on Human Rights.
- Beryl Rawson (1996). *Marriage, Divorce, and Children in Ancient Rome,* Humanities Research Centre.

- Beth A. Simmons (2009). *Mobilising for Human Rights: International Law in Domestic Politics,* Cambridge University Press.
- Bi, Z. and Pandey, S.L.D. (2011). Comparison of Performance of Microfinance Institutions with Commercial Banks in India. *Australian Journal of Business and Management Research*, 1(6), 110-120.
- Brij Kishore Sharma (2005). *Introduction to the Constitution of India,* PHI Learning Pvt. Ltd.
- C. P. Rai (2002). *Child labour: a reality*, Volume 2, Laxmi Shikshan Sansthan.
- Carol J. Adams (2004). *The Pornography of Meat*, Continuum.
- Carol Neel (2004). *Medieval Families: Perspectives on Marriage, Household, and Children,* University of Toronto Press.
- Carolyn M. Sampselle (1992). *Violence Against Women: Nursing Research, Education, and Practice Issues*, Taylor and Francis
- Carsten K. W. De Dreu, Nanne K. De Vries (2001). *Group Consensus and Minority Influence: Implications for Innovation,* Wiley.
- Catalyst (1998). *Women Entrepreneurs: Why Companies Lose Female Talent and what They Can Do about it,* Catalyst.
- Catharine A. MacKinnon (1979). *Sexual Harassment of Working Women: A Case of Sex Discrimination,* Yale University Press.
- Catharine A. MacKinnon, and Andrea Dworkin (1997). *In Harm's Way: The Pornography Civil Rights Hearings*, Harvard University Press.
- Catharine A. MacKinnon, and Reva B. Siegel (2004). *Directions in Sexual Harassment Law,* Yale University Press.
- Cathryne L. Schmitz, Elizabeth KimJin Traver, and Desi Larson (2004). *Child Labor: A Global View,* Greenwood Publishing Group.
- Charles R. Beitz (2011). *The Idea of Human Rights,* Oxford University Press.
- Chitra Banerjee Divakaruni (2000). *Black Candle: Poems about Women from India,* Pakistan, and Bangaladesh, CALYX Books.
- Chowdhury, A. (2009). Microfinance as a Poverty Reduction Tool-A Critical Assessment. DESA Working Paper, 9, 1-11.
- Chris Maina Peter (1990). *Human Rights in Africa: A Comparative Study of the African Human and People's Rights Charter and the New Tanzanian Bill of Rights*, Greenwood Press.

- Christian Tomuschat (2008). *Human Rights: Between Idealism and Realism*, Oxford University Press.
- Christine Loser (2011). *Hindu Nationalism: A Threat to the Indian Democracy?,* GRIN Verlag.
- Christopher M. Bell (2011). *Blackness and Disability: Critical Examinations and Cultural Interventions*, LIT Verlag Monster.
- Claire M. Renzetti, Jeffery L. Edleson, and Raquel Kennedy Bergen (2001). *Sourcebook on Violence against Women*, SAGE.
- Clive Gifford (2009). *Child Labour,* Evans Brothers.
- Colin Barnes and Geof Mercer (2010). *Exploring Disability*, Polity.
- Colin Wringe (1981). *Children's rights: a philosophical study,* Routledge and Kegan Paul.
- Constance Margaret Hall (1992). Women and Empowerment: Strategies for Increasing Autonomy *Education Policy Perspectives*, Taylor and Francis
- Courtney Farrell (2010). *Children's Rights*, ABDO.
- Curtis Francis Doebbler (2004). *International Human Rights Law: Cases and Materials*, CD Pub.
- D. L. Sheth, Gurpreet Mahajan (1999). *Minority Identities and the Nation-state*, Oxford University Press.
- D. Lalitha Rani (1996). *Women Entrepreneurs,* APH Publishing.
- D.Bhaskara Rao, Digumarti Pushpa Latha (2003). *Women, Education and Empowerment*, New Delhi: Discovery Publishing House.
- D.C. Nanjunda (2008). *Child Labour and Human Rights: A Prospective,* Gyan Publishing House.
- Dallas A. Blanchard (1993). *Religious Violence and Abortion: The Gideon Project*, University Press of Florida.
- Dan Goodley (2010). *Disability Studies: An Interdisciplinary Introduction*, SAGE.
- Daniel C. Maguire (2003). *Sacred Rights: The Case for Contraception and Abortion in World Religions*, Oxford University Press.
- Daniel K. Williams (2010). *God's Own Party: The Making of the Christian Right*, Oxford University Press.
- Daniel Moeckli, Sangeeta Shah, Sandesh Sivakumaran, David Harris (2013). *International Human Rights Law,* Oxford University Press.
- David Archard (2004). *Children: Rights and Childhood,* Routledge.

- David Carpenter (1990). *The Minority of Henry III*, University of California Press.
- David Finkelhor, Kersti Yllö (1987). *License to Rape: Sexual Abuse of Wives,* Free Press.
- David G. Hackett (2003). *Religion and American Culture: A Reader,* Psychology Press.
- David M. Beatty (1994). *Human Rights and Judicial Review: A Comparative Perspective*, Martinus Nijhoff Publishers.
- David Wright, Anne Digby, and Digby Anne (1996). *From Idiocy to Mental Deficiency: Historical Perspectives on People with Learning Disabilities*, illustrated.
- Debarati Halder, and K. Jaishankar (2011). *Cyber Crime and the Victimization of Women: Laws, Rights and Regulations,* Idea Group Inc (IGI).
- Deborah M. Merrill (2011). *When Your Children Marry: How Marriage Changes Relationships with Sons and Daughters,* Rowman and Littlefield Publishers.
- Dennis Frederick (2007). *Conquering Pornography: Overcoming the Addiction: A Practical*, Wine Press Publishing.
- Diana E. H. Russell (1990). *Rape in Marriage*, Indiana University Press.
- Dilip Bishwo (2008). *Bhutan: A Shangrila without Human Rights*, Association of Human Rights Activists.
- Diplomacy Marc Gopin James H. Laue (2000). *Between Eden and Armageddon: The Future of World Religions, Violence, and Peacemaking: The Future of World Religions, Violence, and Peacemaking*, Oxford University Press.
- Dr. Mrs. Rajammal P. Devadass (2007). The role of women in education in India, University of Michigan.
- Edward H. Lawson, Mary Lou Bertucci (1995). *Encyclopedia of Human Rights,* Taylor and Francis.
- Edward L. Cleary (1997). *The Struggle for Human Rights in Latin America*, Greenwood Publishing Group.
- Eileen M. Byrne (1978). *Women and Education*, Tavistock Publications.
- Eleanor Flexner, and Ellen Frances Fitzpatrick (1996). *Century of Struggle: The Woman's Rights Movement in the United States,* Harvard University Press.
- Elisabet S. Hauge (2003). Women entrepreneurs: theory, research and policy implications, Hoeyskole Forlaget.

- Elizabeth M. King, and M. Anne Hill (1997). *Women's Education in Developing Countries: Barriers, Benefits, and Policies*, World Bank Publications.
- Elizabeth Podnieks, Jordan I. Kosberg, and Ariela Lowenstein (2005). *Elder Abuse: Selected Papers from the Prague World Congress on Family Violence,* Haworth Maltreatment and Trauma Press.
- Elizabeth Russell Connelly (2000). *Child Abuse and Neglect: Examining the Psychological Components,* Chelsea House.
- Ellen Carol DuBois (1998). *Woman Suffrage and Women's Rights,* NYU Press.
- Ellen Lynn Hall, and Jennifer Kofkin Rudkin (2011). *Seen and Heard: Children's Rights in Early Childhood Education,* Teachers College Press.
- Elumilade, D.O., Asaolu, T.O., and Adereti, S.A. (2006). Appraising the Institutional Framework for Poverty Alleviation Programmes in Nigeria. *International Research Journal of Finance and Economics*, 3, 67-79.
- Emily Davies (2007). *The higher education of women*, A. Strahan.
- Emma Guest (2003). *Children of AIDS: Africa's orphan crisis,* Pluto Press.
- Eugeen Verhellen (1996). *Monitoring Children's Rights*, Martinus Nijhoff Publishers.
- European Centre for Minority Issues (2004). *Mechanisms for the Implementation of Minority Rights,* European Centre for Minority Issues.
- Eva Brems (2001). *Human Rights: Universality and Diversity,* Martinus Nijhoff Publishers.
- F. M. Christensen (1990). *Pornography: The Other Side,* Greenwood Publishing Group.
- Facts on File, and Incorporated (2002). *Crimes against Women*, Infobase Publishing.
- Fareda Banda (2005). *Women, Law and Human Rights: An African Perspective*, Hart Publishing.
- Francis Achampong (1999). *Workplace Sexual Harassment Law: Principles, Landmark Developments, and Framework for Effective Risk Management,* Greenwood Publishing Group.
- Frans Viljoen (2007). *International Human Rights Law in Africa,* OUP Oxford.
- G. S. Bajwa (1995). *Human rights in India: implementation and violations*, Anmol Publications.

- Gail Dines, Robert Jensen, and Ann Russo (1998). *Pornography: The Production and Consumption of Inequality*, Psychology Press.
- Gamini Herath, and Kishor Sharma (2007). *Child Labour in South Asia,* Ashgate Publishing, Ltd.
- Gary Craig, and Marjorie Mayo (1995). Community Empowerment: A Reader in Participation and Development, Zed Books.
- Gary L. Albrecht, Katherine D. Seelman, and Michael Bury (2001). *Handbook of Disability Studies*. SAGE Publications.
- Geoffrey Dale Arnott (2011). *The Disability Support Worker*, Pearson Education Australia.
- Geoffrey Steven Kyeyune (1996). *Street children: why are they out?,* Fountain Publishers.
- George A. De Vos, William O. Wetherall, and Kaye Stearman (1983). *Japan's Minorities: Burakumin, Koreans, Ainu and Okinawans*, Minority Rights Group.
- Georges Kristoffel Lieten (2005). *Child Labour: Burning Questions : Inaugural Lecture,* Amsterdam University Press.
- Geraldine Forbes and Geraldine Hancock Forbes (1999). *Women in Modern India*, Volume 4, Cambridge University Press.
- Geraldine Terry (2007). *Women's Rights,* Copenhagen: Oxfam GB and Pluto Press.
- Geraldine Terry (2008). *Sex Trafficking: Inside the Business of Modern Slavery*. Columbia University Press.
- Geraldine Van Bueren (1998). *The International Law on the Rights of the Child*, Martinus Nijhoff Publishers.
- Geraldine Van Bueren (2007). *Child Rights in Europe: Convergence and Divergence in Judicial Protection*, Council of Europe.
- Gopal Bhargava (2003). *Child Labour*, Volume 2, New Delhi: Gyan Publishing House.
- Graham Pullin (2009). *Design Meets Disability*, MIT Press.
- Guofang Li, Lihshing Wang (2008). *Model Minority Myth Revisited: An Interdisciplinary Approach to Demystifying Asian American Educational Experiences*, IAP.
- Gyanendra Pandey (2005). *Remembering Partition: Violence, Nationalism and History in India,* Cambridge University Press.
- Haque, M.S. and Yamao, M. (2008). Can micro-credit alleviate rural poverty? A Case Study of Bangladesh. Proceedings of World Academy of Science, Engineering and Technology, 36, 1-12.
- Harold Bloom (2006). The American Religion, Chu Hartley Publishers.

- Hayley Fitzgerald (2008). *Disability and Youth Sport*, Taylor and Francis.
- Hector Avalos (2005). *Fighting Words: The Origins of Religious Violence,* Prometheus Books.
- Henri-Jacques Stiker (1999). *A History of Disability*, University of Michigan Press.
- Henry Steele Commager (2008). *Majority Rule and Minority Rights,* P. Smith..
- Herbert L. Bodman, Nayereh Esfahlani Tohidi (1998). *Women in Muslim Societies: Diversity within Unity,* Lynne Rienner Publishers.
- Herma Silverstein (1994). *Date Abuse*, Enslow Pub Incorporated.
- Holly Johnson, Natalia Ollus, and Sami Nevala (2007). *Violence against Women: An International Perspective*, Springer.
- Holly Littlefield (2001). *Children of the Orphan Trains,* Lerner Publications.
- Hossain, M.K (2012). Measuring The Impact of BRAC Microfinance Operations; A Case Study of a Village. International Business Research, 5(4).112-124.
- Hugh D. Hindman (2002). *Child Labor: An American History,* M.E. Sharpe.
- Hugh D. Hindman (2011). *The World of Child Labor: An Historical and Regional Survey,* M.E. Sharpe.
- Human Rights in the Administration of Justice: A Manual on Human Rights for Judges, Presecutors and Lawyers, United Nations. Office of the High Commissioner for Human Rights, International Bars Association.
- Human Rights Watch (Organization) (2003). *Nepal/Bhutan, trapped by inequality: Bhutanese refugee women in Nepal,* Volume 15, Human Rights Watch.
- Human Rights Watch (Organization) (2007). *Nepal, Children in the Ranks,* Human Rights Watch.
- Human Rights Watch (Organization), Women's Rights Project (Human Rights Watch) (1991). *Criminal Injustice: Violence against Women in Brazil,* Human Rights Watch.
- Hurst Hannum (1993). *Basic Documents on Autonomy and Minority Rights,* Martinus Nijhoff Publishers.
- Ian Reader (2000). *Religious Violence in Contemporary Japan,* University of Hawaii Press
- Ibru, C. (2007). Providing Operational Financing for Small Businesses-Challenges and Opportunities. A paper presented at

the Cultural Centre (Main Auditorium), Calabar. 8th November. Retrieved from www.oceanicbanknigeria.comon 13th August, 2012.

- Irobi, N.C (2008). Microfinance and Poverty Alleviation: A Case Study of Obazu Progressive Women Association, Mbieri, Imo State, Nigeria. Master Thesis. Sweden: Uppsala, Sveriges LantbruksUni-versitet.
- Islamic Council of Europe (1980). *Muslim communities in non-Muslim states.*
- Issa G. Shivji (1989). *The Concept of Human Rights in Africa*, African Books Collective.
- Jack Donnelly (2003). *Universal Human Rights in Theory and Practice,* Cornell University Press.
- Jack Donnelly (2012). *International Human Rights*, International Human Rights.
- Jacques Derrida and Gil Anidjar (2002). Acts of Religion, Psychology Press.
- James Griffin (2008). *On Human Rights*, OUP Oxford.
- Jane Fortin (1998). *Children's Rights and the Developing Law, Butterworth,* (Publishers) Limited.
- Jane Fortin (2003). *Children's Rights and the Developing Law*, Cambridge University Press.
- Jane Gallop (1997). *Feminist Accused of Sexual Harassment*, Duke University Press.
- Jane Humphries (2010). *Childhood and Child Labour in the British Industrial Revolution,* Cambridge University Press.
- Jane L. Parpart, Shirin M. Rai, and Kathleen A. Staudt (2004). *Rethinking Empowerment: Gender and Development in a Global/ Local World,* Taylor and Francis.
- Jane Seale (2006). *E-Learning and Disability in Higher Education: Accessibility Research and Practice,* Taylor and Francis.
- Javaid Rehman (2003). *International Human Rights Law: A Practical Approach,* Longman.
- Javaid Rehman (2011). *International Human Rights Law,* Longman/Pearson.
- Jay A. Sigler (1983). *Minority Rights: A Comparative Analysis,* Greenwood Press.
- Jaya Sagade (2005). *Child Marriage in India: Socio-legal and Human Rights Dimensions*, Oxford University Press.
- Jayashree (1999). Human Rights and Working Women: A Source Book for All Working Women in India, Publications Division, Ministry of Information and Broadcasting, Government of India.

- Jean Antoine Dubois, Carrie Chapman Catt (1897). *Hindu Manners, Customs and Ceremonies: The Classic First Hand Account of India in the Early Nineteenth Century*, Courier Corporation.
- Jean Calvin (2006). Institutes of the Christian Religion, Volume 1, P. H. Nicklin.
- Jean-Marc Coicaud, Michael W. Doyle, Anne-Marie Gardner (2003), *The Globalization of Human Rights,* United Nations University Press.
- Jeanne Halladay Coughlin (2002). *The Rise of Women Entrepreneurs: People, Processes, and Global Trends*, Greenwood Publishing Group.
- Jenny B. White (2013). *Muslim Nationalism and the New Turks*, Princeton University Press.
- Jessica Spector (2006). *Prostitution and Pornography: Philosophical Debate about the Sex Industry,* Stanford University Press.
- Joan N. Burstyn (1980). *Victorian Education and the Ideal of Womanhood,* Croom Helm.
- Joan Nordquist (1986). *Domestic violence: spouse abuse/marital rape*, Reference and Research Services.
- Joanne Belknap (2007). *The invisible woman: gender, crime, and justice*, Thomson/Wadsworth.
- Joanne Mariner (2001). *No Escape: Male Rape in U.S. Prisons*, Human Rights Watch.
- Joe Gregory (2005). *Secrets of Successful Women Entrepreneurs*, Cabal Group Limited.
- Joe Lugalla, and Colleta G. Kibassa (2002). *Poverty, AIDS, and street children in East Africa,* Edwin Mellen Press.
- John (jurista) Witte, Johan David Van der Vyver, Van der Vyver, J. D. (1996). *Religious Human Rights in Global Perspective: Religious Perspectives,* Volume 1, Martinus Nijhoff Publishers.
- John Carey (1968). *International Protection of Human Rights: Background Paper and Proceedings*, Oceana Pubs for the Association of the Bar of the City of New York.
- John D. Caputo (2001). On Religion, Routledge.
- John David Skrentny (2002). *The Minority Rights Revoluation*, Harvard University Press.
- John E. Butler (2003). *New Perspectives on Women Entrepreneurs*, IAP.
- John E. Farley (2004). *Majority-minority Relations*, Edition 4, Prentice Hall.

- John Hick (1990). *Philosophy of Religion,* Prentice-Hall.
- John Kabutha Mugo (2004). *Rehabilitation of Street Children in Kenya: Approaches, Quality and Challenges, IKO,* Verlag for Kulturelle Kommunikation.
- John T. Pardeck (2006). *Children's Rights: Policy and Practice,* Psychology Press.
- John Thayer Sidel (2006). *Riots, Pogroms, Jihad: Religious Violence in Indonesia*, Cornell University Press.
- John Wiley and Sons (2010). *Women and Educational Leadership*, John Wiley and Sons.
- John Witte, M. Christian Green (2011). *Religion and Human Rights: An Introduction,* Oxford University Press.
- Joseph W. Slade (2001). *Pornography and Sexual Representation: A Reference Guide,* Volume 2, Greenwood Publishing Group.
- Joyce Hart (2009). *Human Trafficking*, The Rosen Publishing Group.
- Judy Westwater, and Wanda Carter (2006). *Street Kid: One Child's Desperate Fight for Survival*, HarperElement.
- Julia Sloth-Nielsen (2008). *Children's Rights in Africa: A Legal Perspective*, Ashgate Publishing, Ltd.
- Julie K. Ehrhart, and Bernice Resnick Sandler (1985). *Campus gang rape: party games?, Project on the Status and Education of Women,* Association of American Colleges.
- Julie Mertus, Jeffrey W. Helsing (2006). *Human Rights and Conflict: Exploring the Links between Rights, Law, and Peace building,* US Institute of Peace Press.
- Julie Peters, and Andrea Wolper (1995). *Women's Rights, Human Rights: International Feminist Perspectives,* Psychology Press.
- K. Gopal Iyer (2003). *Migrant Labour and Human Rights in India*, Kanishka Publishers, Distributors.
- K. Sasikuma (2000). *Women entrepreneurship*, Vikas Pub. House.
- Kamla Singh (1992). *Women Entrepreneurs,* Ashish Publishing House.
- Karen D. Hughes, and Jennifer E. Jennings (2012). Global Women's Entrepreneurship Research: Diverse Settings, Questions, and Approaches, Edward Elgar Publishing.
- Karen P. DePauw, and Susan J. Gavron (2005). *Disability Sport*, Human Kinetics.
- Karla Fitzhugh (2005). *Prescription Drug Abuse,* Crabtree Publishing Company.

- Kate Walker (2009). *Cordero's Forced Bride,* Harlequin.
- Kathleen Barry (1984). *Female Sexual Slavery*, NYU Press.
- Kathryn Farr (2004). *Sex Trafficking: The Global Market in Women and Children,* Worth Publishers.
- Kaye Stearman (2004). *Child Labor,* Raintree.
- Keith Burgess-Jackson (1999). *A Most Detestable Crime: New Philosophical Essays on Rape,* Oxford University Press.
- Kelly Dawn Askin (1997). *War Crimes Against Women: Prosecution in International War Crimes Tribunals*, Martinus Nijhoff Publishers.
- Kenneth Christie, Denny Roy (2001). *The Politics of Human Rights In East Asia,* Pluto Press.
- Kevin Bales and Ron Soodalter (2010). *The Slave Next Door: Human Trafficking and Slavery in America Today, New Preface edition,* University of California Press.
- Kristoffel Lieten, and Benjamin White (2001). *Child labour: policy options*, Aksant Academic Publishers.
- Kurt Jonassohn, Karin Solveig Björnson (2010). *Genocide and Gross Human Rights Violations: In Comparative Perspective*, Transaction Publishers.
- Laxmi Devi (1998). *Crime Atrocities and Violence against Women and Related Laws and Justice,* Anmol Publications Pvt. Limited.
- Lennard J. Davis (1995). *Enforcing Normalcy: Disability, Deafness, and the Body*, Verso.
- Lennard J. Davis (2006). *The Disability Studies Reader*, Taylor and Francis.
- Leo Grebler, Joan W. Moore, Ralph C. Guzmán, Jeffrey Lionel Berlant (1970). *The Mexican-American people: the Nation's second largest minority*, Free Press.

- Leo Grebler, Joan W. Moore, Ralph C. Guzmán, Jeffrey Lionel Berlant (1970). *The Mexican-American people: the Nation's second largest minority*, Free Press.

- Lettice Kinunda Rutashobya (2000). *Female entrepreneurship in Tanzania: entry and performance barriers, Faculty of Commerce and Management*, University of Dar es Salaam.
- Library Binding (2000). *Child Slavery in Modern Times*, Scholastic Library Publishing.
- Lila Abu-Lughod (2013). *Do Muslim Women Need Saving?,* Harvard University Press.
- Lisa M. Cuklanz (1996). *Rape on Trial: How the Mass Media Construct Legal Reform and Social Change,* University of Pennsylvania Press.

- Lois P. Frankel (1991). *Women, Anger and Depression: Strategies for Self-empowerment,* Health Communications.
- Lorraine Margot Gutiérrez, and Edith Anne Lewis (1999). *Empowering Women of Color, Columbia* University Press.
- Louisa Schein (2000). *Minority Rules: The Miao and the Feminine in China's Cultural Politics*, Duke University Press.
- Louise Shelley (2010). *Human Trafficking: A Global Perspective,* Cambridge University Press.
- Lynn Hunt (1996). *The Invention of pornography: obscenity and the origins of modernity, 1500-1800,* Zone Books.
- Lynn Walter (2001). *Women's Rights: A Global View*. Greenwood Publishing Group.
- Lynn Welchman (2007). *Women and Muslim Family Laws in Arab States: A Comparative Overview of Textual Development and Advocacy*, Amsterdam University Press.
- Lynne Eisaguirre (1997). *Sexual harassment: a reference handbook*, ABC-CLIO.
- Lynne M. Healy and Rosemary J. Link (2012). *Handbook of International Social Work: Human Rights, Development, and the Global Profession*, Oxford University Press.
- M V Pylee (1979). India's Constitution, Asia.
- M.K. Rao (2005). *Empowerment of Women in India*, New Delhi: Discovery Publishing House.
- Mahendra Pal Singh, Vijaya Narain Shukla (2001). *V.N. Shukla's Constitution of India*, Eastern Book Co.
- Mairian Corker and Tom Shakespeare (2002). *Disability/ Postmodernity: Embodying Disability Theory*, Bloomsbury Academic.
- Mamta Rajawat (2004). *Child Labour: The Indian Perspective,* Kilaso Books.
- Marc Weller (2007). *Universal Minority Rights: A Commentary on the Jurisprudence of International Courts and Treaty Bodies*, Oxford University Press.
- Marc Weller (2007). *Universal Minority Rights: A Commentary on the Jurisprudence of International Courts and Treaty Bodies*, Oxford University Press.
- Margaret Moberly (1999). *Fire Bride,* Charisma Media.
- Margaret Schuler (2008). *Legal literacy: a tool for women's empowerment*, OEF International.
- Maria Minniti (2009). *Gender Issues in Entrepreneurship*, Now Publishers Inc.

- Marian Meyers (1997). *News Coverage of Violence Against Women: Engendering Blame,* SAGE.
- Marilyn Shear Goodman, and Beth Creager Fallon (1945). *Pattern Changing for Abused Women: An Educational Program,* SAGE Publications.
- Mariz Tadros (2012). *The Muslim Brotherhood in Contemporary Egypt: Democracy Defined Or Confined?,* Routledge.
- Marjorie Agosín (2001). *Women, Gender, and Human Rights: A Global Perspective,* Rutgers University Press.
- Mark Casson, Bernard Yeung, and Anuradha Basu (2008). *The Oxford Handbook of Entrepreneurship,* Oxford Handbooks Online.
- Mark Gibney (2008). International human rights law: returning to universal principles, Rowman and Littlefield Publishers.
- Mark Gibney, Stanislaw Frankowski (1999). *Judicial Protection of Human Rights: Myth Or Reality?* Greenwood Publishing Group.
- Mark Juergensmeyer, Margo Kitts (2011). *Princeton Readings in Religion and Violence,* Princeton University Press.
- Mark Juergensmeyer, Margo Kitts, Michael Jerryson (2013). *Oxford Handbook of Religion and Violence,* Oxford University Press.
- Mark S. Fleisher and Jessie L. Krienert (2009). *The Myth of Prison Rape: Sexual Culture in American Prisons*, Rowman and Littlefield Publishers.
- Marlene Webber (1991). *Street Kids: The Tragedy of Canada's Runaways*, University of Toronto Press.
- Martha Craven Nussbaum (2006). *Frontiers of Justice: Disability, Nationality, Species Membership,* Harvard University Press.
- Martin Guggenheim (2005). *What's Wrong with Children's Rights?,* Harvard University Press.
- Mary Ellen Richmond and Fred Smith Hall (2007). *Child Marriages,* Russell Sage Foundation.
- Mary L. Boland (2005). *Sexual Harassment in the Workplace*, SphinxLegal.
- Matt Bernstein Sycamore (2000). *Tricks and Treats: Sex Workers Write about Their Clients*, Harrington Park Press.
- Maura McAdam (2013). *Female Entrepreneurship,* Routledge.
- Maxwell Taylor and Ethel Quayle (2003). *Child Pornography: An Internet Crime,* Psychology Press.
- Mejeha, R.O. and Nwachukwu, I.N, (2008). Micro-finance Institutions in Nigeria. MPRA Paper, 13711.Retrieved from http:/ /mpra.ub.uni.muenchen.de/13711 on 23rd August 2011.

- Mercy Tembon, and Lucia Fort (2008). *Girls' Education in the Twenty-first Century*, World Bank Publications.
- Michael D. A. Freeman and Michael Freeman (2011). *Children's Rights: Progress and Perspectives: Essays from the International Journal of Children's Rights,* Martinus Nijhoff Publishers.
- Michael D. A. Freeman, and Philip E. Veerman (1992). *The Ideologies of Children's Rights,* Brill Academic Pub.
- Michael Freeman and Michael David Alan Freeman (2006). *Children's Health and Children's Rights,* Martinus Nijhoff Publishers.
- Michael Haas (2008). *International Human Rights: A Comprehensive Introduction*, Routledge.
- Michael Ignatieff (2009). *American Exceptionalism and Human Rights,* Princeton University Press.
- Michael J. Perry (2000). *The Idea of Human Rights: Four Inquiries*, Oxford University Press.
- Michele Antoinette Paludi, Richard B. Barickman, and Richard Barickman (1991). *Academic and Workplace Sexual Harassment: A Resource Manual,* SUNY Press.
- Mohd Umar (2005). *Bride Burning in India: A Socio Legal Study,* APH Publishing.
- Mridu Rai (2004). *Hindu Rulers, Muslim Subjects: Islam, Rights, and the History of Kashmir*, C. Hurst and Co. Publishers.
- N. Subramanya (2004). *Human Rights and Refugees,* APH Publishing.
- Nab Kishore Behura, Ramesh P. Mohanty (2005). *Urbanization, Street Children, and Their Problems,* New Delhi: Discovery Publishing House.
- Nalini Rajan (2008). *Democracy and the Limits of Minority Rights*, SAGE Publications.
- Nazir Ahmad Shah (1992). *Child Labour in India*, New Delhi: Anmol Publications Pvt. Limited.
- Neera Bharihoke (2008). *Rights of Hindu and Muslim Women,* Serials Publications.
- Neera Burra (1997). *Born to work: child labour in India,* Oxford University Press.
- Neera Burra (1994). *Child labour: impact assessment*, Cornell University.
- Nelien Haspels, and Michele Jankanish (2000). *Action against Child Labour*, International Labour Organization.

- Nicole J. Beger (2004). *Tensions in the Struggle for Sexual Minority Rights in Europe: Que(e)rying Political Practices*, Manchester University Press.
- Noam Chomsky (1978). *Human rights and American foreign policy*, Spokesman Books.
- Obamuyi, T.M (2011). Comparative Loan Performance in Banks and Micro-Credit Institution. *Global Journal of Management and Business Research*, March, 11(4), 60-69.
- Obrad Saviæ (1999). *Politics of Human Rights,* Verso.
- Ola W. Barnett, Cindy L. Miller-Perrin, Robin D. Perrin (2010). *Family Violence across the Lifespan: An Introduction*, SAGE.
- Oriahi, C.I and Aitufe, A.O (2010). Education for the Eradication of Poverty. Current Research Journal of Social Sciences, 2(6), 306-310.
- Orient Blackswan (2005). *Trafficking in Women and Children in India,* Orient Blackswan.
- P. J. Christabell (2009). *Women Empowerment Through Capacity Building: The Role of Microfinance,* New Delhi: Concept Publishing Company.
- P.K. Das (2010). *Hindu Succession*, Universal Law Publishing.
- Paisley Currah, Richard M. Juang, Shannon Minter (2006), Transgender Rights, U of Minnesota Press.
- Palok Basu (2002). *Law Relating to Protection of Human Rights: Under the Indian Constitution and Allied Laws,* Modern Law Publications.
- Pamela Paul (2007). *Pornified: How Pornography Is Transforming Our Lives, Our Relationships, and Our Families*, Macmillan.
- Paramjeet Kaur Dhillon (1993). *Women entrepreneurs: problems and prospects,* Blaze Publishers and Distributors.
- Paras Diwan, and Peeyushi Diwan (1997). *Law relating to dowry, dowry deaths, bride burning, rape, and related offences,* Universal Law Pub. Co.
- Parveen Nangia (1987). *Child labour: cause-effect syndrome*, Janak Publishers.
- Parvis Ghassem-Fachandi (2012). *Programme in Gujarat: Hindu Nationalism and Anti-Muslim Violence in India,* Princeton University Press.
- Patricia Nieuwenhuizen (2006). *Street Children in Bangalore (India): Their Dreams and Their Future,* Het Spinhuis.
- Patrick Thornberry (2002). *Indigenous Peoples and Human Rights,* Manchester University Press.

- Patrick Thornberry, María Amor Martín Estébanez (2004). *Minority Rights in Europe: A Review of the Work and Standards of the Council of Europe*, Council of Europe.
- Paul K. Longmore (2003). *Why I Burned My Book and Other Essays on Disability,* Temple University Press.
- Peggy Reeves Sanday (1992). *Fraternity Gang Rape: Sex, Brotherhood, and Privilege on Campus,* NYU Press.
- Peter Cumper, Steven Charles Wheatley (1999). *Minority Rights in the "new" Europe: The Hague,* Martinus Nijhoff Publishers.
- Peter Davies (1988). *Human Rights,* Routledge.
- Peter Skerry (1993). *Mexican Americans: The Ambivalent Minority*, Free Press.
- Peter Van Ness, Nikhil Aziz (1999). *Debating Human Rights: Critical Essays from the United States and Asia*, Routledge.
- Phil Jones, Sue Welch, and Susan Welch (2010). *Rethinking Children's Rights: Attitudes in Contemporary Society,* Continuum.
- Philip Alston, and Stephen Parker (1992). *Children, Rights, and the Law,* Oxford University Press.
- Philip Jenkins (2003). *Beyond Tolerance: Child Pornography on the Interne,* NYU Press.
- Philip Leroy Kilbride, Collette A. Suda, and Enos Hudson Nthia Njeru (2000). *Street Children in Kenya: Voices of Children in Search of a Childhood,* Greenwood Publishing Group.
- Prabhat Chandra Tripathy (1998). *Crime against working women,* New Delhi: APH Publication.
- Prachi Jaiswal (2000). *Child labour: a sociological study*, New Delhi: Shipra Publications.
- Pramila H Bhargava (2003). *The Elimination of Child Labour: Whose Responsibility?,* New Delhi: SAGE Publisher.
- Premacanda, and Danid Rubin (1998). Widows, wives, and other heroines: twelve short stories, Oxford University Press.
- Priscilla Alderson (2000). *Young Children's Rights: Exploring Beliefs, Principles and Practice*, Jessica Kingsley Publishers.
- Priyam Manisha (2009). *Human Rights, Gender and the Environment*, Pearson Education India.
- R. Scott Appleby (2000). *Ambivalence of the Sacred: Religion, Violence, and Reconciliation,* Rowman and Littlefield.
- R.N. Misra (2010). Women Education and Development, Discovery Publishing House.
- Rachana Kaushal (2000). *Women and Human Rights in India,* Kaveri Books.

- Raghbirlal Bhagatram Sethi (2007). *The Child marriage restraint act, as amended up to date,* Edition: 2, Law Book Co.
- Rajesh Kumar (2000). *Universal's Guide to the Constitution of India*, Universal Law Publishing.
- Rajib Lochan Panigrahy (2006). *Women Empowerment,* Discovery Publishing House.
- Rajmohan Gandhi (2000). *Understanding the Muslim Mind,* Penguin Books India.
- Ram Ahuja (1987). *Crime against Women*, Rawat Publications.
- Ranjana Kumari (1989). *Brides Are Not for Burning: Dowry Victims in India,* Radiant Publisher.
- Rasamandala Das (2012). *The Illustrated Encyclopedia of Hinduism: A Comprehensive Guide to Hindu History and Philosophy, Its Traditions and Practices, Rituals and Beliefs, with More Than 470 Magnificent Photographs*, Lorenz Books.
- Rashmi Agrawal (1999). *Street children: a socio-psychological study*, Shipra Publications.
- Raymond Chandler (2002). *The High Window: A Novel*, Knopf Doubleday Publishing Group.
- Rebecca J. Cook (1994). *Human Rights of Women: National and International Perspectives,* University of Pennsylvania Press.
- Rhoda E. Howard-Hassmann (1986). *Human Rights in Commonwealth Africa*, Rowman and Littlefield.
- Richard Pierre Claude, Burns H. Weston (2006). *Human Rights in the World Community: Issues and Action,* University of Pennsylvania Press.
- Richard Procida, and Rita James Simon (2007). *Global Perspectives on Social Issues: Pornography,* Lexington Books.
- Richard S. Hillman, John A. Peeler, Elsa Cardozo da Silva (2002). *Democracy and Human Rights in Latin America,* Greenwood Publishing Group.
- Richard Wortley, and Stephen Smallbone (2012). *Internet Child Pornography: Causes, Investigation, and Prevention,* ABC-CLIO.
- Rinki Bhattacharya (2004). *Behind Closed Doors: Domestic Violence in India,* SAGE Publications.
- Rob Imrie (1996). *Disability and the City: International Perspectives*, SAGE.
- Robert C. Liebman, Robert Wuthnow (2010). *New Christian Right: Mobilization and Legitimation,* Transaction Publishers.
- Robert McRuer and Anna Mollow (2012). *Sex and Disability,* Duke University Press.

- Robert McRuer (2006). *Crip Theory: Cultural Signs of Queerness and Disability*, NYU Press.
- Robin Warshaw (1994). *I Never Called It Rape,* Harper Collins.
- Rory C. Reid, and Dan Gray (2006). *Confronting Your Spouse's Pornography Problem*, Silverleaf Press.
- Rosemarie Skaine (2002). *The Women of Afghanistan under the Taliban*, McFarland.
- Ross Douthat (2012). *Bad Religion: How We Became a Nation of Heretics*, Simon and Schuster.
- S. P. Agrawal (2001). *Women's Education in India, 1995-98: Present Status, Perspective Plan*, Statistical Indicators with a Global View, Concept Publishing Company.
- S. P. Agrawal, and J. C. Aggarwal (1992). *Women's Education in India*, Volume 1, Concept Publishing Company.
- S. Subramanian (1997). *Human Rights: International Challenges,* Volumes 1-2, Manas Publications.
- Saied Reza Ameli, Arzu Merali (2006). *Hijab, Meaning, Identity, Otherization and Politics: British Muslim Women,* Islamic Human Rights Commission.
- Sally Engle Merry (2009). *Human Rights and Gender Violence: Translating International Law into Local Justice,* University of Chicago Press.
- Sambodh Goswami (2007). *Female Infanticide and Child Marriage,* Rawat Publications.
- Samia Bano (2012). *Muslim Women and Shari'ah Councils: Transcending the Boundaries of Community and Law,* Palgrave Macmillan.
- Samya Burney (1999). *Crime Or Custom?: Violence Against Women in Pakistan,* Human Rights Watch.
- Sandra Fredman (2008). *Human Rights Transformed: Positive Rights and Positive Duties*, Oxford University Press.
- Sandra J. Wells (1998). *Women Entrepreneurs: Developing Leadership for Success,* Taylor and Francis.
- Sandy Hobbs, Jim McKechnie, and Michael Lavalette (1999). *Child Labor: A World History Companion,* ABC-CLIO.
- Santha S., and R. Vasanthagopal (2008). *Women Entrepreneurship in India,* New Century Publications.
- Sara Diamond (1990). *Spiritual Warfare: The Politics of the Christian Right,* Black Rose Books Ltd.
- Selda Altun, Tom Burke, and Jabran Ali (2001). *Stand Up Speak Out: A Book about Children's Rights*, Cooper Square Pub.

- Shane Mountjoy, and Tim McNeese (2009). *The Women's Rights Movement: Moving Toward Equality,* Infobase Publishing.
- Sharon N. Barnartt (2010). *Disability as a Fluid State*, Emerald Group Publishing.
- Shashi Motilal, Bijayalaxmi Nanda (2006), *Human Rights, Gender and Environment,* Allied Publishers.
- Shasta Gaughen (2003). *Women Rights*, Pennsylvania State University: Greenhaven Press.
- Shastri, R.K. (2009). Micro Finance and Poverty Reduction in India (A Comparative Study with Asian Countries). *African Journal of Business Management*, 3(4), 136-140.
- Shelley Lynn Tremain (2005). *Foucault and the Government of Disability,* University of Michigan Press.
- Shireen Hunter, Huma Malik (2005). *Islam and Human Rights: Advancing a U.S.-Muslim Dialogue*, CSIS.
- Shobha Saxena (1995). *Crimes against Women and Protective Laws,* Deep and Deep Publications.
- Shobhan Bantwal (2007). *The Dowry Bride,* Kensington Books.
- Siddharth Kara (2010). *Sex Trafficking: Inside the Business of Modern Slavery,* Columbia University Press.
- Simi Linton (1998). *Claiming Disability: Knowledge and Identity*, NYU Press.
- Simon Watney (1987). *Policing Desire: Pornography, AIDS, and the Media*, University of Minnesota Press.
- Simon Watney (1996). *Policing Desire: Pornography, AIDS, and the Media,* U of Minnesota Press.
- Siraj Sait, Hilary Lim (2006). *Land, Law and Islam: Property and Human Rights in the Muslim World,* Volume 1, Zed Books.
- Soren V. Randall (2006). *Learning disabilities: new research*, Nova Science Publishers.
- Stanley G. French, Wanda Teays, Laura Martha Purdy (1998). *Violence against Women: Philosophical Perspectives,* Cornell University Press.
- Stanley G. French, Wanda Teays, Laura Martha Purdy (1998). *Violence against women: philosophical perspectives,* Cornell University Press.
- Stephen Harold Riggins (1992). *Ethnic Minority Media: An International Perspective*, SAGE Publications.
- Stephen May (2008). *Language and minority rights: ethnicity, nationalism and the politics of language,* Routledge.

- Stephen May, Tariq Modood, Judith Squires (2004). *Ethnicity, Nationalism, and Minority Rights,* Cambridge University Press.
- Steven D. Edwards (2005). *Disability: definitions, value and identity*, Radcliffe Publishing.
- Stuart N. Hart (2001). *Children's Rights in Education,* Jessica Kingsley Publishers.
- Student Services, Inc (1998). *Minority and Women's Complete Scholarship Book*, Sourcebooks.
- Subhas Chandra Parida (2009). *Empowerment of Women in India,* Northern Book Centre.
- Sue Davies, Cathy Lubelska, Jocey Quinn (1994). *Changing the Subject: Women in Higher Education,* Taylor and Francis.
- Susan Deller Ross (2008). *Women's Human Rights: The International and Comparative Law Casebook,* University of Pennsylvania Press.
- Susan Griffin (1981). *Pornography and silence: culture's revenge against nature*, Harper and Row.
- Susan Stryker (2009). *Transgender History,* Seal Press.
- Susan Stryker, Stephen Whittle (2006). *The Transgender Studies Reader,* Taylor and Francis.
- Susanna Paasonen (2011). *Carnal Resonance: Affect and Online Pornography,* MIT Press.
- Sushama Sahay (1998). *Women and Empowerment: Approaches and Strategies,* New Delhi: Discovery Publishing House.
- Sydney Newton, and Julie Gerrits (2010). *Child Abuse,* Crabtree Publishing Company.
- T. S. N. Sastry (2005). *India and Human Rights: Reflections,* Concept Publishing Company.
- Tara Chand (1936). *Influence of Islam on Indian Culture*, Indian Press.
- Tawhida Ahmed (2011). *Impact of EU Law on Minority Rights,* Hart.
- Tessa J. Bartholomeusz, Chandra Richard De Silva (1998). *Buddhist Fundamentalism and Minority Identities in Sri Lanka,* SUNY Press.
- Thoko Kaime (2011). *The Convention on the Rights of the Child: A Cultural Legitimacy Critique*, Sussex Academic Press.
- Thomas A. LaVeist (2011). *Minority Populations and Health: An Introduction to Health Disparities in the United States,* John Wiley and Sons.

- Thomas F. Head, Richard Allen Landes (1992). *The Peace of God: social violence and religious response in France around the year 1000,* Cornell University Press.
- Thomas Risse, Stephen C. Ropp, Kathryn Sikkink (2013). *The Persistent Power of Human Rights: From Commitment to Compliance,* Cambridge University Press.
- Thomas Woody (1929). *A history of women's education in the United States*, Volume 2, The Science Press.
- Tim Dunne, Nicholas J. Wheeler (1999). *Human Rights in Global Politics,* Cambridge University Press.
- Tim Wise (2002). *Dear White America: Letter to a New Minority*, City Lights Publishers.
- Tobias Hecht (1998). *At Home in the Street: Street Children of Northeast Brazil,* Cambridge University Press.
- Tobin Siebers (2008). *Disability Theory*, University of Michigan Press.
- Tom Shakespeare (1998). *Disability Reader: Social Science Perspectives,* Bloomsbury.
- Udai Raj Rai (2011). *Fundamental Rights and Their Enforcement,* PHI Learning Pvt. Ltd.
- Ugoh, S.C. and Ukpere, W.I. (2009). Appraising the Trend of Policy on Poverty Alleviation Programmes in Nigeria with Emphasis on a National Poverty Eradication Programme (NAPEP). *African Journal of Business Management*, 3(12), 847-854.
- United Nations Children's Fund (UNICEF) (2005). *Early Marriage: A Harmful Traditional Practice, a Statistical Exploration,* UNICEF.
- Usha Sharma (2006). *Child Labour in India,* New Delhi: Mittal Publications.
- V. R. Krishna Iyer (1999). *Dialectics and Dynamics of Human Rights in India,* Eastern Law House.
- V. S. Ganesamurthy (2007). *India: economic empowerment of women*, New Century Publications.
- Valentine M. Moghadam (2007). *From Patriarchy to Empowerment: Women's Participation, Movements, and Rights in the Middle East, North Africa, and South Asia*, Syracuse University Press.
- Veena Talwar Oldenburg (2002). *Dowry Murder: The Imperial Origins of a Cultural Crime*, Oxford University Press.
- Vincent Obisienunwo Orlu Nmehielle (2001). *The African Human Rights System: Its Laws, Practice, and Institutions*, Martinus Nijhoff Publishers.

- Vivian Parker Makosky (1991). *Fact book on women in higher education*, American Council on Education.
- Viviane Namaste (2000). *Invisible Lives: The Erasure of Transsexual and Transgendered People*, University of Chicago Press.
- W. James Potter (2003). *The 11 Myths of Media Violence,* SAGE Publications.
- Walter Fernandes (1981). *Caste and conversion movements in India: religion and human rights,* Indian Social Institute.
- Walter M. Kendrick (1987). *The Secret Museum: Pornography in Modern Culture,* University of California Press.
- Werner Menski (1998). *South Asians and the Dowry Problem,* Trentham Books.
- Will Kymlicka (1995). *Multicultural Citizenship: A Liberal Theory of Minority Rights*, Oxford University Press.
- Will Kymlicka (1996). *Multicultural Citizenship: A Liberal Theory of Minority Rights,* Clarendon Press.
- Will Kymlicka (1997). *The New Debate Over Minority Rights, Robert F. Harney Professorship and Program in Ethnic Immigration and Pluralism Studies*, University of Toronto.
- Willi Braun, and Russell McCutcheon (2000). Guide to the Study of Religion, Bloomsbury Academic.
- William M. Struthers (2009). *Wired for Intimacy: How Pornography Hijacks the Male Brain*, InterVarsity Press.
- William Petrocelli, and Barbara Kate Repa (1998). *Sexual harassment on the job: what it is and how to stop it,* Nolo Press.
- William Pinar (2001). *The Gender of Racial Politics and Violence in America: Lynching, Prison Rape, and the Crisis of Masculinity,* Lang.
- Yaduvansh Bahadur Mathur (1973). *Women's Education in India, 1813-1966,* Asia Publishing House.
- Yahaya, K.A, Osemene, O.F, and Abdulraheem, A. (2011). Effectiveness of Microfinance Banks in Al-leviating Poverty in Kwara State Nigeria. *Global Journal of Management and Business Research*, March, 11(4), 12-21.
- Yussuf Naim Kly (1995). *A Popular Guide to Minority Rights,* Clarity Press.
- Zakia A. Siddiqi, and Anwar Jahan Zuberi (1993). *Muslim Women: Problems and Prospects, Aligarh Muslim University, India.* University Grants Commission.
- Zayn Kassam (2010). *Women and Islam*, ABC-CLIO.

Index